CHILD CUSTODY AND THE POLITICS OF GENDER

SOCIOLOGY OF LAW AND CRIME
Editors: Maureen Cain, University of the West Indies
Carol Smart, University of Warwick

This new series presents the latest critical and international scholarship in sociology, legal theory, and criminology. Books in the series will integrate the sociology of law and the sociology of crime, extending beyond both disciplines to analyse the distribution of power. Realist, critical, and post-modern approaches will be central to the series, while the major substantive themes will be gender, class, and race as they affect and, in turn, are shaped by legal relations. Throughout, the series will present fresh theoretical interpretations based on the latest empirical research. Books for early publication in the series deal with such controversial issues as child custody, criminal and penal policy, and alternative legal theory

Titles in this series include

Child Custody and the Politics of Gender – Carol Smart and Selma Sevenhuijsen (eds)

Feminism and the Power of Law – Carol Smart

Sites of Judgement: Essays in the Sociology of Law – Maureen Cain

CHILD CUSTODY AND THE POLITICS OF GENDER

Edited by

CAROL SMART

and

SELMA SEVENHUIJSEN

ROUTLEDGE
London and New York

First published 1989 by Routledge
11 New Fetter Lane, London EC4P 4EE
29 West 35th Street, New York, NY 10001

Typeset by Witwell Ltd, Lord Street, Southport

Printed and bound in Great Britain by
Billings & Sons Limited, Worcester

British Library Cataloguing in Publication Data

Child custody and the politics of gender
1. Children. Custody by divorced parents
I. Smart, Carol, *1948–*
II. Sevenhuijsen, Selma
362.7′95

ISBN 0-415-02669-5
0-415-02670-9

*Library of Congress Cataloging in Publication Data
also available*

Educ

CONTENTS

CONTRIBUTORS

Susan B. Boyd is an associate professor at the Department of Law, Carleton University, Ottawa, where she teaches family law, feminist theories of law, and international law. She is also on the editorial board of *The Canadian Journal of Women and the Law*. Her current research interests include the ideological aspects of the primary caregiver presumption and joint custody, and their implications for feminist strategy. During the 1988-9 academic year she was director of the new Institute of Women's Studies at Carleton University.

Julia Brophy is the family law research officer for Rights of Women which is a feminist advice, information, and research centre based in London. Her major area of interest has been the politics of child custody and the role of law in feminist politics. She has also published work on a range of family law issues. Recently she has written on child care and equal opportunities, has taught on a range of women's studies courses, and has developed community courses for women on both family law and social welfare law.

Martha Fineman is professor of law at the University of Wisconsin, Madison. She is currently working on a book about the interactions of professional and political language or rhetoric in framing the debate about custody rules in the USA. In addition she is editing a book based on papers from the Feminism and Legal Theory Conference which is held annually at the University of Wisconsin Law School.

Regina Graycar is senior lecturer in law at the University of New South Wales, Sydney, where she teaches courses on social security law and law and gender. She is, with Deena Shiff, the editor of *Life Without Marriage: A Woman's Guide to the Law* (Pluto Press), and is currently involved in research on feminist jurisprudence and models of equality.

Nora Holtrust is lecturer in law at the University of Nijmegen, where she teaches courses on women's law. She has published in the area of women and family law and her current research interests include privacy and physical integrity as basic rights.

Delma MacDevitt comes from the Republic of Ireland but is currently living in Italy where she is working in the Facolta di Economia e Commercio, Universita degli Studi Trento. She was formerly carrying out comparative research on legal policies affecting lone parents at the European University Institute at Florence. She is currently researching into the way in which judicial language constructs the family and gender roles.

Kirsten Sandberg is research fellow in the Institute of Women's Law at the University of Oslo. She is currently working on a project on child custody and child welfare law, which includes aspects of the philosophy of law. She is interested in women's law in general, and in particular with women in the third world. The Institute has recently started a diploma course for African women lawyers.

Selma Sevenhuijsen is lecturer in political science in the Department of Political Theory and History at the University of Amsterdam. She has published in the fields of motherhood, women and the welfare state, women and family law, and feminism and political theory. Her current research interests include the connections between feminism and liberal political theory, and the history of feminism and children's interests.

Carol Smart is lecturer in sociology at the University of Warwick where she teaches courses on women's studies, feminism and law, and on sexuality. She has published in the areas of criminology, family law, and social policy, and is writing a book on contemporary feminism's engagement with law and feminist theories of law. She is also editor (with Sol Picciotto) of *The International Journal of the Sociology of Law*. She was formerly the director of the National Council for One Parent Families in London.

Irene Thèry is research fellow at the National Centre for Scientific Research (CNRS), Centre de Recherche Interdisciplinaire de Vaucresson. She specializes in the sociology of law and sociology of the family. Her main interests are a sociological approach to the problem of the legitimacy of state intervention into the 'private sphere' and new forms of family structure, particularly step-families and post-divorce families. She is currently working on the French Revolution of 1789 and family law.

Annick Verbraken is researcher and under-secretary of the Emancipation Council, which is the Dutch government's advisory board on policies on women. She has published in the area of rights of access to children, and on the traffic in women.

Juliette Zipper is a political scientist researching in the Department of Political Theory at the University of Amsterdam. She is currently doing research for her PhD on reproductive technologies and women's reproductive rights. She is an editor of the *Socialisties-Feministiese Teksten*, a yearly anthology of articles in the field of women's studies. She has edited an anthology on motherhood in the Netherlands and Belgium, and has published on violence against women and children, abortion, health politics, and the politics of reproductive technologies.

SERIES EDITORS' PREFACE

The question of how family law regulates family life, and most particularly the lives of women and children, has been of concern to feminists since the eighteenth century. The focus of this concern has shifted, however. At times the main concern may have been domestic violence, or the impossibility of divorce, or the unequal economic status of parties to a marriage, or unequal rights 'over' children. All these different concerns were (and are) interrelated and yet we can detect that at different historical moments some have taken precedence over others. At present we appear to be entering into a new phase of political concern over children, particularly the question of the custody of children on divorce. This book marks part of this renewed focus on children.

It is interesting to analyse why children should have become such a significant part of the 'politics of gender' at the end of the twentieth century. The second-wave women's movement has almost universally demanded better public resources for the care of children, but feminists have also demanded that in the private sphere fathers should take on more of the responsibility of child care. So feminism acknowledged the importance of children and child care to the oppression of women. However, this concern has been rendered more complex by the rising rate of divorce and separation that has led to a situation in which the state has been required to impose a legal (and public) form to the otherwise informal (and private) child care arrangements made by mothers and fathers. To this must also be added the power of the rhetoric of equality, or equal treatment, which has led to a presumption that any recognition of women's special relationship to children is unduly to favour women over men.

The combination of these factors has produced a situation of potential conflict over children; in other words, children have re-entered the public domain of the political and legal. There are two possible scenarios to be sketched out here. One is optimistic and sees that fathers are becoming more involved in child care. It is felt that the conflicts over custody that are erupting can be met by changes in legal procedures to give fathers greater rights. The other is pessimistic and fears that law will seek to impose a model of shared caring on separating couples, irrespective of fathers' actual involvement, and that this will reduce women's autonomy and increase husbands' power to intervene in the lives of former wives. The former sees the problem as one of communication and compromise, the latters sees it as an issue of gender politics in which law plays a crucial, not impartial, role.

This collection of essays reflects this latter concern and, from differing perspectives, documents how legal changes and procedures in countries as far apart as Australia, Ireland, and the Netherlands appear to be reinstating the symbolic father as a central form of authority within the post-divorce family. Recent developments have shattered the link between mothers' interests and children's interests, and mothers are increasingly under suspicion for not putting their children's interests before their own. In this scenario it becomes possible to identify fathers' interests as synonymous with the welfare of children, producing very serious consequences for women. Yet there is no crude conspiracy thesis espoused here; rather, we find a detailed and rigorous examination of different legal systems to try to understand how the courts are dealing with contradictory notions of equality, the interests of children, justice, and social welfare.

While the focus of this book is child custody, this issue typifies a range of developments that are increasingly rendering the operations of the courts and law more complex. Conflicts over children pose, *par excellence*, problems over whether welfare or justice norms should prevail. They highlight the waning role of the judiciary in favour of the professional judgement of welfare officers and constantly challenge the authority of the judge to make such complex decisions. It is precisely these complexities that feminist analysis is required to unravel in order to challenge liberal assumptions that law merely operates as a neutral arbitrator in a context in which power differences are rendered invisible.

In relation to the series as a whole, *Child Custody and the Politics of Gender* represents two main themes. The first is the encouragement of feminist scholarship in the field of law and social regulation. This scholarship marks one of the most exciting developments in this field as it begins to challenge both the form and content of law and traditional legal thinking and doctrine. The second theme is the series' commitment to analytical work that is grounded in the history, culture, and politics of real events and issues. This book spans the divide between theory, empirical work, and policy formulation. In addition to these main elements, this book represents a collaborative effort to overcome national boundaries that differing legal jurisdictions usually manage to render rigid and impenetrable. It is important that feminist scholarship in this field is not hindered by the boundaries that law itself imposes.

Maureen Cain
Carol Smart
January 1989

PREFACE

The idea for this book originally arose out of discussions between Martha Fineman, Selma Sevenhuijsen, and Carol Smart during the summer of 1984 in Madison, Wisconsin. While discussing aspects of family law and the position of women in our respective homelands (USA, the Netherlands, and the UK) it became clear that certain common trends could be discerned in each country. In particular it became apparent that there were developments in the area of child custody and fathers' rights which were profoundly anti-progressive and anti-women. From this point of recognition it was decided that we should organize conferences on the politics of child custody in Europe and North America. Subsequently seminars were organized in the US and Canada, and the European conference was held in the Netherlands. Subsequent to the European conference it was decided to publish this book which is, in part, based on the conference proceedings. However, the scope of the book was broadened to include papers from the US, Canada, and Australia. We also decided to include a paper on reproductive technologies which reflects the way in which the politics of custody are being integrated into a new field of concerns.

This brief history does not explain why the editors of this book thought it was so important to publish a book on child custody from a feminist perspective. The main reason was the recognition that child custody has become a major concern of law reformers and policy makers, who have become alarmed by the consequences of divorce for children. Whilst there may be some causes for concern, it was apparent that the main concerns which are the motivating factors in policy developments are concerns deriving from traditional views of the family and from fathers' rights movements. The problem which we identified was that the question of custody and child welfare in the 1970s and 1980s has developed largely outside a feminist informed framework and has become the terrain of the social work profession, the conciliators, and legal and social policy makers. It is not that the women's movement has had nothing to say on these vital issues, nor that the movement is unconcerned with the welfare of children; rather it is that recent political debates on child custody have been successful in disregarding areas which seem to give voice to women's concerns. As the introductory chapter argues, women's claims are increasingly regarded as selfish demands for unjust legal prerogatives, whilst fathers and children are increasingly depicted as the 'losers' in emotional and material terms. Such over-simplified images can be deconstructed, but it is not an easy task to popularize alternative accounts in the political climates which prevail in many western developed countries.

The consequence of an absence of a feminist dimension in this terrain is that certain concepts like 'the best interests of the child' have come to dominate policy without there being a challenge to the dominance of such vague, but worthy sounding, notions. As Thèry (Chapter 4) points out, these best interests are far from self-evident, yet any opposition to this focus of debate seems to imply that feminists are against the best interests of children. Moreover, to be perceived as being against or indifferent to children's interests (even when this is far from the case) puts feminist arguments beyond the pale. Hence it is difficult to enter the frame of the discussion, let alone to alter its parameters.

Yet this is precisely what is required. Policies affecting children do not occur outside gender politics. Proposals for compulsory counselling on divorce or routine orders for the joint legal and/or physical custody of children have consequences for the position of women *vis-à-vis* men. They may weaken women's economic position after divorce (Weitzman, 1985; Chapter 7 in this volume), or they may create an injustice by rendering women's work in rearing children insignificant (Chapters 2 and 6). The rush to meet the perceived 'needs' of children and to 'rectify' what has become identified as mother preference in custody cases may result in trampling the needs of those people who still carry the overwhelming responsibility for child care, namely mothers.

Notwithstanding this, changes in policy on child custody may not have the appearance of a major threat to feminist ideas or the position of women in marriage. Unlike reactionary changes in abortion law, or in laws governing illegitimacy and divorce, the changes in the field of child custody are complex to unravel and consequences are not immediately apparent. It might even appear that a move towards joint custody reflects the demand by feminists for more paternal involvement in the rearing of children. Yet, as Brophy (Chapter 9) points out, joint custody at the point of divorce does nothing to alter the division of child care labour during the marriage. It is an equal sharing of the work of child care that the women's movement has campaigned for, not purely symbolic laws which enhance men's rights without requiring them to change their practices in relation to children.

It may also be difficult for the women's movement to become sensitive to developments in child custody which occur at the level of court and judicial practice, rather than in the more public forum of law reform. Each custody decision can be isolated from others; women who lose custody, or are 'obliged' to accept joint custody orders, may not realize that they are part of a trend. Custody can easily remain a personal issue rather than becoming a political one.

These are some of the reasons why we thought that a book in this area was so important. However, we also felt it was important to recognize how complex this field is, especially when taking an international perspective. Although this book identifies common trends as far afield as Australia and Canada, France and Norway, it is important not to collapse this insight into a general theory about patriarchy. There are also clear differences which arise from different political, economic, historical and religious contexts. The paper on Ireland (Chapter 8), for example, reveals that the issue of custody can have very different dimensions in a country where divorce is not permitted or recognized.

Finally we regard this book as a starting point for more work in this area. There are many issues that we could not hope to cover in this first attempt. Research has yet to be carried out into issues like the influence of racism in the practice of family courts and domestic jurisdictions. The whole question of state policies which aim to 'stabilize' nuclear families and reassert the authority of the male head of the household needs to be examined in the light of immigration policies which separate families, particularly fathers and children (WING, 1985). Adoption policies are particularly salient here, especially the question of who is allowed to adopt, and which children become 'available' for adoption. This also raises the issue of the international adoption of babies from the third world. Although we discuss adoption in the Irish context in this book, it is clear that these issues need further exploration. Notwithstanding these limitations, we hope that this book will be a contribution towards giving child custody a more central place on the agenda of feminism and towards bringing a feminist perspective to a larger audience.

Carol Smart (University of Warwick, Great Britain)
Selma Sevenhuijsen (University of Amsterdam, The Netherlands)
July 1988

ACKNOWLEDGEMENT

We are grateful to Academic Press for granting us permission to reproduce the paper by Irene Thèry entitled ' "The interest of the child" and the regulation of the post-divorce family' which originally appeared in *The International Journal of the Sociology of Law*, 1986, vol. 14, no. 3/4 pp. 341–58.

Chapter One

POWER AND THE POLITICS OF CHILD CUSTODY

CAROL SMART

> Power is tolerable only when a good deal of its workings are concealed. Its efficacy is proportional to the degree of that concealment. For power, secrecy is not an abuse but a necessity; and this is not only for its greater efficiency but also for its acceptance. (Sheridan, 1980, p. 181)

This is not so much a book about children as a book about power. That is not to say that children are insignificant to the concerns of this book. On the contrary, the chapters reflect a concern with how children are treated during the legal process of divorce which goes beyond platitudes like the 'best interests of the child' or the blanket imposition of an equal rights perspective which ignores the realities of child care. So children are present here; yet the chapters reflect how important it is to clear away much of the rhetoric which surrounds the category of children and the rights of parents, before we can start to formulate policies grounded in the practical realities of the lives of children and their primary carers.

As a consequence, one central concern reflected here is the issue of the allocation of children between women and men through the vehicle of family law. It is no doubt uncomfortable to the philanthropic view of children to associate them so closely with terms like 'allocation' (which posits children as mere objects in a wider frame of material relations) or power (which in liberal terms is the antithesis of love which is, in turn, regarded as the only appropriate emotional condition in which to invoke the concept of the child). However, children form part of a nexus of power within family relations, whether they are loved and cherished or neglected and abused. Parents may or may not deploy the powers at their disposal, but even where the resort to open struggle (as in legal custody disputes or in measures to prevent wives or partners having legal terminations) is avoided, children constitute an implicit site of power relations.

It might be useful at this stage to clarify my use of the concept of power. Power is frequently thought of in negative terms, as a way of controlling those who are weaker than oneself, or in structural terms where classes, sexes, or races have power to oppress other classes, sexes, or races. Power is also depicted as a commodity which is held by an individual or by a representative of a class, gender, or race. In this context power is understood to be power over another individual or collectivity. This power over has inevitably been seen as favourable for those with it, and a distinct disadvantage for those without it. This view of power has sustained liberation movements such as the women's movement, but is increasingly seen as a limited mode of conceptualizing power (see Davis, K., 1987). The problem is that it has tended to create two distinct categories, those with power and those without. In such a formulation women were always those without, they became the eternal victims of those with the power, namely men. Feminist theory has gradually rejected this rigid formulation and, whilst accepting that the category of men have access to greater resources, has increasingly acknowledged that women can exercise power (e.g. Segal, 1987). It is not that women may now have a stake in the power to oppress; rather, the idea of power has changed too. Power may now be theorized as a positive force, one that occurs, as Davis argues, in situations of conflict as well as situations of friendship. So power ceases to be simply 'bad' and becomes an inevitable aspect of all social relationships. With this formulation we are able to recognize that women may also exercise power, that they have power to determine their lives or to make their own decisions. This new formulation of power, which has been stressed in particular by Foucault (Gordon, 1980) does not exclude the old notion of power altogether. It remains possible to see power used in negative contexts; perhaps this is most apparent in the legal context where legal rights do lead to power in the form of power over others without such rights. (I shall elaborate this below in relation to the development of custody rights in Britain.)

This concept of power over is also apparent in relation to children. Both mothers and fathers can be said to have power over children, whether this is economic power, physical power, or emotional power. However, we can also see that the presence of children in a household creates the potential of a power nexus that parents can exploit positively or negatively in relation to one another as a consequence of their social constitution as mothers and fathers. Structurally speaking, children create a specific field of power relations between parents, and the subsequent power claims that parenthood potentiates are linked to the question of gender. (Hence the nature of power claims available to men-as-fathers may be constituted quite differently to those which may be deployed by women-as-mothers.) This power is often taken for granted, only being acknowledged in situations of overt conflict. The point is, however, that this unspoken power relation, which need not be in the negative form, is present even if invisible or denied.

In this chapter I wish to consider briefly the legal structuring of this power and how law has developed different responses as power claims have changed in form and content over time. I shall also consider how gender is central to this process. I shall then consider how the rise of fathers' rights movements and the growing sentimentalization of the father/child bond are posing problems for feminism, especially in the context of Britain which is enduring a so-called return to Victorian values and a renewed celebration of 'natural' family life. Finally I shall point to the significance for feminism of recognizing that the custody of children is not a marginal political issue, but reflects how the (ambiguous) power of women in the category of mother is being eroded.

CHILDREN, LAW, AND THE NEXUS OF POWER

From birth children are dependent upon adults for their physical and emotional survival. This dependency has become manifest in law in the form of parental rights over children. Children (at least young children) are not deemed to have rights; in effect they are hardly recognized as legal persons. Their age and immaturity disqualifies them from taking legal actions to protect their own interests. This means that when parents fail to protect their children's welfare, the state virtually becomes an agent of child protection rather than the advocate of children's 'rights'. So children's recourse to law is couched in terms of protection rather than rights, with the consequence that both the state and parents have the right to do things to children 'for their own good'. This is constructed as operating in the best interests of the child, but it must be recognized that in this process the child, especially the young child, has little influence in determining what is in her or his interests.

To return to the issue of parental rights, this gender-neutral terminology is in fact misleading since the parental rights of mothers and fathers have not always been the same, and in some instances are not the same now. Hence, as Brophy (1982) has pointed out, until the middle of the nineteenth century it was only possible to speak of fathers' rights in respect of legitimate children. Marriage gave fathers complete legal power over their children and in so doing enabled husbands to exercise extensive power over their wives. It is clear that throughout most of the nineteenth century women of all classes could be forced to stay in violent and desperate marriages precisely because to leave (whether through legal divorce or not) would mean leaving behind their children. In such instances the courts were rarely interested in the quality of care that a father would offer; their concern was to protect absolute father right.

It is also clear that the power over wives which absolute father right conferred on married men was not an entirely unrecognized nor an unwelcomed outcome as far as law was concerned. As married women began to campaign for equal rights of guardianship (during marriage) and custody (after separation), the most commonly expressed opposition to these reforms was based on the fear that if husbands lost control over children, they would not be able to prevent their wives from leaving their marriages (Zaborszky, 1984).

> It is notorious that one of the strongest hindrances in all cases ... to prevent wives from lightly separating from their husbands is that knowledge that they will thereby lose their maternal rights. This at all times has been a safeguard to preserve the institution of marriage! (Jahled Brenton, 1828, during a debate in the House of Lords on reform to the guardianship laws, quoted in Pinchbeck and Hewitt, 1973, p. 374)

4

Husbands were also prepared to punish their wives through enforced separation from their children. Take for example the following passage from *Caroline Norton's Defence* (Norton, 1982) which was first published in 1854. Norton was separated from her husband because he was violent towards her. He therefore deprived her of the custody of, and access to, her children aged 2, 4, and 6 years. In fact he gave them to his mistress to look after. Norton wrote,

> Mr Norton held my children as hostages; he felt that while he had them, he still had a power over me that nothing could control. Baffled in the matter of the trial and damages, he had still the power to do more than punish - to torture - the wife who had been so anxious to part from him. I never saw them; I seldom knew where they were. (pp. 48-9)

Such extensive rights over children therefore had the potential to constitute power over mothers; it gave men absolute authority in the family at a time when married women had few legal rights and protections. By the same token it had the potential to reduce women's abilities to make autonomous decisions about their lives and to render children as little more than pawns in a domestic power struggle (see Fineman, Chapter 2 in this volume).

It would be a mistake to assume that absolute father right was an uncontested concept. Caroline Norton's resistance was public, but there were other, less infamous, contestations (see Brophy, 1985). For example in the campaign against wife torture at the end of the nineteenth century, feminists were able to demand reforms of the law such that wives who had taken criminal proceedings against violent spouses were empowered to live apart from their husbands and to take children up to the age of 7 years with them (Matrimonial Causes Act, 1878). Here we see the beginnings of a 'tender years doctrine' in which it was assumed that babies and children under approximately 7 would normally thrive best in the care of a maternal figure. The tender years doctrine became a powerful counterbalance to claims based on fathers' rights.

These shifts were undoubtedly linked to a changing perception of childhood and the construction of modern, 'scientific' conceptions of child development. There is not space to trace this genealogy here; however, it would seem that shifts in 'knowledge' (most specifically the psy discourses - psychiatry, psychoanalysis, and psychology – and pedagogics), combined with increasing pressure from feminists to change the restrictive nature of marriage in the nineteenth century, resulted in the possibility of mothers making new power claims in relation to their children (see Donzelot, 1980; Badinter, 1981; Stetson, 1982). These power claims were not rights based like men's claims to children; rather they were formulated around the uniqueness of motherhood and the supposedly natural (biological) bond between the mother and the child she has borne. They also invoked the idea of the interests of the child, interests which were gradually defined as inhering in the quality of physical and emotional care provided for a child. Under this regime the care a mother could provide became valued and hence created a shift in the power nexus of parenthood (Grossberg, 1983). Such shifts were not unambiguously positive for women, and it would be an oversimplification to imply that the specific construction of motherhood in the nineteenth century did not also result in the production of a confining and dependent role for women (Davin, 1978). However, at the point of marital breakdown, if not during a marriage, the valorization of motherhood gradually modified men's power in relation to children.

WOMEN AND 'PARENTAL RIGHTS'

During the nineteenth century, when women in Britain were beginning to campaign publicly on the issue of child custody and parental rights, it was not infrequently complained that married women – who had followed social convention and expectation – had fewer rights in relation to their biological children than did unmarried mothers. Unmarried mothers had the right in practice (although not in the form of statute law) to sole custody of their illegitimate children from 1841 onwards. For married mothers like Caroline Norton, this disparity must have appeared inexplicable, for why should respectable women have fewer rights than their fallen sisters?

The distinction between married and unmarried women's legal relationship to their children is an interesting one. On the one hand it reveals that the law (and the state) did not take a unitary position on this issue. On the other hand, it is a mistake to interpret the rights of unmarried women as an obvious good or as a form of potential power. Whilst it might have been preferable to unmarried mothers in the middle of the nineteenth century that they should have the right to sole custody rather than the parish or even the putative fathers, this right carried responsibilities which were punitively onerous. The right to sole custody reflected the sole responsibility to support the child and the child's lack of inheritance rights. It was also a right which was meant to reflect the stigma of bastardy and the poverty of the unmarried mother's status. Poor women were, in any case, often forced to put their illegitimate children and themselves into the workhouse in order to survive. Hence the claims that were made by largely upper-middle-class married mothers that poor working-class unmarried mothers had more rights than themselves were really a form of political rhetoric based on a very partial understanding of the practicalities of the latters' lives. Notwithstanding this, this historical anomaly did gradually develop into a real challenge to paternal power and patriarchal power during the twentieth century.

In the 1975 Children Act the common law position of the unmarried mother was codified in statute law. In England and Wales in 1976, 54,000 children were born out of wedlock, and by 1985 the number had risen to 126,000. It would seem that whilst a number of these children were born to women living alone, many were born to women living with men to whom they were not married. (In 1985 65 per cent of illegitimate children had their births registered in joint names which suggested that the parents were in a relationship or possibly living together.) Unlike their nineteenth-century counterparts, many of these women were choosing not to marry in spite of having an ongoing relationship, and some would have chosen not to live with the father of their child. It is at this point that unmarried mothers – having previously been constructed in law as a denigrated category with corresponding 'rights' – were at last able to use their legal rights as a form of power. This power has both positive and negative dimensions. First, it enabled women to lead autonomous lives and to exercise legal rights in a situation where mothers also carried all the responsibilities for child care. In the second instance it allowed women to protect children against abusive fathers, and it protected women against remaining in impoverished relationships through the fear of losing their children. Unfortunately, the fear that increasing numbers of women might opt for 'autonomous' motherhood caused (and continues to cause) considerable alarm. For example, in 1979 the English Law Commission proposed that all biological fathers should have equal parental rights over children regardless of the nature of their relationship to the mother. What the Commission did not comprehend was that such a move would simply extend men's power over women and would do little to protect the interests of children. It was initially blinded to this possibility by its determination that women should not have more extensive legal rights than men, and by the desire to abolish the stigma of illegitimacy. However, the Commission confused two very important issues. The right to sole custody which unmarried mothers have need not be identified as a right of which men are deprived, as if to give anything to women means that men must suffer a loss. The crude calculus of equality with which the Commission worked is inappropriate to situations where responsibilities vary so greatly, and where the quality of daily care provided for a child outweighs more abstract concepts like genetic inheritance. The proposal for automatic parental rights for all biological fathers (had it been accepted) would have put men's rights first on the agenda. The imperative of equality regardless of its consequences would have given little space for the concept of the 'interests of the child' and mothers would have ranked a very poor third in the legal considerations in spite of their role as primary carers of children. Increasingly in the debates on custody in the 1980s, this hierarchy has become explicit, even though the interests of children are meant to be paramount (see Fineman, Chapter 2, Graycar, Chapter 7, and Sandberg, Chapter 5, in this volume).

CHANGING POWER CLAIMS

It is interesting to consider how it has come about that men's claims in the field of custody (of both legitimate and illegitimate children) have become an issue of primary concern. Brophy (1985) has argued that the position of married mothers improved through the vehicle of child welfare. In other words, because mothering became closely linked to the welfare of children throughout the twentieth century, and because the courts increasingly based custody decisions on the criterion of the best interests of the child, mothers benefited indirectly. At least they benefited in so far as their behaviour fitted the acceptable model of decent, chaste, deserted wife.

It was no longer feasible for fathers to assert their rights in the form and language of the Victorian patriarch. Women are no longer legally enthralled by their husbands, and economic independence from men may not be easy, but is not impossible. To reassert absolute father right would, in any case, appear to be contrary to the paramountcy of the welfare of children as currently construed. So claims to children, and indirectly to renewed authority over families and mothers, have taken several new forms and are couched in a new language. Firstly there has been the vehicle of equal rights. Whilst the law has been very slow in responding to equal rights claims by women, it appears to respond with alacrity to perceived inequalities in formal legal rights where fathers are concerned. As Sevenhuijsen (1986) has argued, men's wishes seem to become law with remarkable speed. Hence, fathers' rights groups have argued that there is an unacceptable inequality in the formal position of the unmarried father, who does not have the same rights as the unmarried mother (see De Hondt and Holtrust, 1986b). Married fathers have argued that the courts are biased in favour of mothers and have used fairly scant evidence to try to substantiate this (e.g. Maidment, 1981).

Such claims might not make much headway if it were not for the way in which they have become linked with the second form of power claim, namely that children need fathers. This claim is a direct counter-claim to the strength of the assumption that child welfare is most secure in the hands of mothers. It argues that children need their biological fathers lest they become delinquent and maladjusted (Morgan, 1986; Green, 1976). The consequences of this argument are twofold: mothers who seek divorce are seen as attempting to deprive their children of their fathers, hence they are acting selfishly and possibly against the interests of their children; next, it is argued that fathers must have joint legal custody after divorce, or at least retain generous access to their children, so there remains a father figure to establish stability. This argument now succeeds in placing fathers' rights closer to the interests of children than mothers' claims, and the value of women's nurturing work is increasingly taken for granted or diminished (see Fineman,

Chapter 2 in this volume). The more men's interests and children's interests are seen to coincide, the more mothers are disempowered; not least because for women to argue against joint custody or generous access for fathers can now be interpreted as a sign of selfishness, of a lack of maturity, and hence as a sign that women are not fit parents (see Thèry, Chapter 4, and Boyd, Chapter 6, in this volume).

Mothers, and their supposed 'prerogatives', are becoming defined as the main obstacle to the promotion of father–child relationships. This is not yet a universal trend throughout the UK because there are major regional differences in the courts' attitudes to the role of fathers in relation to children (Priest and Whybrow, 1986). However, the trends which have been identified in North America and in France are clearly noticeable here (see Thèry, Chapter 4, and Brophy, Chapter 9, in this volume). Women are seen to threaten the stability of children through their desire for autonomous motherhood in the case of unmarried mothers, or by petitioning for divorce and sole custody in the case of married women. It is becoming increasingly rare for the behaviour of mothers who resist male authority or surveillance (as opposed to assistance) to be interpreted as legitimate. Should women adopt this stance, they become defined as vengeful mothers, bitter wives, and selfish women. The question of power vanishes and the idea that women might be justified in their actions is subsumed by the trend towards pathologizing mothers who define their children's interests differently from the way the courts and conciliators wish them to (Fineman, 1988). These wholly negative images of mothers are beginning to influence the context in which reforms to the law are contemplated. Mothers who do not want joint custody, or who see their children damaged by contact with neglecting or abusive fathers, are increasingly defined as 'bad' parents. (See, for example, the discussion of the unfriendly parent in Boyd, Chapter 5, in this volume.)

THE NEW FATHERS

The bad mother is now compared to the idealized image of the father who is more than just a good economic provider, but actually becomes involved in the physical and emotional care of his children. Such men no doubt exist. The question is whether they are the vanguard of a real trend and whether they provide a sound basis for reforming laws on custody and access. Lewis and O'Brien (1987) suggest that 'discussion about the "new father" far outweighs evidence to demonstrate his existence' (p. 3). Indeed in their book they present evidence which would indicate that women retain the major responsibility for child care. This is also substant-iated by Piachaud (1984) and Jowell and Witherspoon (1985).

The Lewis and O'Brien comment is very insightful, for the new father is much discussed and is increasingly entering into popular imagery. What should be noticed about many of these recent discussions and images is that they tend to represent men with babies (as opposed to children). Much is made of men's increased attendance at the births of their children – as if this alone heralded the rise of the new fatherhood.

> The man who is there at the birth, who bonds with his baby, bathes it, changes nappies, is not afraid to express his tenderness or push a buggy. He may even swop roles with his wife and let her get back to work.

> The man who leaves his first wife and teenage children (having been nowhere near the birth and never changed a nappy), then marries a much younger woman and goes enthusiastically into the birth-bath-and-potty routine. Many a balding figure now haunts Mothercare in his lunch-hour to the secret fury, no doubt, of his ex-wife. (Libby Purves, 'Searching for the new fatherland', *The Times*, 8 September 1986, quoted in Henwood *et al.*, 1987)

The question is why are we so seduced by these ideas and images? Consider the photographic representations on the following pages. The first one portrays a bare chested young man. He has a well proportioned body and, although we cannot see his face, he gives the impression of being 'attractive'. His masculinity is connoted by his muscular frame and the dark hair on his forearms. He has a very young baby held against his chest in a close and protective embrace. The man is bare chested and the baby is naked, creating an impression of flesh against flesh and inviting the reading of 'flesh *of* my flesh'. The macho image of the man is softened by his tenderness towards the baby. This image is meant for women to consume. Its dominant message would seem to be that, even if men

11

Theater of life, Jan Saudek, © Art Unlimited 1984

appear macho, given the right circumstances they are *really* tender and caring.

The second photograph is also of a young man, who is completely naked, with a naked infant. In this image the sexual potency of the man is enhanced by the presence of the phallus (albeit truncated) and, whilst the messages of the two photographs are not dissimilar, the second one hints more at the link between a

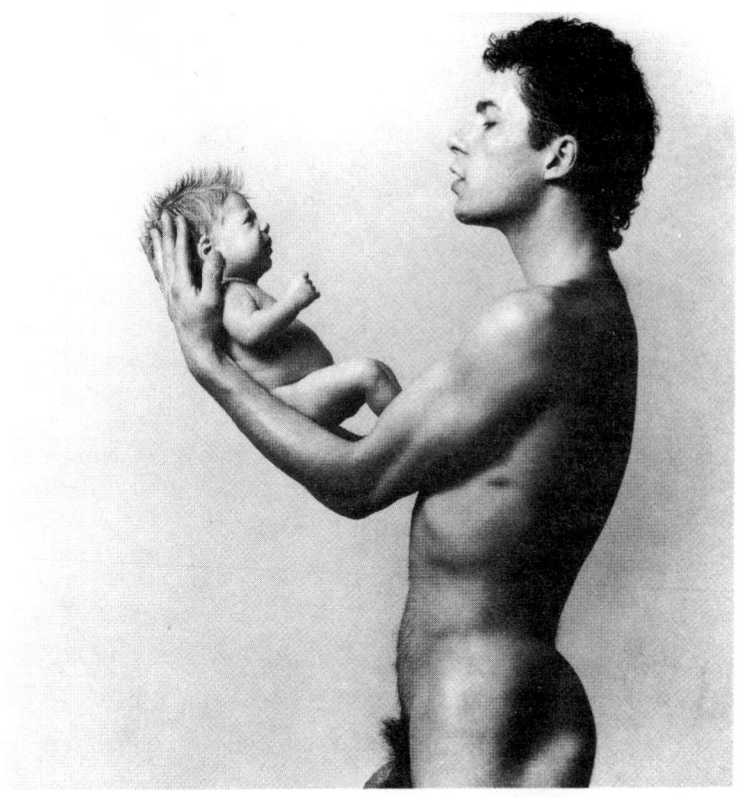

Paul en Benno, Paul Blanco, © Art Unlimited 1984

man's phallic sexuality and his reproductive capacity.[1] This is interesting inasmuch as the link between male sexuality and its reproductive consequences is ironically understated in a culture which focuses this kind of attention almost solely on women. (Although to be sexual it is assumed men must be potent and hence capable of making many women pregnant, contact with, or responsibility for, the actual product of a pregnancy carries a different set of meanings. These responsibilities are traditionally seen as women's.) The other interesting feature of the second photograph is the even more implicit association of a biological or genetic link. The baby is presented as the biological product of the man. His relationship to the child is not presented as particularly caring (even if it is somehow appreciative and self-congratulatory).

We do not expect him to move out of frame to put a nappy on the baby or to feed it. However, there is a kind of proprietorial relationship established here, one that can only be based on the idea that the infant is the man's offspring. The message of the second image does not therefore simply connote the idea of the new caring father, but the more traditional idea of the man as biological begetter with rights – albeit that in this modern version it is a highly sexualized image.

These images appear to offer women the reality of the new father – he is a real man (no hint of wimpishness here) but he loves babies. These are unrelentingly sentimental images which bear little relationship to everyday practices. Yet they do have powerful resonances, perhaps because many women do look forward to shared and equal child care responsibilities. What empirical evidence there is, however, suggests that this is a fairly fleeting sharing of interests (McKee and O'Brien, 1982). The stage of pushing prams and taking photographs palls, and mothers are left to take the burden of the basic work (Piachaud, 1984). These images give substance to a wish which is in no way a reality, and their wider influence lies in the way in which they contribute to the circulation of ideas which assert that the new fatherhood has arrived and needs to be reflected in social and legal policy.

It is interesting to consider the new fatherhood in the context of whether fathers sustain an interest in children placed in the custody of a divorced wife. In the second passage quoted from *The Times* above we are not given any indication as to whether the balding, born-again father is paying maintenance for his teenage children from the first marriage. The chances are that he is not; it is also most likely that he rarely sees the first batch of children. There are relatively few studies which look at the process by which non-custodial fathers become distanced from their children after divorce or separation, the main ones being by Wallerstein and Kelly (1980), Goldstein *et al.* (1980), and Chambers (1979) in the USA, and Mitchell (1985) and Walczak and Burns (1984) in the UK. A common finding in all these studies is the difficulty in maintaining the relationship between non-custodial parents (predominantly fathers) and children. For example, Wallerstein and Corbin (1986) state,

The most difficult and challenging psychological task for parent and child within the post-divorce family is to transplant the parent–child relationship developed within the rich soil of family life into the strange, relatively impoverished and very limited ground that the visiting relationship provides. It is no surprise that a great many parent–child relationships failed to survive the shock of the upheaval and failed additionally to take root outside the family. (p. 113)

Wallerstein and Kelly (1980) also make the point that even where visitation continues over a number of years, frequency does not equate with quality. It is also now documented how access visits by fathers diminish after they 're-partner'. It is interesting to speculate on this process and no doubt it should be recognized that it is difficult to sustain a relationship with children with whom one no longer lives. Re-partnering by men seems to be particularly important to this loss of interest (Weitzman, 1981). It might be argued that this also relates to the invisible power nexus within the family. I have argued above that fathers' relationships with children entail a power relationship with the children's mother. The exercise of access rights continues this power relation, or at least the potential for the exercise of this kind of power relationship. For example, complaints over how the children are cared for, threats to return to court, arriving late to meet the children, returning them late, giving them expensive presents that their mother could not afford may all harass the custodial parent whilst giving the non-custodial parent a sense of control. Notwithstanding that a father may have genuine feelings for his children, access gives him ample opportunity to continue his power relation with his wife or even to create a new potential for the negative expression of this power. However, once a man re-partners, and then has children by his second wife, it seems that he loses interest as one power nexus is replaced by another.

If willingness to support children economically is an index of a continuing interest in children, there is further evidence to suggest that fathers do not feel their responsibilities very heavily. There are indications that many fathers do not readily pay child maintenance for their children and that they could pay more than they do (Chambers, 1979; Weitzman, 1981; Maclean, 1987). The point that these authors make is that, in general, fathers do not fail to contribute towards the cost of child care because they cannot afford to (although remarriage and unemployment often result in inadequate resources to pay maintenance). Indeed Weitzman goes so far as to argue that whilst divorce impoverishes women and children, men's living standards (in the USA at least) rise after divorce. Evidence of this sort goes a long way to repudiate the image of the new father who takes his child care responsibilities seriously. He appears to be interested in his children's welfare only as long as they are part of 'his' household. Divorce, it would seem, does effectively divorce men from their wives *and* children.

It can, of course, be argued that the fathers who feature in the empirical research are the 'old' fathers. These are the men who did not form close bonds with their children, who were not present at their birth, who did not push the prams and change the nappies. It might be suggested that there is a time lag and that these traditional common patterns of loss of interest will change as the new generation of fathers get divorced. Such arguments are not supported by available evidence, however. For example Waller-stein and Kelly (1980) point to the lack of congruence between pre-divorce and post-divorce father–child relationships. It appears that it is very hard to predict the quality of future relationships from past ones. Notwithstanding this, the above argument remains politically attractive. It is also argued that it is because mothers are too powerful in custody arrangements that fathers are 'frozen' out of relationships with their children. Hence fathers' rights movements in the UK, USA, the Netherlands, France, and Australia all maintain that if mothers' legal and *de facto* power could be reduced, then men would remain committed to their children or, at least, feel more responsible. This argument is, in turn, linked to one which maintains that if fathers had more authority and respect in general we could avoid the perceived dangers of autonomous motherhood and could reconstruct the stable family. These ideas prevail in the writings of the New Right.

NEW FATHERS AND THE NEW RIGHT

As Brophy (Chapter 9 in this volume) points out, there has developed an interesting confluence between the ideas of the advocates of the new fatherhood in the liberal legal tradition, fathers' rights movements, and the New Right. None the less, as she points out, it is important to differentiate between fathers' rights movements, the new fatherhood as a popular ideology, and the New Right as a political discourse. The new fatherhood is based on the idea of fathers becoming engaged in what has traditionally been regarded as mothering. Hence the ideal new father does everything a mother would do, and takes on joint responsibilities for day-to-day care. This ideology is sustained in the sort of images discussed above, in films like *Three Men and a Baby*, and in media discussions of the new man. Fathers' rights movements, on the other hand, are not lobbying for the right to change nappies, for a shorter working week, or to reverse child care roles, but for greater legal control over children outside marriage (i.e. after divorce or where there has been no marriage). These are separate issues, yet the fathers' rights movements benefit from images of the new fatherhood because of the presumption that fathers are more involved with the care of their children which gives them political credit in the process of the realization of their goals. This entangling of the new fatherhood and fathers' rights movements is unfortunate for feminism, even though it is arguably of political benefit for fathers' rights. This is because the progressive potential of shared parenting has tended to become overshadowed by the way in which it can be annexed by a reactionary movement which simply aims further to empower men. Mothers who have encouraged shared parenting might now worry that they have conceded legal powers in a context in which they are socially and economically disadvantaged in comparison with their male partners.

From being a progressive ideal in the early days of the women's movement, shared parenting now seems as if it could be a Trojan horse. This transformation has to be viewed in the context of the rise of the New Right[2] in the UK and USA, but also gradually elsewhere in the western world, and the effect that this political movement has had in shifting political horizons in general to the right. The aim of the New Right, which must be distinguished from the ideology of the new fatherhood and to a large extent from the ideas of the fathers' rights movement, is to restore the paterfamilias to his rightful place in the nuclear family (Morgan, 1986; Ehrenreich, 1983; David, 1986; Petchesky, 1984). In so doing the mother needs to be restored to her rightful place too, namely the economically dependent nurturer who, through her vulnerability, will tie the husband tightly to his paternal duties. It is a core element of the New Right philosophy that women should play a vital part in re-establishing the responsibility of men for their families and in stabilizing the nuclear, heterosexual family.

There are two parallel arguments that can be differentiated here because it is easy to assume that the New Right is coterminous with the fathers' rights movement. The first argument is that women should be denied rights such as equal pay, welfare benefits, and abortion facilities in order to render them more needy of men's economic resources in the private sphere. Once returned to this so-called 'natural' state of dependency, it is argued that women will oblige men to become more responsible towards their family duties. Effectively women will have no choice but to force men to support them, since the welfare state will no longer do so if their marriages end, or if they are unmarried mothers. Women are construed as the 'tamers' of men, the anchor points for a restabilized society. In such a scenario divorce becomes less likely, and men as well as women are perceived as having less freedom to leave marriages and abandon responsibilities.

The second argument, which is the core element of the fathers' rights movement, is that men need to be given more legal rights over children because only when their legal powers are restored will men become willing to pay maintenance to children and sustain their fathering role after divorce. This argument does not envisage that men should have greater economic responsibilities for women. Indeed this is exactly where the New Right and the fathers' rights movement part company, since the former includes women in men's responsibilities, whilst the fathers' rights movement is quite content with the idea of women becoming financially independent, or dependent upon the state, after divorce. So the fathers' rights movement ignores the position of women and seeks only to establish a link with children. The New Right unites women and children in the category of men's dependants and as the vehicle of restabilization. It celebrates the idea of a return to 'traditional' roles for men and women. Finally the new fatherhood seems to invoke a new domestic order in which men become idealized nurturers.

Notwithstanding these differences, the new fatherhood, the fathers' rights movements, and the New Right have a symbiotic relationship. The political context of the New Right allows fathers' rights movements to flourish and, while the vision of the maternal father is incongruent with the New Right's vision of

18

men as efficient economic providers and a rigid sexual division of labour, it does accord with the moral vision of the father-dominated household. This coalition of forces is posing serious problems for feminist politics in the UK (and elsewhere) at a time when social and legal policy is undermining the potential for economic independence for women (Smart, 1984; Glendinning and Millar, 1987).

It is also problematic in that it is becoming clear how, once again, the enhancement of fathers' rights will increase their control over women. These developments might be seen as part of a process of 'patriarchal reconstruction'.[3] Taken out of context the fathers' rights movements might pose little threat to the advances made by women over the last century. However, resistance to the changing position of women does take a number of forms which, taken together, can be identified as a process which is weakening the gains that have been made. In the UK the changes in the provision of welfare rights and institutional care for the infirm or elderly are having a disproportionate effect on women. This is because women are required to provide the care that the state no longer offers, and women find themselves as the largest category of persons in receipt of welfare benefits (Scott, 1984; Glendinning and Millar, 1987). Such measures are not aimed at the gains of the women's movement as such, but they undermine it substantially. There are also other examples that could be drawn upon which represent a more direct challenge to the women's movement. For example attempts to reduce women's rights to abortion and to give married and unmarried fathers a voice in whether a termination should be permitted are part of a drive to re-establish men as the source of authority in households. The confluence of such diverse structural, ideological, and political developments as these are altering the context in which men's renewed claims to children after divorce should be read.

It might perhaps be useful to draw upon a recent historical analogy here to establish this point. In the UK in the 1950s and 1960s the courts became increasingly sensitive to mothers' claims to the custody of children on divorce. However, it was only possible to obtain a divorce on the grounds of a matrimonial offence; in other words it was necessary to prove that one party was guilty of adultery or cruelty or desertion, and that the other party was innocent. The courts were faced with a dilemma when 'guilty' wives were obviously the best custodians of the children after divorce. This dilemma is reflected in the following quotations uttered by judges in a range of custody cases (all quoted in Brophy and Smart, 1981):

> I think there is no doubt – and this is not a proposition of law – that from the point of view of common-sense and ordinary humanity, all things being equal, the best place for any small child is with its mother. (*H*. v. *H. and C.*, 1969)

> It could never be in the interest of the child to be entrusted to the care of a woman who had committed adultery. (*Willoughby* v. *Willoughby*, 1951)

> This [good mothering] in itself is not always enough; one must remember that to be a good mother involves not only looking after the children, but making and keeping a home for them with their father . . . in so far as she herself by her conduct broke up that home she is not a good mother. (*Re L. (infants)*, 1962)

The way in which the courts resolved this dilemma was to award 'split orders'. This meant that the mother was given 'care and control', which meant she had the responsibility for daily care (usually of young children); the father was given legal custody, which meant that he retained all the legal powers to make decisions on education, health, domicile, and so on. The mother could do very little without the father's permission; for example she could not change her children's school, or agree to let them have a medical operation. It was gradually recognized that this was an unworkable arrangement which gave rise to conflict which was ultimately damaging to children. But from the point of view of mothers, it was also intolerable in that they remained under the surveillance of their divorced husbands. It was also quite clear that the 'split order' was a kind of punishment because the courts regarded the mother to be inadequate in some way.

The question which this raises is whether we can see the same issues in the movement towards joint legal custody which is the principal demand of the fathers' rights movement in the UK. Joint legal custody would not involve men in the daily care of children, but it would enhance their access rights and would mean that they had to be consulted over major issues concerning the child. This, in itself, might seem reasonable, and indeed there is clearly consultation between many parents who have divorced anyway. The point is, however, whether this should be enshrined in a legally binding court order which becomes the norm in all cases of child custody. As Sevenhuijsen (1986) has argued, where couples co-operate they do not need a court order, but where they are in conflict the court order will only give rise to further conflict. So it is not that the idea of co-operation is problematic, it is the idea that co-operation will be forced on mothers – who continue to be the primary carers of children – in a context in which it can be used as an exercise of power over them. The joint custody order also preserves the idea that in cases of conflict the parties can return to the court for adjudication. In fact parties can do this under sole custody arrangements, but the sole custody order does, in practice, give the custodial parent a greater say in decisions where there is conflict. This operates to prevent the return to an arbitrator. Equality in decision making may have the symbolic, and practical, effect of drawing the court out of the shadows and into the arena of conflict in a much more overt way. This means that the person with the daily care of the child is much more open to surveillance by the courts. The point of divorce opens the 'private' sphere to public scrutiny (Smart, 1984); however, in most cases this scrutiny diminishes after a final court order has been made. Joint custody orders keep this door open, allowing the court the potential to keep reviewing the 'performance' of the parent with the daily care of children (i.e. predominantly mothers). The joint custody movement therefore contains many of the problems of the old 'split orders', except that they are now interpreted as being in the best interests of the children.

RESPONDING TO THE POLITICS OF CUSTODY

One major problem of strategy that feminists face in attempting to improve or protect the position of women and children in the growing conflict over custody is the formulation of a language in which women's and children's needs can be expressed. The question of the formulation of demands may seem secondary, or even superfluous, to the prior task of establishing what these needs might be. However, we already know what these needs are; the problem we face is how to establish their legitimacy, indeed the very legitimacy of any claim by women in this contested area given the existing political climate. In this volume Kirsten Sandberg (Chapter 5) goes into the needs of children in some detail, revealing how even legislation which pays lip service to the best interests of the child may operate against these very interests by inducing long drawn out procedures and creating uncertainty. Martha Fineman (Chapter 2) points to the need to recognize the importance of women's nurturing skills, and that the move to an abstract notion of welfare and equality should not render this work invisible and valueless. All of the chapters point to the vulnerability of women in the court process, and how this is being increased as new standards and norms for deciding upon custody issues are being introduced. Yet the image of how the law deals with issues of custody is quite contrary to the empirical picture that is presented in the chapters in this volume. The dominant image is one in which women are unjustifiably favoured, in which fathers are excluded to their detriment and the detriment of the children, and where the interests of the children have been misconceived. The problem that feminism faces is, therefore, not to remake the wheel by inquiring (again) into what the needs of women and children are, but to find a way of articulating these familiar needs in a form which is identified as legitimate and which can counter the strong ideological package constituted by the coalition of the New Right, the fathers' rights movements, and the imagery of the new fatherhood.

There are two formulations which have been open to feminism in the past. These are the discourse of rights (especially equal rights) and the discourse of child welfare. In the areas of guardianship (during marriage) and of child custody (after divorce) both of these discourses have been deployed, although the welfare principle has been dominant. Whilst married fathers had greater rights than mothers to exercise the prerogatives of guardianship (indeed it was not until 1973 that married women were accorded equal guardianship rights over children in marriage), in the field of custody the welfare principle has been paramount for most of the twentieth century. However, it was open to feminist campaigners to point to the undervaluation of motherhood in a legal regime which embraced unequal parental rights during marriage, so the rights discourse did not vanish completely from feminist rhetoric. The discourse of rights is also still retained in situations where there is a conflict between parents and the state, for example where social services wish to take a child into care. None the less, the welfare principle tends to take precedence over rights in questions of custody. Hence there has been the tendency for custody conflicts between divorcing parents to become focused on which parent can provide most adequately for the welfare of the child (in the future) rather than on which parent has the most legitimate rights.

This development has had a major consequence for the visibility of the mother's position in custody disputes. If she should enter into the conflict on the basis of a rights argument as a counter claim to the fathers' rights lobby, it would be presumed that she is negligent of the welfare of the weakest members of the family, namely the children. The assertion of rights by mothers has become synonymous with an assertion of selfishness. (Indeed, there is some evidence that any claim to rights by mothers has frequently been treated in this way (Brophy, 1982).) In the present this is connected to the shifting political framework of the 1980s in which the demand for rights in general has become redefined as antisocial and self seeking, rather than as socially progressive. In the specific instance of mothers, the rights claim has also been undermined by the fixed idea that to claim rights for mothers is to put the interests of women above the interests of children. This is seen as particularly offensive in a context in which it is presumed to be 'natural' for mothers to put their interests last. But it is also invidious in that it has led to a presumption that for children's interests to be met, mothers' interests must be forgone. That their interests might coincide in many instances is obscured. Rights then are increasingly perceived as 'unjust prerogatives' (see Holtrust *et al.*, Chapter 3 in this volume), a general example of this tendency being the way in which the right to strike has become redefined as an unfair burden on employers and an obstacle to free trade. Not all rights claims are disqualified in this way, however. The right to family life when this means a nuclear heterosexual family with a man as head of household is still maintained as a basic human right. Indeed we can discern a hierarchy of rights in which rights to specific forms of family life are justified whilst certain individual rights of choice and autonomy are redefined as destructive of the very right to family life.

The alternative discourse available in this field is the welfare discourse. However, as Thèry (Chapter 4 in this volume) reveals, it is not open to mothers to define the specific meaning of the welfare of children either in individual cases or in general. The concept of welfare, which has been deployed by feminists in the past, is no longer open to such a range of competing definitions. It is now secured by the welfare agencies and is less open to 'popular' redefinition. In this context it is the professional who is relied upon to divine the best interests of the child, and not the primary carer who is, by definition, seen as having vested interests. It is in an interesting Catch 22 situation that women now find themselves. If they do not invest emotionally and materially in their children they can be seen as bad mothers and undeserving of custody. But if they do invest then they are seen as having vested (and therefore selfish) interests in the decision on custody. This position therefore disqualifies them as impartial commentators on the welfare of their children and their claims for custody become treated with suspicion. In this way it becomes increasingly difficult for women to intervene in the process of defining the best interests of children.

These two discursive frameworks of rights and welfare have operated to restrict the formulation of demands for change because they have come to dominate the process of policy making. It has become almost impossible to formulate issues about custody outside these two parameters, yet since both fail to give legitimacy to the material position of mothers it is paramount to find a new mode of articulation. One attempt that has been made to circumvent these limitations is the idea of introducing a primary carer principle into custody decisions. This idea, which is discussed in detail in following chapters, offers a way out of the impasse of the rights *versus* welfare discourse, whilst remaining consistent with the overall concern for children. It also gives space for a recognition of the work of women in raising and caring for children. One of the most important aspects of the primary carer principle is that it can provide security for those parents who do most of the child care (predominantly women, although this need not remain so), and for the child. The primary carer principle would recognize the *status quo* and give benefits to those who do the caring without imposing an inflexible set of norms which presumes that only women can or should be the primary carers.

As a principle for conflict resolution the primary carer principle meets the needs of those parties who can be the most vulnerable in legal disputes, but it does not 'confiscate' rights from men. They would be in a position to change their behaviour in relation to child care which would, in turn, alter their position in law. But of equal importance is the fact that this principle does not seek to construct or impose an 'ideal' patriarchal family structure on existing households. The primary carer looks at how child care has been arranged. It does not seek to create symbolic legislation to attach men more securely to their children, nor does it seek to create an equal division of labour after divorce where none existed before. The principle puts the courts in the role of conflict resolution, not in the role of social engineering. Quite simply it would reduce the temptation for courts and welfare officers to meddle in the lives of women and children whose only reason for being subject to such official scrutiny is their involvement in the legal process of divorce. The primary carer principle is obviously not a panacea which will eliminate all conflicts in this increasingly contested area of child custody, but it goes a long way towards meeting the needs of those who are most vulnerable without imposing an inappropriate rights argument. It also restricts the ever expanding terrain of welfare discourses without abandoning a central concern for children's needs. Finally it is significant to the whole issue of power. It restricts the negative form of power, which is men's power over women which derives from their material status and from law's investment in men's symbolic role in the family. It also enhances women's power to act in the interests of children, to provide care and nurture without the fear that they will lose their children on the basis of a decision which reflects new fashions in psychological or legal thinking rather than the material conditions of child care.

The problem with the prevailing debate on child custody is that it refuses to acknowledge that there are power relations inherent in these familial relationships. Where they are acknowledged they are assumed simply to be bad, as considerations which should be expunged as damaging to the ideal of post-divorce family life. This is to misconstrue the situation facing men, women, and children in such a way that the interests of those who have fewer resources or opportunities to exercise power are simply neglected. We must deconstruct notions like the 'best interests of children', or the ideology of the new fatherhood to ensure that legal and social policy does not relegate caring and nurturing by women to the lowest priority whilst redefining women's objections as individual pathologies or selfish vested interest.

NOTES

I am very grateful to Selma Sevenhuijsen, Julia Brophy, and Martha Fineman for their invaluable comments on earlier drafts of this chapter. I am also grateful for their sisterly support.

1　It should also be noted that this sexualized image can have a different and more sinister meaning. The man's sexuality may be read as being directed towards the infant in a way that implies the potential for child sexual abuse. In this sense these images can be distastefully ambiguous and can cause considerable distress to incest survivors.

2　It is not easy to define the term the New Right, not least because it does not form a discrete political grouping, and because many of its core ideas are not exactly new (Green, 1987). However, it represents a coalition of views which have gained political ascendancy in the west since the 1970s. It combines economic policies such as monetarism, with social policies on welfare, health, and housing which embody notions of reducing government support and encouraging privatization and individualization of provision. It also entails the development of policies and discourses on the family, sexuality, and morality, with so-called fundamental issues like sexual behaviour being foregrounded as major political (as opposed to private) matters. The New Right has therefore become associated with the idea of a remoralization of society, and hence its focus (direct and indirect) on women who are largely identified as their most appropriate individual agents of remoralization.

3　I am grateful to Selma Sevenhuijsen for suggesting that the term patriarchal reconstruction would be useful in this context.

CASES

H. v. H and C. (1969). All England Law Reports, vol. 1, p. 263.
Re L. (infants) (1962) All England Law Reports, vol. 3, p. 4.
Willoughby v. *Willoughby* (1961) Probate, p. 184.

Chapter Two

THE POLITICS OF CUSTODY AND GENDER:

Child Advocacy and the Transformation of Custody Decision Making in the USA

MARTHA L. FINEMAN

INTRODUCTION

In recent years, increased political attention in the United States has focused on the family as an institution in a state of crisis and transition. Advocates of various reforms assert that the stresses of modern life, particularly the high divorce rate, will certainly change the family. The family is viewed as an institution in a transitional stage and, as such, is the subject of ideological struggle within the context of the political system (Fineman, 1980).

The assumptions underlying a variety of suggested reforms in the rules that govern families reveal the tensions in conflicting attitudes concerning the institution. Separated out for particular concern have been the children, anointed as the 'victims' of the dislocations in the modern family. For example, moral and political concerns over the implications of the no-fault, freely accessible divorce systems adopted by the states have tended to centre on the resulting precarious position of the 'children of divorce'.

Characterization of children as the innocent victims, in need of protection from their parents' licentious ways, is typical of professional reformers' rhetoric in this age of no-fault divorce. Not surprisingly, there is a strong underlying anti-divorce aspect to much of this rhetoric and the reforms it supports. While there is no longer serious consideration of the idea that the law should prohibit or make it difficult to divorce, the terms of the dissolution and the structuring of post-divorce relationships are going to be dictated and monitored by the state. In the custody area this is manifested by rules that seek to preserve as much as possible the pre-divorce power and authority relationships between fathers and their children (Fineman, 1988). Even though access to divorce has been eased and women's economic position improved, the state's supervision of the termination process and its imposition of substantive standards regulating the post-divorce mother–child unit have been greatly increased.

This increased state regulation of the post-divorce family has occurred against the backdrop of significant social and legal developments that have characterized the establishment of, and response to, the women's movement in the United States. During the 1970s there were successful attempts in most states to make laws 'gender neutral'. Such campaigns were particularly significant in the family law area where gendered rules had been the norm. The push for degendered rules was considered a symbolic imperative by feminists concerned with law reform even when it was recognized that such reforms might actually result in removing an arguable advantage for women, as in the case of maternal preference rules for deciding custody cases (Fineman, 1983).

It is interesting to note how much more successfully the equality model has been adopted and implemented in the context of family law as compared to more general laws. As equality and the concurrent concept of gender neutrality have been incorporated into divorce decision making, the old, tested gendered rules that permitted predictable inexpensive decisions to be made in most cases without protracted litigation have been set aside. One problem confronting the newly formally-degendered family law system is the need to create new gender neutral factors or processes to handle the cases (Chambers, 1984). The need for an authoritative articulation of alternative standards has set the stage for political and ideological battles.

In addition, the women's movement's push for equality in the family and workplace generated various backlashes. For example, the economic reforms concerning property divisions at divorce met with resistance. Stringent proposals for state and federal provisions for the collection of unpaid child support were argued for with rhetoric that labelled delinquent fathers as 'deadbeats'. This generated defences by newly formed fathers' rights groups that linked men's failure to get custody to refusals to pay child support. These groups appropriated and successfully employed the feminist rhetoric of equality to force reforms in the family law area, such as mandatory joint custody, which were not particularly beneficial to women and children (Fineman and Opie, 1987). Joint custody legislation has become increasingly popular in the United States and many statutes permit it to be imposed by courts even if one parent objects.[1]

Fuelling the success of the fathers' rights groups have been various professionals involved in the divorce process who viewed the traditional rules as imbalanced in favour of women. These professionals used the images of excluded (but worthy and caring) dads to fashion a professional standard of 'shared parenting' after divorce. This new norm was to be implemented via the mediation skills of these same professionals (Fineman, 1988).

This chapter considers one aspect of this political struggle over the control of custody decision making at divorce. I am particularly interested in two developments: first, the construction and articulation of a need for independent, legal child advocacy at divorce; second, the designation of certain professionals as the source of wisdom in regard to appropriate advocacy for children. I argue that these developments reveal ideological changes in society's perception of the mother–child bond that occurred as a by-product of the move to gender neutral family law.

The institutionalization and professionalization of the concept of child advocacy has been one development that has operated to justify the way states currently regulate custody decisions at divorce in favour of increasing control by men over their children's and thus their ex-wives' lives. The proposals for reforms in this area also reflect competing perceptions of large segments of the legal and non-legal professional communities about the functioning of families and individuals within families, about the implications of divorce, and about the appropriate role of the legal system in the creation and imposition of social norms. This chapter will critically analyse these developments.

I will first consider the factors which set the stage for the development of the concept of independent child advocacy and how that concept has been put into operation. I will then examine two foundational assumptions underlying the concept of in-dependent child advocacy. The first assumption is that the child should be considered as separate from the parent. The second is

29

that it is possible to define children's interests independently when they are conceptually separated and set apart from parental interests. I conclude ultimately that the presentation of independent child advocacy as a necessary and desirable goal in the divorce process in fact operates to empower certain professionals, greatly increasing the power of fathers in the process, but cannot realistically be viewed as providing benefits to children. In order to avoid these tendencies, I suggest that nurturing behaviour be recognized and rewarded by the adoption of the 'primary caretaker' rule for determining custody at divorce. This rule values caretaking and dilutes the power of the helping professionals in custody decision making.

THE POLITICS OF CUSTODY

The need for advocacy

The ideal of child advocacy in divorce was the creation (at least initially) of the legal profession[2] and was presented as the integration of legal and social science skills (Stone, 1982). In part, the creation of the role was the early recognition on the part of judges and family court personnel that the best interest test was not functioning well in the traditional adversarial court context.

The creation of something like the child advocate position was an inevitable product of the general unease generated by the widespread acceptance of no-fault divorce and by the breakdown of the best interest of the child test.[3] The best interest test became unworkable when the old rules of thumb, such as a maternal preference, which were used to implement it were attacked as unacceptable standards for custody decision making. The emphasis on gender neutrality, which occurred in part as a result of feminist agitation, called into question the desirability of the presumption that children belonged with their mothers unless they were unfit.[4] Gendered considerations began to fade from favour as a way to make custody decisions, and were even attacked as unconstitutional in some states.[5]

The determination of fault had also earlier provided a way for the traditional legal process to resolve custody issues. The adulterers, wife beaters, and others that the court found at fault, lost custody of their children. As gender and fault disappeared from the process it became apparent that the best interest test had worked, in part, because these other references had served to resolve most cases. Increasingly, the best interest of the child test, degendered and free from fault, began to be viewed as unworkable in any context by the judges and attorneys who had to employ it (Mnookin, 1975). The search began for other sources of decision making (Chambers, 1984).

For purposes of this discussion, the significance of the continued use of the best interest test in the context of post maternal-preference and post fault is found in its theoretical separation of the child from the family. When the courts operated with the norm of maternal preference, the child was conceptually aligned with the mother and, in the absence of compelling evidence, it was presumed that she acted in her child's interest. The designation of the 'innocence' when divorce was based on proving 'fault' could also be viewed as functioning in the same way, namely as an allocation device. The consequence of removing these 'easy' indicators has meant that we must focus on the child only, as an independent individual, with interests which may differ from both of his or her parents'. It is this development that has clearly created the need for an advocate for the child, as distinct from those who represent the parents or family.

The resort to non-judicial decision makers in order to apply the best interest standard masks the severe problems with the substantive test. It does not solve them and, in fact, allows the best interest test to remain functional long after it should have been discarded. The best interest test has tremendous symbolic appeal, however, focusing as it does on the 'child'. In addition, attacks on the test are easily deflected within the context of the current paradigm that views families as mere collections of individuals whose interests are often in conflict. Attempts to change the test to make it more predictable are met with charges that parents' interests are being substituted for those of children. Continued adherence to the best interest test has serious consequences, however. It has necessitated a continuous search for alternatives to the court as the legal decision maker in custody cases. Judges are uncomfortable with the lack of specificity in the test and resorting to the helping professions as assessors of what constitutes the best interest of a child has become a widespread practice (Okpaku, 1976; Levy, 1985).

The failures of legal institutions

The two legal institutions which have been instrumental in the development of the idea of an independent advocacy function in regard to children's interests at divorce are the courts and the legislatures of the states. Both of these legal institutions make legal decisions in different ways and with different constraints, all of which impact on the institutions' respective abilities to address custody issues in a coherent manner. Courts, for example, are traditionally considered inappropriate to formulate major policy directives because they are institutions which resolve disputes between individuals. As a result, the courts define and resolve custody questions in individual cases by focusing on the rights or obligations of the individual members. The current best interest of the child test encourages this.

The best interest test necessitates a comparison of parents' qualities and a determination as to which of them would be the preferable custodian. The test is so fact and circumstance specific that it defies any articulation of universal standards other than that embedded in the test itself – namely that the court is making the determination which is in the best interest of this specific child. No wonder the courts have welcomed the idea of an independent child advocate under the best interest test! A child advocate, particularly when that advocate is also an attorney, allows the adversary nature of the proceeding to operate while presenting a neutral actor with the task of ensuring that the child's interests are not sacrificed to the parents' anger. With gendered decision making no longer permissible and no other societal norm emerging as the replacement for the preference for maternal custody, courts must search for efficient ways to make individual custody decisions. The child's advocate presents a procedural solution which allows courts to conclude, somewhat complacently, that the child's interests are in fact brought to light and protected.

Legislatures, in contrast to courts, have the capacity to perform as broad policy making bodies, but are susceptible to political pressures and the creation of simplistic, universally imposed, idealized norms. This tendency has been demonstrated in the entire spectrum of divorce reform, from marital property rules to the establishment of a preference for joint custody (Fineman, 1983; Fineman, 1986; Fineman and Opie, 1987). Legislatures have been particularly responsive to the equality rhetoric of the fathers' rights groups in the divorce area. Equality as a model for decision making has symbolic as well as political appeal. In the case of child advocacy, many states' legislatures now require separate representation for children when custody is contested, and a few have proposed that such advocacy be provided whenever a divorce involves children, even if there is no contest over custody.[6] In the latter situation, merely the fact that there are children is considered sufficient to trigger the need for advocacy. The situation of divorce provides the *prima facie* need for child advocacy independent of whether there is conflict between the parents.

Complicating the inherent problems with legislatures or courts as rational policy and decision making institutions is the fact that doctrinal family law during the past several decades has rejected the idea that the family has 'rights' associated with it as a unit or as an 'entity'. The thrust of law concerning the family in the USA currently reflects an adherence to the notion that the family is nothing more than a collection of individuals, each with specific individuated and potentially conflicting 'rights'.[7] Therefore the real unit of modern concern for family law and policy, and the legal institutions which implement them, is the individual. Laws focus on single issues isolated from other circumstances in order to 'help' specific family members. Family law has begun to reflect an assumption that the family may be harmful to an individual's (economic, emotional, and physical) health (Fineman, 1980).

In order to minimize the evils inherent in divorce the law focuses on and identifies the rights of the individuals. When the individual is a child, we have created a situation which mandates the use of state authority to intervene in a 'protective' manner. Children as one set of individuals with separate and potentially conflicting rights and interests from their parents need an 'advocate' and the state is the logical supplier of persons to assure that role.

In the best interest of the child

Gender neutrality and the custody debate The power and persuasiveness of the attack on gendered decision making in the custody area has had more profound impacts than merely making the legislatures' or judges' tasks more difficult. In fact, it seems that the force of the gender neutral logic has been extended beyond explicitly gendered rules to those that merely operate to produce results which tend to favour one gender over the other (Fineman and Opie, 1987).

This fetish with gender neutrality has had important implications both for the articulation of what substantively constitutes 'the best interest of the child' and for what safeguards are considered necessary to achieve it. For example, rules that focus on the performance of nurturing or caretaking tasks as the basis for preferencing parents have been attacked, not because they are explicitly gender biased, but because in operations they will act to favour women who traditionally perform such tasks.[8] Nurturing as a decisional value, even though it is not inherently gendered and is potentially a choice for both men and women, is thus devalued. The search is not only for language, but for factors that are gender neutral.

This expanded version of neutrality favours fathers. It removes, by labelling them gendered, the things women typically tend to do for children, which are grouped under the term 'nurture'. Neutrality in this regard, in the context of an active and operating gendered system of lived social roles, is anti-maternal and is hardly gender neutral in its impact.[9]

In addition this expanded concept of neutrality operates to set the stage for increased state control over custody decisions. Experts, from the legal as well as the helping professions, are necessary to construct and implement new degendered standards and procedures under the best interests test (Okpaku, 1976). The rationale for this increased intervention is, of course, the presence of children. Children are used politically as the imprimatur for the development of processes and rules which conceptually alienate children from their parents and place their future in the control of state designated experts.

ο *Concern for the child and the custody debates* The control over decisions concerning the custody of children has been increasingly viewed as appropriately removed from parents and placed within the public or political sphere. This shift in the perception concerning the locus of legitimate custody decision making is evident through a variety of transformations in the way that the issue is discussed and understood. For example, increasingly, the mere presence of children at divorce, whether there is conflict over

QUESTIONS ABOUT THE CURRENT PARADIGM

There are two critical problems lurking within the idea of a child advocacy that I want to explore. The first problem is with the creation and acceptance of the child as an independent client separable from his or her parent and in need of advocacy services at divorce. Even were the need for such advocacy clear, however, there is a second problem concerning the process for the articulation and definition of the child's best interest. The very fact that the client is also a child raises questions about the feasibility of accomplishing this difficult task.

The creation of the child-client

When one takes a serious historical look at the academic literature that underlies the notion of an advocate for children in divorce cases, one is struck by the fact that neither the arguments for, nor the arguments against, the institution have changed much over the past several decades (Okpaku, 1976). Essentially the assertion is made that children need representation, that they are victimized by divorce, and that the traditional adversary process does not protect them and may even further victimize them (Hansen, 1966; Litwack *et al.*, 1979–80). There has been little conceptual development beyond this assertion, however. There is no consensus about the functions that a child advocate should perform or even who should serve as the advocate. It is an ideal that continues to be ill-defined. None the less, because of the political context of current family law reform efforts, it is an increasingly powerful ideal, even if idiosyncratically implemented in the form of a variety of asserted 'child centred' reforms which are ineffectively criticized or controlled.[11]

The focus of advocacy The child is now viewed as a free floating entity who is the focus of the custody proceeding. Like all assertions of 'rights' in the United States with its constitutional tradition, the language used in advancing arguments for child advocacy is symbolically powerful and compelling. This is particularly true because the term 'child' is highly sentimentalized in our culture. For example, in an early Family Court 'Bill of Rights for Children in Divorce Actions', the first right listed is that of the child 'to be treated as an interested and affected person and not as a pawn, possession or chattel, of either or both parents'. The justification for child advocacy is set forth in the form of a right attached to the child:

> recognition that children involved in a divorce are always disadvantaged parties and that the law must take affirmative steps to protect their welfare, including the appointment of a guardian *ad litem* to protect their interests.[12]

Note that this bill of rights emphasizes children's need for, and right to, protection from their parents. This protection is to be implemented through a legal advocate. The right of the child to advocacy is one to which the state must respond. Intervention is not only desirable but inevitable. The entire argument is built upon the unquestioned assertion that children were being used as 'pawns', or were viewed as 'property' by their parents.[13]

The acceptance of children as victims, which is evidenced by the rhetoric surrounding discussions of divorce and is manifest in the interpretation of the best interest test, is the ideological basis upon which the arguments for increased state involvement implemented through extra-judicial actors have been constructed. The result is that a battery of experts who are presumed to act in the best interests of children is added to the process. Furthermore, both the questions and the solutions concerning any individual child are developed independent of parental decisions or initiative. The description and characterization of the problems facing the child, the important judgements which must be made, and the solutions which are suggested, are all in the hands of the professionals. The rationale for this is that the parents, experiencing divorce, can no longer be trusted to act in the child's interest. If a child's future cannot be entrusted to his or her parents, then a child advocate is essential. The fact that they are enmeshed in an adversarial contest alone is sufficient to deem them incapable of acting in their child's best interest. They are assumed to be only concerned with their own self-serving ends.

The advocates A significant component of the modern, de-gendered, regulatory, and highly interventionist view of divorce, is the notion that the state's historic interest in protecting children establishes a legitimate avenue for the exercise of state control through judgements at divorce about parenting behaviour. This judgement process is dependent upon the designation of additional professional personnel for intervention into families.

If judges need to make decisions based on considerations of what is in the best interest of the child, but feel unprepared to do so, they must look elsewhere for answers. For the most part they have looked to members of the 'helping professions', but legal specialists acting in the child's interest have also been employed. It is not surprising that since the conceptual separation of the child occurs in the context of a divorce proceeding, which is always a legal proceeding, child advocacy in the divorce context has become increasingly understood to be a requirement for separate legal representation. The best interest of the child test, therefore, is a substantive rule which, in order to be appropriately implemented, has the effect of creating a 'client', the child, for the legal advocate. At the same time, the formalization of the idea, and the designation of a child's advocate, allows the best interest test to remain the substantive standard. In these ways, the procedural innovation of the child advocate masks the substantive test's inadequacies. It replaces discredited social norms, such as maternal custody, with a legal actor characterized as neutral, thus insulating the test from effective attack.

Implications of the paradigm

There are two questions which we should ask. The first is whether or not it is accurate, or helps discussion of the issues, to cast children as victims of divorce. The second question to consider is, even if children are victimized by divorce, does this necessitate the establishment of separate, independent legal advocacy? The first question should give rise to additional ones. For example, if it is true that, typically, parents during the divorce process are so self-absorbed as to use their children as 'pawns', is it not appropriate that child advocates should be required in all divorces where there are children? After all, pawns are not only sacrificed in games that end up in court, but are equally at risk in negotiated or non-contested cases.[14]

Further, and most importantly, if it is true that a large number of parents can comfortably be presumed to have the tendency to sacrifice their children's well-being in this way, is not the real conclusion we should reach that there are a lot of people out there who are unfit parents, unable to separate out their own needs and act in their children's best interest? Could they ever be trusted to do so? Can a parent who views his or her children as 'property', or treats them as 'pawns', be expected to convert and be non-exploitative with the granting of divorce decree and custody award?

The second question about the ability of child advocacy to remedy victimization also raises additional considerations focused on what purpose, either ideologically or politically, such advocacy actually serves. The typical characterization of the problem places a lot of faith in professionals and assumes that, at best, parents involved in the vast majority of custody cases become temporarily incapable of acting in both their own and their children's interests. I am not sure we should be satisfied by unadorned assertions of wanton parental self-absorption and blatant sacrifice of children's interests, no matter the degree of professional assurance or force with which they are made.

The net result of the uncritical acceptance of the child-as-victim construct is state sponsored substitution of informal non-legal professional decision making for that of parents or that of the courts. The significant input into the custody decision making process is no longer through parents, but professionals, inaccurately designated as 'neutral' or 'disinterested', and legitimated by the notion that they alone are capable of acting in the best interest of children. Furthermore, the locus for the decision making is no longer the judge, but these same professionals. I am far from convinced that this development is necessarily to the benefit of children, and have serious doubts as to whether it is even desirable.

¶ *Construction of the child-client's 'best interest'*

Related to the observation that the terms of the substantive legal test for custody have created a climate where we easily accept the conclusion that there is a necessity for child advocacy is the question of how this child's best interest is to be ascertained. When the child is perceived as separate or independent – a client in need of separate counsel – there must be some way in which to assess what the content or goal of the representation should be. How does the child's advocate in the divorce proceeding determine what is in the child's best interest, and act to advocate that interest?

If the advocate is a member of the helping professions the assumption is that he or she possesses the skills to make the best interest determination. Normally, however, these professionals are not advocates within the context of particular cases, but are viewed as expert, neutral witnesses. Thus professional assessments are conceived of as evidence to assist in the determination of best interests, but another actor is necessary to perform the advocacy role in the adversary context – to represent the child. In most instances this advocate is a lawyer.

The presence of an attorney as the child's advocate creates problems that transcend (while they also complicate) the problems associated with the involvement of mental health professionals who customarily perform evaluations. This is particularly true because of role confusion between these professions, coupled with uncertainty as to whom and what is represented.

The function of the legal advocate Even if one accepts the idea of a need for independent child advocacy, a critical problem is connected to this perceived need for legal representation or an adversarial 'champion'. Once we establish a need, we must consider the problem of the appropriate function of the independent child's advocate. This creates a dilemma for the advocate which is dependent upon the acceptance of the characterization or creation of the child-client as potential victim of his or her parents. If this is true, then parents cannot be trusted to provide objective or neutral information about the child and his or her interests. All information from them is suspect. The advocate must construct a vision of the child's best interest – that which is to be represented or advocated – independent of parental input.

Since the modern conceptualization of the process has already eliminated parents as sources of this best interest determination and the desire for gender neutrality has made suspect social and informal empirical observations about mothers and nurturing, we are left with three potential sources of determination. The easiest to dispose of quickly are the suggestions that we look to the child to ascertain what solution should be advocated. The legal advocate could ask the child which parent he or she prefers, and then advocate whatever result the child indicates. This is roughly how an attorney would act in representing a competent adult client. Since many children are unable, or unwilling, to express a preference as between competing potential custodial parents, and since some research indicates that it even may be harmful for older, competent children to choose between parents at divorce, the children's choice approach is not considered a viable option, at least for children under the age of 14 or 15.[15]

The vast majority of the supporters of legal child advocacy do not adhere to such a narrow view of their responsibility. They do not conceptualize the role of the child advocate as being an advocate for the child, *per se*, but as an advocate for the child's best interest. This is a distinction of considerable importance. Instead of merely representing the child's preference, such an approach demands that the child's legal advocate undertake the task of making an assessment or evaluation of what is in the child's best interest that is independent of, though it may consider, the child's wishes as to his or her custody.

The advocate and ascertaining best interest How can the legal advocate make an evaluation of what is in a child's best interest? In practical terms the requirement of independent advocacy means that there are two non-parental contenders for primary determiners of the best interest of the child at divorce. There is a need not only for the advocacy, but also for the construction of the child's interest. The societal signals which would indicate that in most instances this would lead to a maternal preference are to be excluded by the demands of gender neutrality. Structurally, we are then presented with a choice between the two types of professionals who hover around the divorce process – the legal advocate on the one hand, and the helping professional on the other.

The legal professional may make the decision, acting as both an investigator and collector of information, and thereafter as an informed expert who has examined the evidence and reached a conclusion, of what is in the best interest of the child. This choice creates the necessity for the legal advocate to investigate, to collect information from both experts and non-experts about the child and family, and to make a judgement about what should be the appropriate placement. The legal advocate acts in this regard as an investigator and as an expert within the legal process. The role of advocate is one with a substantive dimension.

Not only has a client been created for the legal advocate, but the characteristics of that client necessitate that one primary function for the legal advocate is to construct this client's interest in a manner which, to a large extent, is independent of the client's direction. In this instance, where the legal advocate is making an independent assessment of the quality of evidence accumulated, he or she is no better equipped than a judge to make such an assessment, and would seem, for that reason alone, to be unnecessary to the process.

By contrast, the legal advocate's role may be more limited and the various mental health professionals, who have increasingly become more significant in the divorce context, will explicitly serve as the arbiters of the child's best interest. In this process, the legal advocate often acts as nothing more than the advocate of the opinions of expert helping professionals (psychological, psychiatric, or social work) as to what is in the child's best interest (Levy, 1985). The legal advocate then operates to represent the experts' conclusions and, in effect, the mental health professional becomes the substituted client (he or she who speaks for the constructed child-client – the vehicle through which the child's best interest is realized).

Increasingly the conclusions of experts in this area have been centred on imposing the ideal of shared parenting after divorce. In a gender neutral world perceived to require the devaluation of nurturing, they have undertaken the task of bringing fathers back into the post-divorce picture. This has resulted in the creation of professional norms which would give custody to the 'most generous parent', or the parent most willing to share the child with the other parent. A desire for sole custody has now been labelled 'pathological' and is to be discouraged or punished by legal rules which mandate post-divorce co-operation and sharing (Fineman, 1988). The child advocate is part of a larger process whereby professional norms such as these are incorporated and made operative within the context of the legal system. The child advocate ends up representing the professional ideal.

Function of the independent advocate in practical terms There is an important additional problem with the concept of a legal advocate as a child's independent advocate. It is not clear why one needs a legal advocate to interpret and assess expert and other information and reach a conclusion as to the best interest. Is this not what a judge would usually do? What does an attorney for the child add in this process? In some instance, perhaps, some witnesses not called by a parent might be produced, or an expert employed who was not consulted by either parent, nor scheduled by court personnel. One wonders how often such a positive contribution by the legal advocate occurs, however, and whether the information placed before the judge in such cases is typically dispositive, or merely cumulative.

Although there are few benefits, there are real dangers in accepting the child advocacy model. Where the legal advocate represents the helping professional's opinion as to the child's best interest, the presence of an attorney designated as the child's advocate may in fact give added, undue weight to professional advice that should be only one factor in fashioning a judge's opinion. The legal advocacy aspect of the role may result in the social worker or psychologist functionally being the ultimate custody decision maker when the child's attorney uses professional recommendations to establish his or her assessment of what is in the child's best interest.

A primary issue in the current construction of the various roles in custody decision making should be the consideration of whether the legal advocate can be independent of the mental health professional. It is a powerful combination when social worker and child's attorney agree, for whatever reason. In addition, the judge's role may be compromised. The presence of the child's legal advocate may present an easy way out for the judge. It provides the judge with an additional referent - another neutral actor who is cast as representing only the child's interest and, for that reason, allows the illusion that his or her conclusions can be safely trusted.

POLITICAL IMPLICATIONS OF THE ACCEPTANCE OF THE IDEA OF CHILD ADVOCACY

As stated earlier in this chapter, the crux of the problem, and what necessitates the development of institutions like the guardians *ad litem* or children's legal advocates, is the evolving substantive standard which applied in its contemporary gender neutral manner is so amorphous, undirected, incomprehensible, and indeterminate as to be meaningless without a substantial extra-judicial implementation team. The only response to a degendered, no-fault divorce system, short of scrapping the best interests of the child test, is the creation of alternative decision makers, and the referral of all substantive decisions to them. There are problems with this no matter which professional is the source of the best interest determination. The problems for a legal advocate are extreme, however. The legal advocate, as the advocate of best interest, will inevitably be in the position of merely parroting idealized notions of what is in all children's best interest according to the current theories of mental health professionals.

The legal advocate functions to give the illusion of neutrality to the decision making process. They allow the system to limp along without serious reassessment of the political and practical roles played by mental health professionals and other child advocates. As a result the definition of what is in the best interest of a child is arrived at through the use of processes and standards which enhance the position and power of these same professionals. Custody decision making and the rules that govern it are more than just making individual decisions regarding placement of children. Submerged in the rules and processes are political and ideological conflicts between 'mothers' (or nurturing and caretaking values) and 'fathers' (or independence and financial security values); between the professions of law (or advocacy and adversariness as values) and the helping professions (or treatment and therapy as values); between the moralists (who would burden the divorce system so as to impede or discourage divorce and to punish those who seek to divorce) and the secularist (who would seek to implement rules that ensure no one loses too much if he or she decides to leave a marriage). The illusion and pretence of objectivity and neutrality, of which the legal advocate is but one part, serves the interests of those empowered by the *status quo* and the bias in professional opinion making.

A LIMITED ROLE FOR THE CHILD'S LEGAL ADVOCATE

In spite of the problems with the idea of child advocacy addressed in this chapter, I do think that those concerned with children's welfare could perform two valuable and needed political functions. First, in individual cases, someone designated as a child advocate could bring legal values, such as due process and a preference for public decision making, back into a process that has become so informal and non-legal as to operate often according to the whims of politically unaccountable professionals, or to be driven by professional fads and biases.

Second, on the level of law reform, the potential child advocate could lobby for the replacement of the best interest of the child test with a more determinative substantive rule – one less dependent on the helping professionals, more attentive to the traditional legal decision making, and more responsive to the parent who performs the actual child caretaking responsibilities. As the substituted rule, I suggest the primary caretaker rule which rewards past care and concern for children and minimizes the role and power of the helping professionals in custody decision making.

The primary caretaker rule has been criticized as merely being the old maternal preference in gender neutral terms because it would operate within our current social situation to award custody more often to mothers than to fathers. It seems to me that the fact that this is offered as a criticism shows how far we have strayed in the United States from real concern for children to a desire to adhere to simplistic notions of equality between spouses at divorce. The primary caretaker rule is gender neutral on its face and men can change their behaviour if they want to have an opportunity to get custody. The rule values nurturing and caretaking and rewards it. This is appropriate.

In addition, one advantage of the primary caretaker rule is that the evidence on which it relies can be gleaned in open court according to our notions of due process and publicly accountable decision making.[16] It avoids the need for speculation, assessments about psychological consequences of attributes, and refocuses responsibility for the decision on the parents and, if they cannot agree, on the judge who must make the factual finding as to who has cared for the child. Therefore, the rule takes decision making away from the helping professionals.

There have always been voices of doubt raised about the effectiveness of the current system with its reliance on predictions about the future well-being of children based on scanty evidence of questionable validity. The legal advocate could best serve the interests of children by not viewing him or herself as only a part of a best interest team. The legal advocate should not be aligned with any other professional, but should remain sceptical and critical of them all. The helping professional experts would be presumed to be useful only to weed out or identify those parents who are clearly unfit to care for their children. Providing that the tests and methods of such professionals are reliable, they can tell us who falls below a legally defined bright line. Their opinions as to the superior parent – the one who most resembles their professional ideal and which in current practice would be the best interest recommendation – should be viewed as just an opinion. At most it would be entitled to no more respect than any other opinion; optimally it would be excluded as irrelevant in most custody determinations.

The legal advocate's function would, in those few cases where necessary, ensure that the helping professional's opinion was not overvalued in contrast with information more relevant to the determination of who had acted as the primary caretaker – that supplied by teachers, neighbours, and others who have more extensive exposure to the individual child. The legal advocate would act as a check on the private informal decision making process. In this way, professional biases (such as the current ones favouring shared parenting or creating a custody preference for the 'most generous parent') would be recognized as a professional bias, an ideological conclusion, and subjected to vigorous and critical probing. This would truly be in the child's best interest.

When experts do testify, the expert's education and experience would be explored by the legal advocate. Supervision and a critical assessment of the fact gathering process of the mental health professional would be essential functions for the legal advocate in fulfilling his or her responsibility to the child. The goal would be to expose, and thus examine, the process of reaching a non-legal professional opinion. What has been lost under the current practice of deferral to the helping professions are legal procedural values such as due process and public decision making, in addition to the undervaluing of nurturing and caretaking. The current referral to extra-judicial personnel may make us feel at ease because we can believe that some professional is appropriately taking care of the custody business, but that illusion may not work in the best interest of the children.

CONCLUSION

My suggestion that the limited role for those concerned with children and the divorce process be confined to bringing custody decision making back to a more traditionally legal model is not meant to convey the impression that the legal system is without substantial, wide-reaching flaws. Judges and attorneys may also be moved by fads, subjected to pressures, and operate from biases. I do believe, however, that the imperfect legal system historically has created better rules for women and children than the equally imperfect child-centred, therapeutic, mental health professional system that is now dominant.

The therapeutic/child advocacy model has had two extremely negative effects. In the first instance, it is premised upon the conception of the child as separate, independent, and removed from his or her mother. This individualization concept permeates our thinking about mothers and children. In its extreme form, it allows us to create, and then dissect, something termed the 'maternal–foetal conflict', a concept that places a woman in an adversary role with the foetus she carries.[17] In the divorce context, individualization compels us to appoint an advocate in order potentially to define and represent a child's interest against his or her mother or nurturer.

In the second instance, the therapeutic/child advocacy model has enhanced the role of professionals as decision makers in a degendered system. Nurturing and caretaking have become suspect and devalued because they are gendered and, thus, typically will favour mothers over fathers in deciding custody. The legal system's traditional fact finding methodology is compatible with valuing, nurturing, or sacrificing for children. Neighbours and family members can testify as to who cared for the child as a matter of historic fact and, if the decisional value is nurturing, decisions can be made quickly and reasonably well in most cases. Deprived of such a value reference, the system has had to resort to professionals who supply their own set of norms under the guise that they are neutral and are alone qualified by temperament and training to act as advocates for the child.

As it has evolved, any claims for the specialness of the relationships between mothers and children have been eradicated from the system under the dictates of gender neutrality. The professional child advocate now acts with the social sanctity once afforded to mothers by preferring them as custodians. The process has become bureaucratized, is made more technical, and the stage is set for massive intervention by the state through professionals, all of whom justify their usurpation of decision making authority as in the best interest of the child.

NOTES

1 See, for example, Florida Statute § 63.13 which establishes a presumption of shared parenting, regardless of parent objection, unless the party opposing such a disposition establishes that joint custody would be detrimental to a child.

2 The potent idea of a legal advocate for children in divorce actions can be traced back to a series of articles, which constituted a campaign by judges in the United States to provide protection for children from the adversary model. An early proposal was for a 'friend of the child' to be assigned (Drian, 1962). Judge Hansen made the issue into a 'campaign' (Hansen, 1966).

3 The best interest of the child test involves a comparative balancing of the strengths and weaknesses of the parents. Factors such as health, wealth, education, and moral conduct have all been considered. The test is indeterminate, and easily manipulated by judges and lawyers. Appellate review is rare since the test is very fact specific and the trial judge has wide discretion to conclude which parent will act in the child's best interest.

4 Gender neutrality remains the popular variety of feminist reform. A cogent discussion of the historic and contemporary conflict between strict equality, or 'rule equality', and special treatment, or 'result equality', in British feminist thought, is provided by Smart and Brophy, 1985. Within the context of American feminism, see Fineman, 1983.

5 See *Ex Parte Devine*, 398 So. 2d 686 (Ala. 1981); 'State divorce statutes chart and summary sheet introduction', *Family Law Reporter* (BNA) 5-6 (24 March 1986).

6 The state of Wisconsin, for example, has recently begun a formal legislative study of a proposal for automatic appointment of a guardian *ad litem* whenever a divorcing couple has a child.

7 For a further discussion of this perspective, see Fineman, 1980.

8 This has been the position of Judith Areen, an influential family law casebook author who, in the teachers' manual which accompanies her *Family Law Cases and Materials* (second edition), concludes:

> On balance I find the primary caretaker approach ... objectionable because it does not look first to the needs of the children, and because it is at the same time unnecessarily hostile to men because

more gender neutral reforms [i.e. economic reforms] could be adopted to offset inequities in bargaining power.

I believe a more appropriate way to offset financial disadvantage is by direct modification of statutes governing child support, alimony and division of property, not by a presumption that is not gender neutral in impact. (Areen, 1985, pp. 122, 124)

9 For a fuller explanation of this phenomenon, see Fineman and Opie, 1987.

10 Traditional doctrine, even post-fault, attempted to instil a non-interventionist value in custody decision making. See, for example, Uniform Marriage and Divorce Act § 402 and 409 (1970) which respectively suggested, retaining the tender years doctrine as the allocation mechanism for initial decisions and allowed modifications only in limited circumstances.

11 Probably the best contemporary illustration of this is the movement toward mandatory joint custody. For a discussion of this development see Fineman, 1988.

12 Hansen, 1966. See also Foster and Freed, 1972.

13 The idea that children are used as 'pawns' or 'bargaining chips' in negotiations between divorcing parents is fairly widespread in the USA. It is found in professional literature as well as in the more polemic fathers' rights communications. For example, Wallerstein and Kelly asserted:

> Psychologically, an individual's rage against an ex-spouse, often expressed in litigation in which the child is the pawn, can apparently remain undiminished by the passage of time or by distance. The fight for a child may serve profound psychological needs in a parent, including the warding off of severe depression and other forms of pathological disorganization. (Wallerstein and Kelly, 1979, p. 472)

14 To make the irony of this statement clear, let me be explicit in stating my belief that the mere presence of children, or even a contest as to custody, is not itself sufficient to justify the coercive intervention measures which attend contemporary practice. A better approach, as discussed below, is to adopt a sensible rule to guide decision making, thus decreasing litigation of the issue, and to use guardians *ad litem* sparingly.

15 Most states admit evidence of the child's wishes, if the child is competent to testify. This approach was advocated by the authors of the Uniform Marriage and Divorce Act. Uniform Marriage and Divorce Act § 402 (1970).

16 Judge Neely anticipates that the evidentiary hearing on who is the primary parent would only last a few hours, and that the witnesses will be neighbours, teachers, etc., not experts (Neely, 1984, p. 181). See also Fineman, 1988.

17 See for example Gallagher, 1987.

Chapter Three

RIGHTS FOR FATHERS AND THE STATE:

Recent Developments in Custody Politics in the Netherlands[1]
NORA HOLTRUST, SELMA SEVENHUIJSEN, AND ANNICK VERBRAKEN

INTRODUCTION

This chapter was inspired by unease about the acclaim in recent years with which the media, jurists, and politicians in the Netherlands have received proposals for joint custody. Joint custody is now put forward as the ultimate realization of the principle of equality and the legal emancipation of women. It is suggested at the same time that not only can custody be legally shared but also the day-to-day care of the children. In this way it is argued that women will be able to emancipate themselves after divorce. In our view, this is a one-sided way of looking at things. This rush to apply the principle of equality to divorce and unmarried motherhood gives one food for thought, especially while the state is certainly in no hurry to develop a similar policy in the fields of employment, social, and fiscal rights for women, which would allow for the sharing of child care within marriage. Moreover, those who initiated the legal changes are not to be found in women's movement circles or in the Emancipation Council,[2] but rather in what has been called the 'rights for fathers movement' and lawyers sympathetic to their ideas and demands.

Such political-strategic statements are, however, not sufficient on their own to construct a feminist stand on the current issues surrounding custody. We need to delve deeper into the nature of the problem itself. During the political struggle in the 1970s about access to children, the women's movement was reasonably successful in bringing a 'power approach' to the political debate and to considerations by parliamentary decision makers (see Komité Vrouwen en Familierecht, 1982). By 'power approach' we mean the view that access should not solely be viewed from a perspective of the so-called 'interest of the child', but also from a perspective of the social organization of mothering and fathering, and the broader power relations between men and women. A power approach questions the role of law in enforcing day-to-day relations and contacts, and debates the meaning of 'rights' in this context. It asks for a discussion of the reasons and motives for a strong state intervention in this field, and looks for problems that are solved or created by the proposed reforms, especially the effects for women. We feel that it is urgent to develop such an approach now in the field of custody as well. This means that the question which becomes important is what 'custody' in the present relationships involving child care and child rearing really means. Which relationships do the proposed legal changes concern, what are they going to solve, and what will the changes mean for women who wish to divorce or wish to become mothers outside marriage or without being otherwise legally tied to a man?

We shall consider these questions by examining the proposals and arguments put forward by a number of leading jurists. The most influential definitions of custody as a political issue are created by lawyers, in jurisprudence, and interpretation in legal journals. These definitions play an important part in and around parliamentary debates. We shall examine the most important explicit and implicit presuppositions of legal discourse and their relationship to feminist arguments which stress power relations.

The chapter is meant to be explorative. We wish to chart an area that is relatively new for the theory and strategy of modern feminism. We seek to show what is at stake and where a feminist vision should be developed which goes beyond superficial ideologies of equality, but takes equality as an ideal seriously at the same time.

The Dutch legal system provides for the sole custody of children in extra-marital situations. Because women usually provide day-to-day care for their children, they are almost always awarded custody after divorce and they then become the single bearers of parental authority. For several years this system of sole custody has been under strong political pressure, of which the first sign was the political struggle in the 1970s around access to children after divorce. (Verbraken, 1981.)

On 4 May 1984 a decision by the Supreme Court allowed the continued existence of joint legal custody after divorce if both parents so desire. Since then some lower district courts have applied this policy to situations in which no marriage or other form of cohabitation existed but in which the man has 'recognized' the child.[3] Following these decisions, jurists increasingly have called for changes in the legal system of custody and the Minister of Justice has responded accordingly by announcing a bill. The debate among jurists and developments in jurisprudence show that the regulation of parenthood and the corresponding rights and obligations is undergoing a radical change in the 1980s.

In 1986 the Minister of Justice published a draft Bill on Parental Authority and sent it to several advisory bodies. The main lines of this proposal are the following.

1 After divorce joint parental authority essentially comes to an end.

2 Parents can ask the judge for joint legal custody if they both want it. The option of choice for joint or sole custody is thus introduced.

3 Unmarried parents can, if they both wish, enter a note of their intention to share parental authority in the custody register. In this way they obtain joint legal custody. There is, however, a requirement that both parents have a legally recognized family tie with the child, which means that the unmarried father must have 'recognized' the child. This means that the possibility of joint custody is not open to lesbian couples or step-parents.

Part one of this chapter deals in a nutshell with the most important developments in the political debate on custody since the parliamentary debate on access in 1981. European law is an important element in this debate. Not only articles in legal journals, but also jurisprudence show an increasing tendency to invoke European treaties in order to win recognition of legal familial relationships between fathers and children as a fundamental human right. Parts two and three deal with custody after divorce and custody without marriage respectively. These matters are often brought together under the heading 'extra-marital parenthood' and there is a tendency to regulate them from the same perspective, namely that of rights and obligations deriving from blood ties or the idea that every child should have a legal father. However, these are entirely different relationships and also different legal rules, which is why we shall deal with them separately.

FROM FATHERS' RIGHTS TO HUMAN RIGHTS

Shifting arenas and definitions

The first Dutch bill on access to children was designed to regulate access to the child after divorce for the parent without legal custody (Second Chamber 1978–9, Bill no. 15,638). At first the bill seemed likely to go through without problems, but this changed after intervention by the women's movement, quickly followed by other organizations. A lengthy struggle, which also involved the media, followed between both interest groups and official institutions. The fathers' rights movement advocated regular and generous access as the norm, regardless of the circumstances, and emphasized that access should be legally enforceable.

Sanctions were considered indispensable because difficulties concerning access were presented as the result of the custodial parent's (i.e. the mother's) unwillingness to co-operate (Ten Dam and Wegelin, 1984). Feminists stated that this image of unwilling mothers was based on sexist imagery and countered this stereotype with women's experiences; for example, the fear that forced access merely confronts mothers with fathers who in many cases were or are still bad parents, even to the extent of abusing their children. In addition it was pointed out that women, the daily nurturers, are burdened by enforced contact with their husbands and the consequences for their children. They are also confronted with welfare workers, therapists, and psychologists, who blame a poor father–child relationship on the mother's inability to come to terms with the grief of her divorce. It was alleged that consultation with fathers and their right to participate in decisions concerning the child(ren) would also lead to endless negotiations and bargaining with ex-husbands. In short, feminists maintained that the right to access was more a confirmation of patriarchal conceptions – in which fatherhood means surveillance, relationships are legally enforceable, and a world without fathers is unthinkable – than the voluntary continuation of the ties between father and child after divorce.

Between the parliamentary debate on the Bill of Amendment in the Second Chamber and its defeat in the First Chamber in

December 1981, feminist contributions to the public debate have received a good deal of recognition, because to many it had become quite clear that this was a matter of fathers' rights to which the interests of the child were made subordinate. Indeed, it could be seen as a victory for the women's movement that the bill was so heavily criticized in the First Chamber, was suspended, and eventually removed from the agenda altogether. But the real victory would have been recognition by the Minister that the women's movement's considerations were legitimate, followed by a decision at cabinet level to review the right to access in a different light. A first step would have been an official policy memorandum such as was produced for example on sexual violence. For every political issue, and the corresponding decision making processes, centres around the definition of the problem: how is the problem described and within what framework?

The parliamentary debates had already made clear that the victory was temporary. The Minister of Justice announced that the Dutch were living under the 'tyranny of a legal construction', meaning sole custody after divorce. It was his opinion that the Dutch people, because of this legal construction, had never accepted the idea that access after divorce should be a normal matter. According to him, therefore, Dutch law should return to the nineteenth-century system in which the parental authority of both parents continued to exist after divorce. Access would then be a normal part of custody and should be regulated as such. This sort of reasoning, namely that problems in the relationship between two people are the result of the legal construction in which it is embedded, has since come to lead a life of its own. Over the past few years, rights for fathers have been established with increasing frequency, but not through parliamentary debate and public political decision making. The arena of decision making has changed. The most important arena has become the courtroom, because it is there that Dutch law is examined in the light of European treaties. Developments in family law have therefore become relatively invisible, occurring outside the usual channels of political debate such as the media, interest groups, and political parties.

This shift corresponds with the 'discovery' of human rights. Shortly before the public debate on access in the Second Chamber, the European Commission on Human Rights declared a complaint by a Dutch father admissible. He had been refused a request for access to his minor son by a Dutch court. When this decision was brought to his attention by the Christian Democratic MP Korte van Hemel (now junior Minister of Justice), the Minister of Justice declared that the amendment then under debate should conform to section 8 of the European Convention on Human Rights which guaranteed the right to the protection of family life. He then confronted MP Ria Beckers of the radical Party PPR with the statement that her view of enforceable access, as a bitter struggle between parents which is not in the interest of the child and therefore undesirable, is directly opposed to the Convention on Human Rights. This was an indication that rights as defined in international treaties were to become an important weapon in the struggle for fathers' rights (see Holtrust and De Hondt, 1986). In the next section we shall indicate how 'human rights' as a political concept were to play a decisive role.

Human rights as a political concept

Like fundamental constitutional rights, international human rights in treaties provide guarantees for the individual against the state. An example of a treaty is the European Convention on Human Rights of 1951, which originated in the Council of Europe as a reaction to the gross violation of human rights during the Second World War. When the Convention was compiled there was some difference of opinion as to whether the right to protection of family life actually belonged in it. This was eventually included in section 8, probably because of the Universal Declaration of Human Rights of 1948 which sees the family as the fundamental unit upon which every society is based and which therefore deserves protection. The Convention is aimed explicitly at the protection of the individual; implicitly it reproduces the family model from the Universal Declaration.

The text of section 8 of the European Convention reads as follows.

1 Everyone has the right to respect for his private and family life, his home, and his correspondence.

2 There shall be no interference by a public authority with the exercise of this right except such as is in accordance with the law

and is necessary in a democratic society in the interests of national security, public safety, or the economic well-being of the country, for the prevention of disorder or crime, for the protection of health and morals, or for the protection of the rights and freedom of others.

The European Convention on Human Rights contains supra-national law which is of a higher order than national law; national law must be in conformity with it. National legislation can be examined in the light of the provisions of the Convention. Citizens with a direct interest can appeal to the European Commission or the European Court, both at Strasbourg. The divorced father discussed above lodged a complaint with the European Commission that Dutch law on access constituted a violation of human rights. If the Commission finds the complaint admissible it then refers it to the European Court or to the Committee of Ministers.

Section 8 has a horizontal effect; that is to say, it affords the right to persons to protection of their family life *vis-à-vis* other persons. It is standing jurisprudence of the European Commission that 'family life' includes the right to access after divorce. This interpretation is broader than what is usually deemed 'family life' in the Netherlands. Even after family ties, and therefore actual family life, have been broken, as in the case of divorce, the ex-family members are still deemed to have a 'family life'. The Court must evaluate the different 'family lives' of those concerned and can establish access against the will of the mother-custodian if her reasons for refusing access are deemed unfounded. This implies interference, even active intervention, by the 'public authorities' in the private family life of the mother. And was that not what section 8 was originally all about?

In Holland, the European Convention has a direct effect, i.e. Dutch courts can apply the convention directly without transformation into national law. Over the past years the direct application of section 8 in cases of access and custody has become increasingly popular with lawyers. Section 8 can play a part in a number of ways and in a number of situations. The section provides for the right to access for the parent without custody, but it also protects the family life of the child in the sense that the parent without custody could lose the right to access in the interests of the child. There could therefore be a collision of rights, in which case the court must weigh them against each other; the interests and rights of the child are the most important.

This line of reasoning in court decisions has been taken over in a new amendment on access which was presented to the Second Chamber on 2 May 1985. According to the memorandum accompanying the Bill of Amendment, the right to access is based on section 8 of the European Convention on Human Rights.

The draft Bill on Revision of the Law of Affiliation which was published in 1981 has become the means of carrying the blood ties between father and child into the sphere of human rights. The legal debate on the draft bill has been almost entirely concerned with what it does propose to leave unchanged, the legal character of recognition. The draft maintains the rule that the man who did not beget a child can nevertheless recognize it as his own – the so-called legal act theory. It also maintains the requirement that a man can only recognize a child as his with permission from the mother. The opponents of the legal act theory maintain that an illegitimate child can only be recognized by the man who begot the child. These advocates of 'the truth principle' hold that the requirement of maternal consent should be abolished.[4]

Finally, since 1984 Dutch courts have awarded joint custody to divorced or unmarried parents if they so desire. If only one parent were to have custody, this would be a violation of section 8 of the European Convention, or so the reasoning goes. It was this possibility that started the legal debate with which we shall now deal.

CUSTODY AND PARENTAL AUTHORITY DURING MARRIAGE AND AFTER DIVORCE

A short history

As we have seen, since 1901 the 'tryanny of a legal construction' has ruled the Netherlands, i.e. after divorce only one parent is awarded parental authority of the child or children. Parental authority by one parent only is called custody. So custody in Holland is always sole custody and has almost the same content as parental authority.

In the nineteenth century, authority by one parent was nothing special, for both in and after marriage (divorce) it was the father who had authority over the children. In 1901 the Minister of Justice proposed to change the term paternal authority into parental authority, but the Second Chamber was only willing to consider such a change 'if the man remains the organic head of the family' (De Vries and Van Tricht, 1903, p. 82). This meant that the only real change in the distribution of parental rights between men and women was the fact that from then on women could be awarded custody after divorce. Before then the father automatically retained parental authority after divorce. Only the party to whom no blame attached (adultery being the most important ground for divorce) could sue for divorce. In practice this meant that the court could commit the children to the care of the mother while the father retained his legal power over them and could, for example, decide where they were to live. After 1901 the parent to whose care the children were committed was also awarded parental control. Care and control were now in the same hands and were defined as custody.

The minister defended sole parental control by the father within marriage as follows:

> Under normal circumstances the influence of the wife will be strong enough to counter the legal authority of the husband. If opinions differ, however, one of them must decide. . . . And if, in the end, the legal decision must rest with one parent, who shall demonstrate on reasonable grounds that this parent should be the mother? Those who desire such a change must perform that demonstration. (De Vries and Van Tricht, 1903, p. 56)

As far as sole custody after divorce is concerned, the minister remarked:

> the wise and well-meaning father or mother with custody will listen to the arguments in the interest of the child without amendments to the law. The unwise or ill-meaning will merely frustrate all cooperation. (De Vries and Van Tricht, 1903, p. 222)

An amendment in 1947 gave women one-quarter of parental authority. Parental authority has always covered both the person and the property of the child. The mother was now permitted to participate in decisions concerning the person of the child. But it remained necessary to have only one captain on the bridge; if opinions differed, the father was to decide. A new regulation was added, giving the mother the right of appeal to the court if she disagreed with the father's decision.

In 1977 the Second Chamber requested a survey of all legal rules and regulations which could be considered a violation of the principle of equality of men and women (see Anders Geregeld, 1978). As a result of this survey a bill appeared in 1980 aimed at 'removing a number of inequalities between men and women in family law and the law of persons and in a number of other fields' (Bill no. 16,427; see De Jong, 1981). One of these inequalities concerned the difference in parental authority between the father and the mother.

When this bill was passed on 1 January 1985, joint parental authority within marriage became a fact. The court has the same referee function it has had since 1947. If opinions differ, both the father and the mother may request a ruling by the court. The problem of two captains on the bridge has been solved by appointing an admiral – the state – in the guise of the court and aligned institutions such as Councils for the Protection of Children and pedagogic welfare organizations. Although, when taken at face value, this amendment may sound like progress, we must not forget that parliament did not agree to it within the framework of a substantive debate on parental authority.

The Supreme Court and custody after divorce

In 1982 a married couple in Amsterdam in the throes of divorce proceedings requested that the district court award them joint custody of their child. Although they no longer lived together, the parents shared the day-to-day care and upbringing of the child to their mutual satisfaction. Both the district court and the Court of Appeal waived the request; the mother was awarded custody. The Supreme Court however determined that sole custody in this case constituted interference in family life as meant by section 8 of the European Convention.

According to section 8, such interference is permitted if provided for by law. The Dutch legal regulation in this case is the law on custody after divorce. According to the Supreme Court this rule is usually justified in the interests of the child, which is entitled to the protection of those interests. Such protection becomes necessary in cases of divorce, considering the tension which is to be expected between parents. However, the Court said this could be different if the parents,

> as had been contended in this case ... consider themselves capable of maintaining good relations with regard to the continued sharing of the day to day care and upbringing of their child and therefore have requested joint custody of that child. (Supreme Court, 4 May 1984)

In such cases the Supreme Court rules that termination of joint parental authority must be examined in the light of the interests of the child. In short, what this decision boils down to is that the law on custody need not be applied if the conditions set out in the decisions are met. But at the same time, the interpretation 'if these conditions are met' and the quest for exact procedural requirements to establish these 'facts' has led to protracted debates among legal scholars. In these debates concepts like 'care' and 'consent' are given content and meaning.

The normative effect of jurisprudence

Although courts make decisions in concrete cases, these often have a normative effect. This is especially true of decisions by the Supreme Court. As the (legal) interpretation of a decision may differ according to the interpreter, who will not usually be willing (or indeed able) to take the concrete case with which the decision deals into account, one decision may have far-reaching consequences after a while. This can be seen in the legal literature which clearly tends to 'stretch' decisions by the Supreme Court.

According to a number of legal scholars, the Supreme Court's decision of 4 May 1984 does not necessarily mean that joint custody after divorce requires that the parents share the care of the child. Hammerstein-Schoonderwoerd (1984), for example, wonders what is wrong with allowing parental authority to continue even though the parent concerned hardly sees the child. According to Doek (1985, p. 214), joint parental authority is well suited to what he calls 'classic divorce situation'. Jansen, a senior civil servant in the Ministry of Justice, repeatedly uses the words 'day-to-day care and upbringing', but if one parent has 'less facilities' (in other words not enough time to take care of the child because of an important job) then there is nothing wrong with joint parental authority. One might wonder what he means by day-to-day care and upbringing, for he contends that the image of 'mothers actually taking care of the children and fathers seeing to the financial side of things, is not representative of most families' (Jansen, 1985, p. 211).[5] Indeed, this division of labour is already apparent in the fact that women often need maintenance or social security payments after divorce, while it is rare to find a man in this position. Jansen however does think that 'it would, in itself, be desirable if fathers were to be given more opportunities for taking care of their children during the day'. But, he immediately adds, 'this division of roles must not be prescribed by law, even if such a thing were possible. For then the State would have to create the financial conditions – and that we might as well forget at once' (Jansen, 1985, p. 212). With which remark the door is closed once again.

Loss of face and inequality

Advocates of joint custody after divorce as a general norm defend their point of view with two arguments. First, they are concerned about 'loss of face' for the parent who is awarded supervisory custody only. If joint custody is awarded after divorce, then neither parent need feel that he/she has had his/her 'crown knocked off' (Rood-de Boer, 1984a, p. 1,280). Jansen speaks of one parent becoming 'the great decider' while the other is 'reduced to looking on'. The argument which refers to loss of face is often cited in other countries too (and criticized): 'Members of the legal and mental health professions place considerable importance on this ego-boosting function of joint custody' (Miller, 1979, p. 365). It will become clear that we are not so impressed by the argument of loss of face for men (for this is what it often boils down to in practice) as a reason for amending the law on custody.

The second, more implicit argument, concerns the principle of equality. Those who use it refer, for example, to a recommendation of the Committee of Ministers of the Council of Europe (number R(84)4) which advocates the equality of parents *vis-à-vis* each other (Jansen, 1985, p. 207). Men and women, and therefore fathers and mothers, should be treated as equals. Mothers are seen as privileged above fathers because they are more often awarded custody of the children after divorce, while fathers have to be satisfied with access and paying maintenance. This is presented as discrimination against fathers. But discrimination means the unequal treatment of equal cases for which there is no justification. To preach formal equality in the absence of actual equality is also discrimination. Until now, there have been no large-scale political objections by men to women taking care of the children during marriage. Why should that task after divorce suddenly become a privilege? Moreover, in most cases there is nothing to show that women are awarded custody against the will of their husbands. Most men never request custody and it is disputed in only 10 per cent of all divorce cases. In these situations the father is awarded custody as often as the mother (see Gisolf and Blankman, 1980; Luthin, 1984).

The point is, of course, that equality is a difficult criterion for matters in which inequality will remain the usual practice. Children usually live with one parent after divorce and it remains to be seen how practical the new trend of having them live in two houses is, or what children themselves feel about this arrangement. The principle of equality in custody decisions and its application may mean injustice. For at what point is equality to be considered, and how? Should it be measured during marriage, at the time of divorce, or in the future? And what counts – the educative qualities of the parents or the material conditions which the father and mother can provide? There can be no justification for removing children from the care of the mother against her will after divorce if the (tacit) arrangement during the marriage was that she took care of the children and the husband took care of the income.

A better criterion for awarding custody might be the primary caretaker principle. It is a gender-neutral criterion based on the notion that it is of great importance to maintain the ties which the child has developed during the marriage with the parent who provided primary care and nurturing. It is not based on stereotyped ideas about motherly love, but on the legitimacy of the child's need for continuity. It will indeed mean that mothers will, at present, be awarded custody more often, but men are eligible on exactly the same footing (see Polikoff, 1982; Sandberg, Chapter 5 in this volume).

Meanwhile, joint custody seems to fulfil a sort of symbolic function for continuation of shared child care after divorce in situations in which a man and a woman shared the same care during marriage. These are situations in which it is reasonable to share legal authority but in which it is not necessary. For here the only question is: Who represents the child as legal representative? These situations require no more than solid arrangements, general rules for how to act if opinions differ, and trust in the person awarded legal custody. But here too 'authority' seems of special value for men who feel uncertain about the continuation of their relationship with their children. It is high time that debates on joint custody, co-parenthood, and shared authority provide some clarity on the difference between taking care of children, demanding authoritarian rights, and the symbolic function of legal provisions.

Agreement between parents

It sounds fair that if two people are agreed, it should be possible to share parental authority. This is a strong appeal to the liberal doctrine of free will and free choice. The question is, of course, what we can expect of an 'agreement' between parents caught in the throes of divorce proceedings. Let us take a very necessary and critical look at the conditions for agreement and for procedural rules designed for the expression of free will. For 'free will' and 'consent' are not free floating concepts: they derive their meaning from the context of the courtroom and the legal procedures and battles around it (see Pateman, 1980). According to some legal scholars, joint custody need not be requested by both parents. It is sufficient if one files the request and the other does not object, while court intervention is deemed unnecessary if the parents are 'mutually agreed' (Hammerstein-Schoonderwoerd, 1984, p. 624; Elzinga, 1984). Doek (1985) however would have the parents file a joint request in which they state why they feel capable of coming to a good working arrangement, so that the court and the Council for the Protection of Children can, if necessary, examine the matter in full.[6]

It is not unreasonable to suppose that a refusal to agree to joint custody will also be subject to examination by the court if 'equality' were to become the norm. Such proposals subject women to the jurisdiction of the state and control by welfare workers, for at present, at least, it will be the men who file the requests and the women whose interests lie in sole custody.

This tendency to 'juridification' is also present in the rules which some legal scholars propose for situations of mutual disagreement after joint custody has been awarded. According to Doek (1985) it is not necessary then to 'fall back' on sole custody. Recent legislation, which provides for an appeal to the court as a referee in matters of dispute during marriage, is produced out of a hat to serve its purpose after divorce as well. Parents with conflicts may then 'put their conflicts before the court in order to obtain a solution'. It would seem that in the future parents must also 'agree' to seek adjudication. In reality it will probably look very different. Women who occupied an unequal position of power during marriage will be faced with the following dilemma: either they share custody, so that they are still unable to make their own decisions; or they opt for sole custody and are told that they lust after power or, worse, deny their children a father.

The fact is that many bargains occur during the negotiations which automatically accompany every divorce. We can well imagine this practice being extended to custody matters if 'joint or single parental authority' becomes a matter of choice (if you agree to joint authority, I won't request sole custody). Suppose that a mother has 'agreed', whether or not under pressure, to share parental authority. The father keeps his busy job. Can the mother now force him to work less so that he has more time for child care? Can a mother move house if she finds a job somewhere else, or because she feels like it? Who has the decisive vote on which school the child attends? Suppose the father wants the child to go to a church school, while the mother chooses a state school. What will the court take into consideration? The father's choice, dictated by religious beliefs, although he does not actually take care of the child; or the mother's, even though it may not be one of principle and merely dictated by the fact that the school is round the corner?

The advantage of joint custody after divorce is supposed to be the fact that the court need not intervene in (disintegrating) family life. But if the family has disintegrated, there will be an increasing appeal to the courts. For joint parental authority does not only mean that the father's supervision and control of the mother and the children continues after marriage. It gives him an extra weapon: he can request that the court nullify the mother's decisions. It will mean extra work for the courts and welfare workers, but also for others such as school directors and medical institutions, for they will be obliged to listen to a second representative of parental authority. The father figure, whom the child 'needs, according to many' as Jansen says, is first and foremost a 'deciding figure', with all that it entails.

During the past years, fathers who felt themselves 'de-fathered' or passed over after divorce have given the judiciary a feeling of helplessness; the courts do not know what to do. Yet it would be better to face the problem, instead of devising quasi-solutions (the institutionalization of joint custody) which entail the risk of increasing the problems for all concerned (including the courts).

PARENTAL AUTHORITY OUTSIDE MARRIAGE

Dutch law on 'illegitimate' children (i.e. children born out of wedlock) provides for independent motherhood for women. An unmarried mother automatically has a legal familial relationship with her child and she has also automatically sole custody, except when she is not of age. The father can obtain a legal familial relationship by voluntarily recognizing the child as his, for which prior written consent from the mother is required. Recognition is a legal act, i.e. it need not correspond with the biological truth. After recognition, the mother retains custody of the child. This means that in situations in which there has never been a marriage, women almost always have formal control to decide in matters of child care; they are the legal representatives of the child.

As we described on pp. 54–8, since the Bill on the Law of Affiliation was published in 1981, legal scholars tend to advocate basing affiliation with regard to fathers on blood ties too; begetters should be registered. Some authors see no reason to link registration with enforceable consequences. Jansen and Doek, on the other hand, advocate 'biological truth' as a principle, because it makes rights for fathers possible. Access for, and maintenance by, fathers should become the rule, they say, perhaps linked to parental authority or some form of supervision or consultation. The 'advocates of truth' see the requirement of the mother's consent for recognition as a barrier to the rights of fathers.

In the following we shall examine current arguments and historical backgrounds in the matter of consent and authority, in order to reach the basis of a feminist argument which takes into account power relations between the sexes and the relationship between nurturing and authority.

Maternal consent: from right to privilege

The Bill on the Law of Affiliation of 1981 retains the requirement of maternal consent for recognition of the child by the father. This is in keeping with the theoretical options upon which the bill is based, for it opts for the 'legal act theory' as a basis for legal affiliation between father and child. The Minister of Justice De Ruiter who proposed the bill put the following liberal argument of free will forward with regard to the matter of consent:

> From the position of the mother it is unacceptable that a man could establish a legal relationship with her child against her will. The establishment of a legal relationship with a child requires freely given consent by both the woman and the man. (Herziening van het Afstammingsrecht, 1981)

There is still room, therefore, for 'independent motherhood' in De Ruiter's proposal.

The requirement of consent by the mother for the father to recognize his child does not fit with a system of rights for fathers based on the 'biological truth'. The advocates of such a system do not speak the liberal language of free will and consent. Instead they have introduced the 'right of the begetter to recognize his child'. This would mean, for example, that a known sperm-donor in cases of artificial insemination, or a man who has lived with a woman at one address during the period of conception, would have the right to recognize the child or at least to be registered as its begetter. By taking this right as their starting point, the 'advocates of truth' manage to convey the impression that there is something outrageous about requiring the mother's permission.[7] They paint an image of women of evil intentions against well-meaning, excluded men.

Hammerstein-Schoonderwoerd, professor in family law, states for example in the legal journal *Nederlands Juristenblad*:

> But should the begetter, who does wish to bear the responsibility for his child, *be denied the right by the mother* [our italics] to legally recognize that child and so establish a legal familial

relationship with it? (Hammerstein-Schoonderwoerd, 1982, pp. 704)

And a former member of the Supreme Court, in an article in the same journal speaks of a 'veto, for which the woman need give no reason'. She has her own ideas on what motivates women:

> It is certainly imaginable that a woman would refuse her consent for the father to recognize the child, because she objects to him, or because she has joined the feminist movement, in short, reasons that fit the 'I'm alright Jack' era, but those reasons are in themselves insufficient to warrant passing over the interest of the father – and the child – concerned. (Minkenhof, 1982, p. 830)

Minkenhof also speaks of a fundamental right of the father to recognize his child, and she even doubts whether the legal requirement of consent is still valid here, considering section 8 of the European Convention and the Marckx decision.

Jansen and Doek complete this train of reasoning in the *Nederlands Juristenblad* of 16 February 1985. They argue that if blood ties form the basis of family life and kinship (and they refer to European law in order to make it seem inevitable), then the begetter who wishes to determine his paternity legally must be free to do so. The most important barrier to that freedom is (as was to be expected) the requirement of the mother's consent, 'a cherished acquisition, especially in feminist literature' (Jansen, 1985, p. 209). Jansen is much taken with Minkenhof's suggestion that the legal requirement of consent is no longer valid in the light of European law (and hints at a test case). But as long as the matter remains undecided, the courts in his view should be authorized to examine the mother's reasons for refusing. Doek poses the historical question of whether the legislator would consider it in accordance with the European Convention that the mother could refuse her consent to the biological father with whom she lives 'without stating any reason' and could therefore prevent the establishment of a legal familial relationship between the child and his or her father: 'On what grounds should the unmarried mother have such a right (which the married mother has not)?' (Doek, 1985, p. 217).[8]

To put it briefly, the mother's consent has been redefined from a liberal requirement of freely given consent to a misplaced privilege by which unmarried mothers can prevent men from exercising their constitutional rights, but for which they need give no reason. Doek's statement makes it abundantly clear how we should view the matter – in the light of political strategies (also in other fields) aimed at creating a state-regulated extra-matrimonial marriage. Affiliation must be viewed in the light of rights for men and the necessity of guaranteeing extra-matrimonial paternity, now that an increasing number of women are bearing children outside legal marriage.

Although the present generation of feminists is likely to distrust motives of protection in law, we must realize that the requirement of consent does protect women in situations in which oppressive behaviour by men plays a part, such as abuse or incest, or in situations in which men use 'access' to the child as a weapon against the woman. The introduction of examination of motive by the court would mean that the onus of proof would rest upon the individual woman in such cases. A structural problem, for such is the official public policy view of sexual violence, would then be pushed on to individual women who would become involved in endless legal proceedings and examinations by different agencies. From this point of view the government should be reluctant to do away with legal institutions which have some protective effect.

There are other reasons too why feminists should demand that legislation does not do away with the requirement of consent. The right of the begetter to recognize his child can only function in a system in which the corresponding legal obligation to name the begetter has been introduced for the woman. One can learn from West German law that this obligation is usually embedded in a state regulated system of kinship obligations and claims (see Bahr-Jendges and Bubenik-Bauer, 1984). There the mother of a child born out of wedlock is placed under supervision of the Jugendamt (an institution for the protection of children). This supervision remains until the mother has named the begetter so that the Jugendamt can then arrange maintenance for the child and matters of inheritance. Mothers used to be able to avoid this by depositing the name of the begetter with a solicitor. Now the mother with a reasonable income, who does not desire maintenance from the father nor social security from the state, remains under supervision. Mothers also lose part of their social benefit if they refuse to name the father (see Finger, 1983; Oberlies, 1983).

As far as the Netherlands is concerned, this is a point to be remembered. Municipalities are now obliged to claim social security paid to a divorced woman from the ex-husband. This could easily be extended to cover children born out of wedlock if obligatory registration of begetters is introduced, as the 'advocates of truth' would like to see. That way state interests (namely to spend as little as possible on social security) would create yet another barrier to the economic independence of women.

It would be a good thing if the advocates of paternity registration, in the belief that children must be able to trace their father, were to consider the side effects which might very well turn out to be the main effects. The motive to 'know your father' does not automatically lead to a system of registration – mothers could tell their children themselves.[9] This would not apply in cases of artificial donor insemination, but there are not (yet) many advocates of donor-registration in the Netherlands.

But apart from issues concerning violence, financial matters, or the side effects of registration, feminists should discuss the question of whether women can claim a right to choose the means and circumstances under which they bear children. The French Minister of Justice has advocated such a right as a fundamental or human right.[10] Arguments around a 'right to choose' were developed in campaigns around abortion and contraceptives, and it remains to be established if they can be applied to custody matters as well.

The validity of a more generalized claim for autonomy in issues concerning motherhood seems only limited, especially as long as it takes recourse to special characteristics of women as individuals (see Kingdom, 1985; Petchesky, 1984). The language of natural rights excludes the possibility of speaking in terms of collective responsibilities, relations between people, and especially power relations between men and women, where feminist strategies refer to (see Sevenhuijsen, 1986). The political disadvantage of a discourse of 'rights' is that it can provoke an endless chain of counter claims of 'rights', which is part of an unpredictable juridification of relations around human reproduction. Besides this, a 'right to choose circumstances' supposes active public policies which make childbearing a viable option for women, that does not restrict them in other activities, and creates possibilities for sharing child care with other persons, including fathers.

The problem is that recent neo-liberal policies in most western European countries are not going in the direction of creating collective responsibilities and public services. Instead they reconstruct a 'private' responsibility for child care, as part of strategies that strengthen the market as well as the family. In such conditions the claim for a fundamental right to choose is essentially a defensive strategy *vis-à-vis* the fathers' rights movement and their claim of social relations on the basis of biological links. A 'right to choose' then would mean that the courts should have to weigh the fundamental rights of women who bear children against the claim of protection of family life of men on the grounds of begetting or providing sperm.

Authority over children born out of wedlock

As we have already said, in Dutch law the woman who bears a child out of wedlock automatically has sole custody over her child. This legal rule makes independent motherhood for women possible, but it was never designed with 'rights' for women in mind. The regulation of custody was always closely linked with the regulation of recognition by the father. Until 1947 the unmarried mother had to recognize the child in order to establish a legal family tie; no recognition, then no legal custody. In nineteenth-century law it was unclear whether illegitimate children came under paternal authority or custody. This was changed in 1905; since then sole custody has been the rule for all situations outside marriage. An automatic legal relationship between mother and child was not considered necessary, from the point of view that mothers always recognized their children before the father anyway; they were unable to consent to recognition by the father until they had recognized the child themselves.

The introduction of automatic family ties in 1948 is to be seen against the background of the increasing surveillance of unmarried mothers in the course of this century. Institutions for the care of unmarried mothers were worried about children being 'given up without rules and regulations', which was possible as long as no one could be quite sure who the mother was. By abolishing recognition by the mother, giving up of children could be regulated more satisfactorily.

The ruling as proposed by the draft Bill on the Law of

Affiliation, by which the man who has recognized the child can share authority with the mother (with her consent), has been heavily criticized in legal literature. It is maintained, on the one hand, that men will have too great an authority. De Langen (1982), a professor of juvenile law, objects to the fact that the draft bill introduces yet another category of children who will be confronted with courts and institutions for the protection of children if their parents become involved in problems and conflicts with each other. She also maintains that it remains to be seen whether the addition of a person with authority over the child will mean an improvement for children who have been alone with their mothers for any length of time. Moreover, she doubts whether a new category of adults should be assigned rights at a time when many are calling – without much success – for a reappraisal of the significance of parental authority from the (legal) point of view of the child. In her view the woman will often receive short shrift from the courts in decisions regarding her child, while she runs the risk that the man with whom she shares parental authority will request intervention by the Council for the Protection of Children, enforced therapy, or custody.

> The only person who really seems to benefit from these provisions, is the man, who, while taking upon himself no obligations with regard to the child, nevertheless acquires a great deal of power over the child, and therefore, also over the woman. (De Langen, 1982, p. 1,135)

On the other hand, some authors advocate extending the possibility of sharing authority even further than men who have accepted paternity or are registered as fathers. Hammerstein-Schoonderwoerd would like to see this circle enlarged to include all persons who share any aspect of child care with the mother, for example her brother or her woman friend. In her proposals, authority is detached from biological or legal affiliation (Hammerstein-Schoonderwoerd, 1982). In their articles in the *Nederlands Juristenblad* of February 1985, neither Jansen nor Doek are very explicit on this matter. In their view the enforceable consequences of affiliation extend in any event to the maintenance obligation and the right to access. This means that they maintain that the begetter of the child should have legally enforceable access to it and also an economic responsibility (partly enforceable through municipal claims for social benefits on ex-husbands). Jansen states explicitly that authority is not necessarily the automatic consequence of affiliation (so that determination of paternity 'does not necessarily threaten the mother'). But what is meant by the phrase 'not necessarily automatic'?

The proposal contained in the draft Bill on the Law of Affiliation to make joint parental authority possible outside marriage has already been applied by the courts. In 1984 the lower district court in Tilburg was the first court to award joint parental control to two unmarried parents who did not live together. The court considered rejection of their request to be unjustifiable interference in family life (section 8 of the European Convention). The court referred to the Supreme Court's decision on joint custody after divorce. On 21 March 1986 the Supreme Court confirmed, in two cases, that unmarried parents can have, on their request, legal joint custody. If the normative effect of the Supreme Court's decision is extended to all aspects of the extra-marital situation, this will mean, at least if some of the authors mentioned above have their way, that a request for joint custody by the father which is not disputed by the mother will be considered to be joint request. It is also possible that the mother's motives for refusing to agree to joint custody will be subject to examination by the court.

The Department of Justice has since published a draft bill, in which the possibility of joint parental control for unmarried parents is introduced. In this proposal only the mother and the recognized father can share parental control, so earlier proposals for shared control between, for example, two women are ruled out. The proposal contains no condition of joint care for obtaining shared control. The only condition is that both parents jointly request the arrangement (*Wetsvoorstel*, 1986).

Again, political decision makers should take into consideration whether extra-marital joint custody is really necessary. In any event it is not necessary in order to share the day-to-day care of the child. In a sole custody system the people concerned (for example the parents) can always make mutual arrangements with regard to such day-to-day concerns and with regard to the way in which decisions are to be made, even in case of disagreement. Present or future family life need not be prevented by sole custody. If there is disagreement on the way in which the child should be brought up, it is often better that one person makes the decision without becoming involved with courts and welfare agencies. Joint custody is no improvement for the courts, either. Instead of one decision to award sole custody after divorce, the court may now receive appeals for help again and again from married, unmarried, or divorced parents, unable to solve their disputes within the limits of their joint authority. For women and children the regulation is not always an improvement as over and over again they can be subject to the jurisdiction of the state, to compulsory 'family' therapy, and 'welfare aid'. They will lose the legal autonomy which they possess. In the meantime the first persons to regret their agreement on shared control have returned to court with a request to annul the agreement and be awarded sole custody again.

CONCLUSIONS

Of course there are situations in which a man and a woman can share both child care and parental authority harmoniously. In these cases the granting of equal rights can indeed have the stimulating effects of continuing shared care which proponents of 'emancipation policy' expect from it. But the sharing of authority is not a condition for the sharing of day-to-day care, and the law is better tailored for situations of conflict than for situations of harmony. Introducing joint authority without doing something about promoting joint care is, from a political point of view, the continuation of patriarchal traditions rather than a contribution to emancipation.[11] For centuries mothers have had to put up with men having supervision over the way in which they cared for their children. Not until 1901 did a limited number of women (divorced or not married) acquire an independent right to authority, at least if they also took care of their children. Within marriage, until 1985, men had more parental rights than women. It is a great improvement that maternal capacities are no longer automatically linked to supposed natural female capabilities. As a result, however, politicians act as if this in itself has meant equality, but they fail to delve deeper into the social organization of motherhood and the power aspects to which it is related.

The image of the 'bad mother' keeps emerging as a guide for future legislation. Mothers who wish to divorce, but not to share parental authority with their ex-husbands, are represented as 'bad mothers' who deny their children a father and prevent men from being fathers, or as mothers lusting after power. Unmarried mothers are depicted as the essence of selfishness, the supposition being that they want children for their own enjoyment only and also want to have the sole say in their upbringing. They are the focus of all sorts of public unease and fear about a world without fathers. Ironically, married mothers are now expected to be grateful; they may at last share parental control with their husbands. Their behaviour and their circumstances are held up as an example to their unmarried counterparts.

Looking at the whole matter from this perspective, it becomes visible that the legal debates contain many elements of the disciplining of motherhood, irrespective of whether all proposals become encoded in law. The debate gives an opportunity for leading persons publicly to pronounce their views on motherhood, femininity, and the need for fathers. This remains a discourse in which women themselves have little say. At the same time feminism is continuously marginalized or made suspect as soon as it deviates from the straight road towards equality or voices doubts about the basis or effects of principles of legal equality.

It is clear that women will not benefit from the further unbridled development of the jurisprudence of the Supreme Court, which has been based, until now, on a one-sided interpretation of European Law and 'human rights', especially if that development turns out to be the model upon which the national legislative body, parliament, styles its new legislation. The rhetoric of the human rights argument becomes so powerful that other considerations on desirable arrangements in the sphere of child rearing and parenthood are becoming illegitimate and a 'real' public debate becomes impossible. This new style of rhetoric can, for example, be perceived in a new draft bill on parental control, in which it is proposed to speak only in terms of parental care. The difference between care and control is eradicated here. Parents can in this proposal share parental 'care', without questions being asked about who is looking after the child or with whom the child lives.

It is striking that all the details of family law are being remodelled in separate bills, without a broader discussion on the relations of child rearing and the principles that should guide it. As long as the confusion on the effects of custody arrangements lasts, from a feminist point of view it would be better if the Dutch legal system were not changed. The present system at least affords women a chance of independence and legal autonomy, as well as some protection. If the system is revised in the short term, it should at least contain the necessary guarantees for 'rights' of women.

This means for example that the option of sole custody should be presented as 'normal' a choice as the option for joint custody. In the modelling of divorce procedures there must be solid guarantees that women are not obliged to agree to joint custody because of more or less subtle pressure. The court should not be permitted to examine the reasons a woman may have for refusing to agree to a request of joint custody. It should be possible to fall back on sole custody if an arrangement of joint custody does not work, without having to provide elaborate motives and without the courts having to examine them. The mother's consent before recognition of a child by a man should remain in law, for example by recognizing it as a fundamental right of women in the light of voluntary relationships and reproductive freedom. Finally, feminists should think through – leaving legal aspects aside for a moment – what we want from fathers and what sort of fathers we want for our children. We are still waiting to unmask patriarchal fatherhood.

NOTES

1 This chapter is a modified translation of an article which was originally published in 1986 and which was meant as an active intervention in the debate described here: Nora Holtrust, Selma Sevenhuijsen, and Annick Verbraken, 'Rechten voor vaders en de staat. Recente politieke ontwikkelingen rondom ouderlijke macht', in Sevenhuijsen, S. *et al.* (eds) (1986) *Socialisties-Feministiese Teksten 9*, Baarn, Ambo, pp. 10–35. Changes in jurisprudence and other legislative developments afterwards have been included as much as possible.

2 The Emancipation Council (Emancipatieraad) was installed by the Dutch government in 1974 and consists of experts in emancipation who advise the government on all aspects of emancipation policy. Until 1981, official emancipation policy was mainly based on concepts of equal chances and 'role change'. Recently the central focus has been slowly changing into a programme aimed at altering hierarchical power structures. Issues around sexual violence, child custody, and economic independence have been influential in this change (see Dijkstra and Swiebel, 1982).

3 To create a legal family tie with a child born out of wedlock a man has in Dutch law to make a legal recognition in the registrar's office. The

only prerequisite for this act is the mother's consent: there is no need for a biological proof of paternity. Legal recognition is a voluntary act, which cannot be enforced upon begetters.

4 Ironically they use the Marckx case in order to define the blood ties between father and the child as a human right. In this case the European Court ruled for an unmarried Belgian mother, Paula Marckx, who complained that Belgian law is a contravention of section 8 of the European Convention because it does not allow legal family ties between an unmarried mother and her child until after she has legally recognized it (see De Hondt and Holtrust, 1986b).

5 Doek and Jansen are important spokesmen of the fathers' rights movement. Some female legal scholars also follow part of their reasoning, e.g. Minkenhof and Rood-de Boer.

6 Rood-de Boer, however, contrary to Hammerstein-Schoonderwoerd, Doek, and Jansen, does posit the requirement that 'parents must be actually able to continue to share responsibility'.

7 This attack was launched at the annual Meeting of the Association for Family and Juvenile Law on 27 November 1981. Reports of the meeting were published in *Tijdschrift voor Familie en Jeugdrecht* (*FJR*), 1981, 6, pp. 182 passim.

8 In the meantime, in 1987 two district courts have already done away with the requirement of consent by the mother. In one case according to the court the mother has no reasonable interest in preventing recognition of the child by the father. In May 1988 the Supreme Court ruled that a mother is not under all conditions allowed to refuse her consent for recognition. Her consent can be replaced by a sentence of the court. The Supreme Court again applied the human rights argument. Section 8 of the European Convention is supposed to imply that a biological father and his child have in principle a right to legal family ties. Only the protection of the rights of others is allowed to curtail these rights.

9 Research has shown that mothers usually do; see Holtrust and De Hondt (1987).

10 Badinter formulated this point of view during a debate in the Council of Europe on reproductive technology and human rights in 1985.

11 We use the term 'patriarchal' here in its literal meaning; it refers to the social and political relations in which the power of men as fathers is embedded.

Chapter Four

'THE INTEREST OF THE CHILD' AND THE REGULATION OF THE POST-DIVORCE FAMILY

IRENE THÈRY

We are faced in France with an apparently paradoxical situation. Like many other countries, France has experienced widespread upheavals in family life since the late 1960s, both in behavioural patterns and in dominant images of family life. One of the decisive factors has undoubtedly been the great rise in the divorce rate; according to recent statistics, nearly one marriage in three will end in divorce (in Paris, one in two).

These figures do not take any account of the breakdown of *de facto* unions, where, in fact, we have also seen a qualitative change, with particularly important effects on women's lives; in nearly 90 per cent of cases, custody of the children is awarded to the mother. But French feminists have had little to say about divorce or its consequences; there has been little attempt to mobilize opinion or to analyse these developments, even though the Divorce Reform Law of 11 July 1975 was discussed and voted on at a time when feminism as a social movement was at the height of its activity.

Some scattered efforts did take place (e.g. permanent centres for divorced women), but their broader implications were not examined, despite analytical works by a number of individuals (cf. Delphy, 1974; Dhavernas, 1978; Boigeol and Cammaille, 1978). Nowadays the groups mobilizing around divorce are almost exclusively associations of fathers (although some groups have become mixed), who are fighting the legislation and criticizing dominant legal practice from a perspective which cannot be reduced simply to a defence of male interests. In other words, divorce and its aftermath occupy only a small corner in the thoughts of those feminists who dispute the traditional division of

78

masculine and feminine roles, despite the fact that divorce serves to reinforce this division in many ways. Numerous explanations could be advanced to account for this situation but that would require a lengthy exposition. Here I will confine myself to making two necessarily schematic points.

First, when I speak of the 'feminist movement' I use a useful but inexact term. There has never been a unified feminist movement in France, rather a movement of feminisms, with divergent and contradictory aims and objectives. It is not surprising that the supporters of 'womanhood' may be satisfied in the long run with a situation which seems to give them the advantages of women (they want custody of the children, they get it) even if it means mixing up feminine privileges won by women with the reproduction of gender roles. The silence of feminism may indicate a level of acceptance of this attitude.

Second, the relative lack of interest must be understood in the context of a greater and more profound lack of interest in the family as an institution. While for many years feminist analyses have addressed domestic production, sexuality, and the position of women in the labour market, those feminists interested in the institution of the family, its history, recent evolution, and regulation by civil and social codes, have remained few and isolated.

A full debate about the origins of this situation in France would require an analysis of the theoretical foundations of the different currents in feminism. Here let me just say that I am one of those who belong to the opposite camp. My particular interest stems from the realization that divorce as a social phenomenon has important implications for the lives of women today and their social position, and I think that the regulation of divorce is a revealing symptom of the present day evolution of norms and images in family matters.

The divorce reform of 1975 was part of a package of very important reforms which, from the mid-1960s onwards, firmly recast French family law inherited from the 1804 Napoleonic Code. Successive laws on matrimonial settlements (13 July 1965), adoption (11 July 1966), contraception (28 December 1967), parental rights (4 June 1970), affiliation (3 January 1972), voluntary termination of pregnancy (17 January 1975), and divorce (11 July 1975) are generally interpreted as being both indices and causes of the gradual abandonment of the moral, patriarchal domestic order which the Napoleonic Code symbolized. We are said to be witnessing a sort of dilution of familial norms in favour of a liberal, pluralist regulation, which recognizes the diversity of domestic situations and gives individuals an increased independence in their 'private' choices. Thus family law has ceased to be the defender of the family order, but rather a more flexible, more 'administrative' law, whose main aim will be to ensure respect for the respective rights of individuals in respect of their personal liberty. This perspective is the predominant view among French women lawyers. However, it is of little assistance in helping us understand what is actually happening on a social level as a result of the establishment of new modes of family regulation. I shall try and defend the hypothesis that we are witnessing not a dilution but a reformulation of familial norms; the more important to grasp in that it is not necessarily expressed explicitly in terms of prescriptive and proscriptive utterances.

This reformulation of norms is complex and may appear incomprehensible, yet even a partial analysis of the ways in which it works is essential in a feminist perspective. Once again, it is a case of distancing oneself from what 'goes without saying', what appears as 'natural' social organization. Yet even the definition of 'natural' is not static: on the contrary, it changes all the time. What does it mean today? In my research I have attempted to make a modest contribution towards an answer by providing a study, albeit circumscribed and limited, of the use of a very controversial legal concept – 'the interest of the child'.

'THE INTEREST OF THE CHILD': SIMPLE 'ALIBI' OR EFFECTIVE REGULATORY INSTRUMENT?

The history of French divorce legislation is long, complex, and tormented. Divorce was introduced at the beginning of the French Revolution (1792), reorganized in 1804 on less liberal lines, then abolished at the time of the Restoration by the 'De Bonald' law of 1816. Proponents and opponents of the notion of the indissolubility of marriage were equally balanced throughout the nineteenth century and it was not until 1884 that divorce was reintroduced. The 'Loi Naquet' of 1884 authorized divorce only on grounds of fault and made provision for awarding custody of children to the 'innocent' spouse. Nearly one century later the Divorce Reform Law of 11 July 1975 introduced divorce by mutual consent and provided that the sole criterion in custody decisions was 'the interest of the child'.

A much criticized criterion

The appearance of this criterion, first in case law, then in the Civil Code, is linked to the gradual calling into question of 'paternal power', which historians have seen in terms of two main dynamics: on the one hand, the increasing intervention by the state in the sphere of the family in the name of the protection of the child, in particular the child 'at risk', following a logic of social control (Meyer, 1977; Donzelot, 1977); and on the other, a transformation in the representation of domestic relationships, the functions of the family, parental duties, and the recognition of the child as a distinct person (Perrot, 1982; Ariès, 1975). Thus, reference to the general interest justifies state intervention in family life while, simultaneously, reference to the interest of the individual recognizes an area designated 'private'. The contemporary notion of 'the interest of the child' that now permeates family law and child law has been built up through the contribution of these divergent logics.

Over the past few years in France, as elsewhere, the practice of referring to 'the interest of the child' as a criterion in judicial decision making has been much criticized and disputed. There are three levels of argument that can be distinguished.

1 For some it is not so much the principle nor the general criterion as such, but rather the dominant meanings which have been attributed to it. They therefore offer a 'good' interpretation of the interest of the child to counter the 'bad' interpretation. Proponents of joint custody, for instance, see such a 'bad' interpretation of the principle in the legislation ('the child is placed in the care of one *or* other of the parents', Civil Code, Article 287). For them this interpretation of the needs of the child runs contrary to an even deeper interest – to keep both his or her parents. Throughout a whole range of such debates each position claims its particular version of 'the interest of the child' as the only one in accord with the current state of knowledge in the social and human sciences.

2 At a second level, there are those who dispute the criterion itself. Its indefinable character is seen as giving free rein to the subjectivity of the decision makers. Family law is once again shown to be constitutionally incapable of formulating norms to limit the arbitrariness of its decisions. They criticize the way in which reference to 'the interest of the child' is abused, and call for research into objective principles of decision making (Carbonnier, 1962).

3 Finally, at a third level, there is another group who criticize the criterion itself, not as a subjective and 'empty' concept, but, on the contrary, as a concept overflowing with political and social objectives which, further, have very little to do with the person of the child. They point to the symbolic power (*profit symbolique*) conferred by referring to the 'interest of the child', a term which for them has thus functioned primarily as a means of linkage in the legal discourse, espousing 'all forms, all ages, all causes' (Chauviere, 1982).

These three levels of criticism have a common thread in seeing the criterion as an alibi; an alibi for dominant ideology, an alibi for individual arbitrariness, an alibi for family and more general social policies for which the law serves as an instrument. In my opinion we need to go beyond these critiques, which all assume (implicitly or explicitly) that there is such a thing as 'the interest of the child' *per se*, which can be stripped of instrumentalizations. Rather we need to examine the relationship between the use of such a criterion and the changing methods of regulation in family affairs. I put forward two hypotheses.

1 'The interest of the child', as a judicial criterion, is only apparently indefinable and empty. To the extent that it functions as a device for decision making this 'key concept' must be invested with at least sufficient weight that decisions do not appear purely gratuitous and arbitrary. That is what legitimates judicial intervention – the authority of the judiciary itself as institution. It is not a question of denouncing 'the interest of the child' as a mask, an alibi, or a discourse tacked on to a legal process which in fact operates under different premises. Rather one must seek to discover the values and images which inform the criterion in a particular context and the specific processes of regulation implied by its use.

2 'The interest of the child', whatever the content assigned to it, never concerns the child and its needs considered in isolation, but, on the contrary, views the child in the context of a system of relationships. In divorce, what is evaluated and regulated is not the life of the child but the totality of the familial arrangements after divorce. In other words, the criterion of the interest of the child, precisely because it is unique and exclusive, acts as a principle for regulating the post-divorce family, possibly even to the detriment of the infant in the case.

The discourse of judges and lawyers who claim to take into account only the interest of the child (as opposed to the interests of each of the parents) should be countered by showing that, when they speak of the child, they are always and inevitably speaking of something else – the father, mother, the family itself. Therefore, we need to understand the reasons for this unspoken assumption and its effects on the procedural moves in attributing custody after divorce. We come back again to the problem we defined at the outset. The issue is not the status, position, or role of the children, but rather that of the adults and in particular the mothers. To admit that the real function of 'the interest of the child' is to permit the setting up of a reorganization of the family unit after the marital breakdown is entirely pertinent. Far from being a detour, it is the very heart of the matter. Thus we must analyse how such a reorganization is achieved, how it is justified, and what this means for the representation of paternal and maternal roles. What does it imply for the women concerned and for all women, whether or not they are divorced, whether or not they are mothers?

From 'divorce as preservation' to acceptance of marital fragility

If 'the interest of the child' is not a simple alibi in legal discourse but a tool, an instrument of regulation, with its own efficacy, then it is important to analyse why the juridical norm has needed to incorporate such a notion. The period from the 1884 law to the 1975 law has in general been interpreted as the transition from 'divorce as sanction' (fault based divorce) to 'divorce as failure' (irretrievable breakdown, Roussel et al., 1983; Commaille, 1982). The notion of the fragility of the matrimonial relationship has progressively replaced the principle of indissolubility, which held that divorce should not be granted unless there was a recognized case of fault, and that the guilty party would be punished by not having custody of the children; in other words, the child as 'object' would be offered to the innocent spouse in recompense.

However, one wonders whether too much has been made of this contrast. Do the terms 'object', 'property', so frequently used with reference to the former status of the child of divorced parents, accurately render the actual social and juridical status of the child in 1884? The child has never been an object (only a slave is an object) and was not the property of its parents. Rather the child was seen as a component of the family and thus subject to the authority of the paterfamilias, which is quite a different relationship and supposes obligations on his side. In the nineteenth century a series of laws were passed to limit and control the exercise of paternal power. By 1884 the notion of 'the interest of the child' was already largely constituted and in use (Le Guidec, 1973). Moreover, the 1884 divorce law does take it into account in that Article 302 of the Civil Code refers, albeit in a secondary way, to 'the greater advantage of the children'.

To believe that the blamelessness of the spouse as primary criterion for awarding custody meant that the law simply ignored the interest of the child would be to introduce into the old Napoleonic Code an unnecessary incoherence. Quite simply, the law presumed that this interest *a priori* lies with the innocent party. The interest of the child and the interest of the innocent spouse are merged in a single entity, 'the interest of the family'. This perspective implies that divorce is perceived as a means of maintaining the family by the expulsion of the guilty scapegoat.

What is not present is any concept of the 'parental alternative', i.e. a choice between parents, in relation to custody; the child simply remains within a partly 'decapitated' family. If its interests are not invoked, it is not because they are ignored, but because it would be beside the point – the presumption is that it is in the interest of all children to live within their families, whether or not that family is deprived of one of its parents. Seen in these terms, 'divorce as sanction' is equally 'divorce as preservation'; that is, the preservation of the family unit, under the authority of the parent who has not failed in his or her duties.

Understanding the notion of the innocent party in these terms, not as a negation of the child's interest but as a particular interpretation of it, we can thus see that the family after divorce is perceived in terms of family continuity. The family functions rather as it would have functioned on the death of one of the spouses. The innocent party is charged with remaining faithful to the matrimonial relationship, albeit now dissolved. Hence the stigmatization of remarriage (Rondeau-Rivier, 1981). Paradoxically then, the basic concept embodied in the 1884 law is the indissolubility of the matrimonial relationship; the guilty party is shut out from the family and suffers virtually a 'social death'.

Very quickly, however, this model of divorce was to be broached. Initially in exceptional cases and then more and more frequently, the weight attached to the role of the mother and to the mother–child relationship came to justify awarding custody to her, irrespective of any fault on her part. The mother thus came to appear as the best guarantor of family continuity, with the mother–child relationship perceived as 'naturally' indissoluble. Conversely, the indissolubility of the marriage gradually ceases to be considered the natural guideline to judge the inevitable exceptions and to regulate them in the interests of preserving the moral and familial order.

What this amounts to, through the increasing reference to the maternal role in the regulation of divorce, is a real mutation in the concept of family relationships. It is no longer the couple and the initial marital commitment which is the basis of the family and its durability, but the parental relations between mother and child. Thus the post-divorce family ceases to be a preserved family and becomes recognized as a different family from the initial unit, a specific type of family with its own organizational modes. It would take too long to retrace all the stages in the recognition of the post-divorce family as a specific type of family unit; in particular, the discourse on the 'child of divorce', a virtual stereotype of the 1950s and 1960s, which shows that 'the aftermath of divorce' is a matter of course and that the interests of the child are no longer confused with the interests of the innocent parent (Thèry, 1985).

From the middle of the 1960s (1964 to be precise) the divorce rate began to rise sharply and continues to rise today. The now routine quality of divorce indicates that the fragility of marriage has come to be seen as an integral element of life. It is no longer a matter of managing the exceptions by reference to the norm but of admitting that the norm has changed. Hence the introduction of divorce by mutual consent in 1975. At the same time, the legislation confirms the evolution in jurisprudential thought and the fact that 'the interest of the child' has become the exclusive criterion in the award of custody. But it would be naive only to see this as a sign of the greater attention accorded the needs of the child, its difficulties, and its 'rights'. What is particularly interesting to note is that this criterion should be presented as claiming to exclude any consideration of the needs, interests, or rights of parents. The concept of 'the interest of the child' necessarily develops into a general image of what the 'good' post-divorce family organization should be, indicating one or more model(s) of family life after divorce. Which one or ones? That is what we must examine.

THE POST-DIVORCE FAMILY: IMAGES AND DOMINANT VALUES

Here I would like to present some of the results of empirical research which I conducted in 1982–3 concerned with the judicial use of the criterion of 'the interest of the child'. I examined all the files concerned with altering custody arrangements after divorce decided by the tribunal in Paris in 1981 – in all, 235 files. The methodology consisted in systematically collecting and classifying the arguments developed by the different actors in the proceedings (the parties themselves, the lawyers, magistrates, social workers, experts) which refer to 'the interest of the child' and then relating those arguments to the information available in each case – sex and age of the children involved, time elapsed since divorce, the sex of the custodial parent, etc. A file comprising seventy-four variables (forty-nine information variables, twenty-five argument variables) was constructed and subjected to statistical analysis – multiple correlation and factorial analysis of correspondence. (For details of the methodology and results, see Thèry, 1983, 1985.)

It is the results concerning parental roles which are most relevant to the question of the concept of the post-divorce family unit and its regulation. The analysis enables us to isolate the following.

1 The evaluative processes of the judges.
2 The dominant values in the post-divorce family.

3 The double logic put to work in the system of regulation.

Let us look at these points in order, in brief outline.

The evaluative processes of the judges

One of the clearest findings of the research is that the findings run contrary to the prevailing discourse of practitioners (judges and advocates). According to this discourse, they decide each case on its merits on the facts of each individual situation. The findings also oppose the prevailing discourse of the opponents of the use of this criterion 'the interest of the child', the understanding of it as an 'alibi' for the individual arbitrariness of each judge. It is possible to isolate the evaluative criteria of the interest of the child; the main decision making criteria which prevail within one jurisdiction and which limit the power of each individual judge. Three main principles can be isolated.

1 Respect for parental agreement – 179 applications were uncontested. In all these cases the judge concerned respected the parental agreement, without really trying to ascertain whether or not it conformed to the needs of the child. It was in 'the interest of the child' that the parents not be in conflict. The judge ratified the proposed solution.

2 Respect for the wishes of the child – 111 files were based on the uncontested wish of the child, ninety-one expressing a wish to change custodial parents, twenty wishing to retain the present situation. Without exception the judge decided in conformity with the wish of the child (only twenty-three children out of a total of 301 were heard by the tribunal).

3 Recognition of the *status quo* – ninety-four applications for changes in custody were based on a *de facto* change in situation, which had preceded the judicial process. The judge 'legalized the situation' in ninety-two cases; one request was withdrawn by the plaintiff (the child had returned in the course of the proceedings to the custodial parent's residence); one was modified; only one of the two children concerned changed their custodial parent.

In total, out of 235 files, there were only fifty-one where the judge tried to determine the 'best solution' by comparative evaluation. Thirty-three of these were decided following the intervention of a social worker or an expert psychiatrist, whose recommendations were followed in 100 per cent of the cases. There were only eighteen files where the magistrate gave judgement according to his 'personal conviction'. Thus the image of the all-powerful magistrate appears to be a stereotype which has no basis in fact; in the large majority of the cases the judge has at his disposal guidelines and constraints which considerably limit his power, but which increase the authority of his decision.

However, the existence of these three clear criteria for evaluation does not resolve all problems: far from it. Each raises many questions, and rightly so. What does parental agreement mean? Is the wish of the child the same as the interest of the child and to what extent is this wish induced by the parent? Does respect for the factual situation not risk it becoming a *fait accompli*? Are the criteria used by experts (psychologists, psychiatrists) legitimate, or are they leading to a 'therapization' of conflictual divorce? Without engaging in this debate (see Thèry, 1985), let us just say at this stage that the norms exist, that it is important to recognize their existence, in the long run, to dispute them and thereby abandon the myth of 'the interest of the child' as an empty concept.

The post-divorce family: dominant values

The analysis of arguments allowed us to extract twenty-four classes of argument, of wide diversity, which can be classified in three sub-headings: norm arguments (arguments of principle, expressed abstractly), circumstantial arguments (description/evaluations of a situation which assumes values without mentioning them by name), and symptom arguments (presented as tacit signs of the adaptation or non-adaptation of the child to his or her situation). Beyond their diversity, the arguments employed present certain dominant characteristics, which indicate reference values. Three main types can be distinguished.

The stability value

This is the number one value; it is omnipresent in the discourse of all the actors in the proceedings. Any change is interpreted as a potential disturbance, which implies that earlier decisions will not be modified except for serious reasons. Thus a change in the custodial parent's circumstances will only work against this predisposition towards the *status quo* where the child's life is radically disrupted. But if the custodial parent wants to live abroad, for example, then it is the non-custodial parent who assumes responsibility for the stability and lifestyle of the child (Thèry, 1985, pp. 5–63).

In another sense, 'stability' is seen as the equivalent of 'morality' and normality: 'I have a stable home' is the argument most frequently employed by parents in describing themselves. The stable home, also called a normal home (a house, a man and wife and children) is highly valued, whereas, conversely, the accusation of instability has begun to displace the former accusation of immorality, but it plays exactly the same role.

The weighting accorded to stability effectively ensures the stability of judicial decisions by discouraging demands for change. Thus the priority given to the mother in the divorce proceedings is carried over, even when the regulation of the marital situation is no longer part of the demands and specific problems of the organization of the post-divorce family. My results, for example, lend no support to the widespread idea that fathers were demanding custody of adolescent children; there is no correlation between the age and the sex of the children and the frequency of demands for change of custody on the part of the fathers, at least in my sample (Thèry, 1985, pp. 64–5).

The reference to the stability is embodied in two different situations, which constitute the two main normative models of post-divorce family life: in the one, what is sought is marital and familial stability reconstituted after the break-up; while the other stresses agreement of the original parents and stigmatizes any conflict as 'an avatar of the marital conflict'.

Model 1: stability and the development of the new union

I found with some astonishment that it was very rare to find any arguments which made reference to the 'natural' competence of the mother or the father; only fourteen requests (out of 235) were predominantly based on the idea that the mother is indispensable to the young child, or that 'paternal authority' is necessary for an adolescent. That seems a very small proportion, if one is seeking a link between the gender division of parental roles to gain custody. But this makes more sense once one grasps the dominant model of the post-divorce family as a reconstituted family, that is as a substitute for the initial family. It is this new family which is to guarantee the return to stability and a place within the social norm. This is in line with the theses developed by W. J. Goode on the pressure to remarry (Goode, 1965, pp. 203-16). Hence the parent living alone, whatever their sex, is suspect; suspected of emotional and sexual instability, suspected of being incapable of overcoming the marital crisis linked to divorce. It is as if only a new union (legitimate or *de facto*, remarriage does not discriminate) guarantees that divorce could be overcome. It is as if the divorce never happened; one can make a clean sweep of the past. The 'good' parent, as a model, is one who is presented to the child as the guarantor of a future independent of the effects of the previous family history. Moreover, the good parent is one who needs nothing, above all not the presence and love of his or her child; a genuine taboo imposes silence on the needs of the parents, especially their emotional needs. To risk evoking them is immediately to be suspected of being a 'vampire' parent over-investing in the child one's own frustration and weakness, thus to be punished by the refusal of custody (Thèry, 1984).

Thus there is a real reversal of traditional models. The stigmatization of remarriage and the prescription of fidelity have given place to the stigmatization of solitude and the prescription of 'remaking one's life', i.e. finding a new partner. Note however that one of the effects of this model is to blur the 'givens'; a fair number of the changes from maternal to paternal custody are principally justified by the presence of the father's new spouse, presented as a maternal substitute. In other words, the biological mother-child relationship is not the sole reason for favouring women and, paradoxically, some awards of custody to the father serve to reinforce the sexual distinction of parental roles, for they are in fact shifts from the mother to the father's second wife. (Thèry, 1983).

Model 2: stability and the stigmatization of parental conflict
Traditionally, one knows that the law does not exactly hold back from stirring up conflicts between the ex-spouses and that this has contributed to contradictory decisions in which the child ends up being passed back and forth from one home to another like a ping-pong ball (Goldstein, Freud, and Solnit, 1973).

But on this model, too, we can see a complete reversal of values. Not only, as we have seen, do judges decide cases in conformity with parental agreement where it exists, but any conflict is stigmatized as harmful to the child and a symptom of the incapacity to overcome the marital crisis. Parental conflict is never seen in terms of disagreements linked to the post-divorce situation but rather equated with a resurgence of the marital conflict. Divorced parents in conflict are essentially ex-spouses still in the grip of their emotional wrangles. Such an image is very dubious, clearly because it gives a unilateral and reductionist interpretation of the disagreements. But its function is to legitimate a genuine norm of goodwill which can be expressed in the form: 'The parental couple should be separate from the breakdown of the couple's relationship.' Two types of divorce are thus highlighted: the 'good' divorce, where the parents are in agreement on the future organization of the family; and the 'bad' divorce, at its worst pathological and pathogenic, the conflictual divorce.

The double logic in the regulatory system

In his analysis of the social regulations applied to the family, Jacques Commaille highlights the plurality of logics and the contradictions which result from 'going beyond any theoretical model in terms of simple causal relations to seek a model which integrates the principle of a complex structure of causalities' (Commaille, 1982, p. 24).

The different meanings given to 'the interest of the child' in the context of a legal procedure designed to award custody are a striking example of the plurality of logics. To the question 'Who can determine where "the interest of the child" lies?' there are four possible answers – the parents, the child itself, the judge, the social workers whose job it is to carry out inquiries or provide expertise. These four responses are presented as simple effects of diverse domestic situations. The parents are the ones best placed to evaluate the interest of the child; if they do not manage to agree, the judge takes over, possibly relying on the expressed wishes of the child; and in the cases of stalemate, the skills of the expert are invoked to help sort out the knots of conflict and to begin to resolve them. The coherence of this 'reactive system' is however only apparent. What happens is that these different and contradictory meanings are treated as if they were part and parcel of the notion of 'the interest of the child'.

1 The interest of the child can be assimilated to whatever the parents agree. In this instance, neither the 'needs' nor the wishes of the child are really put into the balance against a solution which best suits the parties, as we have seen, for example, in the case of the joint decision to remove the child abroad. Seen thus, the interest of the child is scarcely distinguishable from the parental interest. Paradoxically, parental interest is seen as only a formal reference point, whereas, far from indicating a point of view independent of that relating to the child, it in fact conflates the child's needs with the options, choices, and wishes of the parents. Thus, although it might be assumed that in the course of the proceedings the judge will make sure that this agreement is not contrary to the objectives of parental authority (to protect the child's education, welfare, and morality), in fact this process of verification is a formality. The judge only has at his disposal the version of facts presented by the parties and in any case has no power to oversee the enforcement of a judgement imposed on the parents contrary to their joint wishes. In such cases, despite the marital breakdown, the presumption which operates is the same as when parental authority was exercised jointly, namely that the parents are the ones best placed to judge the interests of the child.

2 Second, the interest of the child can be equated with the child's own wishes. Here, from the bundle of factors which constitute the 'advantage' of the child, it is the emotional and relational factors which carry weight. The equation 'wish–need–interest' of the child could however be disputed on its own principles. Making the child responsible in a situation of which it is the subject, and which runs counter to its basic wish for the couple to stay together, is contrary to the principles which justify the legal incapacity of the minor; it assumes the child is able to determine for themselves where their long-term interest lies.

3 When it is the judge who resolves the conflict, he makes reference to a third concept of 'the interest of the child'. What is brought into play here is that bundle of needs and specific rights associated with the idea of childhood as a stage of life – the need for stability and security, the right to education, the right to keep in touch with both parents, and the wider family and friends. These needs and rights are thus presented as basic, universal rights which can then justifiy refusing custody to one of the parents. In this case the respective needs and interests of the parents are

rejected as irrelevant to an evaluation of an interest of the child, which transcends the individual domestic situation at issue. The paradox of this procedure, which makes the judge the child's representative, is that this sense of 'the interest of the child' is also the most controversial, the most open to debate, since it deals in prevailing values in the field of the family and education and yet is left to the subjective appreciation of the judge.

4 Finally, 'the interest of the child' can be understood in terms of family dynamics to be referred back to the family crisis in which the divorce is both a result and a factor. The prevailing perspective among specialists called on to intervene via social inquiry reports or expert reports prioritizes the psycho-emotional dimensions of domestic separation. The interest of the child is run together with the capacity of the adults to accept their situation and their past. Therapeutic support is thereby justified not only at the time of the proceedings but sometimes before and after, in the guise of 'follow-up' of particular separated families.

These four responses, each one stressing a particular aspect of 'the interest of the child' and recognizing the authority of one competent source over the others, reveals not only the plurality but also the disarray, the incoherence, and the contradictions of the sociolegal system of post-divorce regulation. Overarching the infinite diversity of combinations which the complexity of this notion of 'the interest of the child' allows, one can discern the double logic of abstentionism and interventionism.

On the one hand, and undoubtedly more often than not, family law and family justice recognize individuals as autonomous, in the original meaning of the word; that is, as individuals, be they parent or child, who, in creating their own rules, are responsible for the organization of their own lives. It is these choices which are ratified by the judiciary. The transcending norm of The Family is superseded by the plurality of family units and domestic models and, fundamentally, when the flowering of the person and the individual values can justify 'a general movement for the recentering of law on the individual' (Perrin, 1983, p. 221). To the extent that this shift occurs, then the determination of the interest of the child will appear to spring from the private domain of individual liberty.

On the other hand, and again more often than not, intervention in particular families and intrusion at a very personal level is now legitimated by the juridical-legal system, which calls increasingly on the intervention of clinical psychologists, social workers, and psychiatrists, whose skills are drawn into the service of a para-legal regulation of family conflict. This intrusion is moreover usually regarded as acceptable by the divorced spouses themselves and perceived as a support. There are signs of this movement towards deregulation in the development of the practice of mediation in certain countries and in particular in the USA (Ietswaart, 1980; Kelly, 1984), in experiments into family crisis therapy in Sweden, in place of traditional methods of information (Oberg and Oberg, 1984), and, more generally, in the development of assistance on divorce in France and elsewhere.

As its name indicates, such a deregulation of divorce does not mean 'minimal intervention' by the judiciary, but the displacement of this intervention and the transformation of procedures. Indeed, the growing integration of the judicial institution into a 'continuum of structures (medical, administrative, etc.) whose functions are essentially regulatory' (Foucault, 1976, p. 19) is transforming the judicial institution itself. That is to say that the double logic (abstentionist/interventionist) noted in the post-divorce situation cannot be reduced to a clash of strategies and professional codes of ethics, a negotiation of power sharing between law and medical experts leaving each delimited area through sharing of abilities and roles.

The real effect of the mechanisms of regulation is to exacerbate the contradiction by polarizing the two categories of divorcing spouses (in the sense of parties subject to divorce proceedings): those for whom the law rubber-stamps their autonomous decisions; and those upon whom control and regulation are to be imposed. There seem to be few intermediate solutions, at least judging by the very small number of files which we have examined which, in cases of conflict, did not require the implementation of any investigative measures. Thus we have on the one hand a 'lax' judicial system (no doubt because the courts are overworked), and on the other, for the minority, the heavy machinery of social inquiry and expert reports. Consequently, by making the conflict a sign or a symptom of risk-laden divorce, reference to 'the interest of the child' will create among the divorced a sub-population of 'divorced people at risk' as a result of the procedure.

THE SUBSTITUTE FAMILY AND THE ENDURING FAMILY – THE TWO LOGICS OF THE POST-DIVORCE FAMILY

We have analysed the prevailing values in the current image of 'the interest of the child' in its essential characteristics – stability, security, overcoming the marital and family crisis, refusal to instrumentalize the child. The ambiguity of these notions allows them to be used to justify very varied, even opposing, solutions, varying with whether primary competence is allotted to the parents, child, judge, or experts in evaluating this interest. In each instance, these values are organized according to an overriding logic. We have thus noted that the reference to the 'parenting couple' can have two meanings: biological father and mother (whose agreement is the only thing preventing the instrumental use of the child); or the couple formed from one of the parents and a new spouse seen as a parental substitute (the reconstituted home being the best guarantee of the restabilization of the child).

At a more general level, one can distinguish two opposing poles in relation to the 'interest of the child': a logic of substitution which prioritizes the household; and a logic of durability based on the biological family and its history.

Divorce as total split and the logic of substitution

In the files which we have analysed the dominant image seems to be that of a total break in the continuity of the family: the marital breakdown implies a dissolution of the nuclear family; the child must break with its own history. In place of the home which has disappeared the child is given the substitute of one of the reconstituted homes following the requirement of the parental alternative. Calling this the logic of substitution implies that the new home signifies that the marital and domestic crisis has been overcome and the custodial parent is once again in a stable situation. In the end, the child's new equilibrium is only completely assured by the substitution of a new family for the disrupted family, thereby offering the child the gift of a secure life, on a material as well as a psychological and emotional plane. The coherence consists in the following arguments.

1 The development of the concept of the 'normal home' and the idea that the child has need of a major point of orientation.

95

2 The value attached to the new union, the functional perception of parental roles, the image of the second spouse (or companion) as a parental substitute.

3 The perception of stability as a stable way of life, necessary to the child's needs to 'have a childhood' and in particular to settling into school life.

According to this substitution, stability and security are understood through social relationships; 'the interest of the child' views its mode of life by reference to what it would be in a unified nuclear family. The substitute family is fundamentally different from the nuclear family since biological relationships are no longer to be the foundation of the 'natural' family organization. Thus the substitution argument implies:

1 the parental alternative, with parental authority awarded to the sole custodial parent and a strong differentiation between the role of custodial and non-custodial parent;

2 the redefinition of the child's relations with one of its parents (the one with access);

3 the building up of important relationships between the child and the substitute parent who represents a possible second spouse.

In other words, divorce is seen as seriously affecting kinship relationship, in order to facilitate a new family life. The effects of divorce may thus be minimized by a conflict-free transition in the daily life of the child. Paradoxically, the continuity of relationship between the child and one of their biological parents allows (and requires) making a clean break with the past without compromising the psychological and emotional balance of the child.

This model can be clearly distinguished from the traditional model of the maintenance of the original family around the 'innocent' spouse. The remarriage or the new union are no longer shocking: quite the contrary. The setting aside of one of the parents is justified, *a posteriori*, because of the functional way in which parental roles are perceived: the parent–child relationship only has importance and worth to the extent that it appears in daily life; the substitute family is seen as the sole means of offering anew the benefit of a normal home, despite the breakdown of marital relations; it follows that one or other of the biological parents can continue in place. Hence this 'parental alternative' approach is quite different from the opposition between the innocent and the guilty party.

For the system to work, parental agreement is necessary, in contrast with the traditional model (one knows that justice does not fear to fan the flames of conflict). This agreement is an agreement of mutual non-interference, implying that each parent accepts their new status. If visiting rights and 'staying over' progress without problems, there will be no disturbance of the new home. Even the complete disappearance of the non-custodial parent would not affect the organization of the post-divorce family unit, since s/he does not assume the status of secondary parent, and may divest him/herself of his/her interest in the child – is even encouraged to do so.

At the opposite pole is the other logic representing a minority view. It presents divorce as a transition in a none the less continuous history and presents divorce as a reorganization of the already existing system of relationships.

Divorce as reorganization and the logic of durability

In this perspective, the marital break-up, where it involves the separation into two households, paternal and maternal, is not perceived as splitting up the family. Divorce is a transition between the original family unit and the reorganization of the family, which remains a unit, but a bipolar one.

In the context of the theory of the durability of the family the following issues are raised.

1 The right of the child to keep his two parents, to love them both, and to benefit from the two separate attachments.

2 The idea that a substitute parent can never replace the biological parent.

3 The perception of stability as first and foremost psychological and emotional, as a stability achieved despite the breakdown (and not a stability recovered after the breakdown).

In this logic, stability as a prime concern of the child is a function of the unity of the biological family, still preserved, and the continuity of the family history. It does not derive from the unity of the household. Anything which can assimilate the child's current relations to his parents with what it was before the breakdown is perceived as being in 'the interest of the child'. To see the father and mother as equal and complementary is to ensure the permanence of the family and thereby the child's welfare.

This model implies:

1 the refusal of the parental-alternative, in favour of joint parental authority;

2 effective care and control of the child by both parents on an equal basis.

In the post-divorce scenario, the mode of family life is seen to be understood through practical arrangements; the child has two points of reference, two households, between which it comes and goes. This specificity can be organized in such a way as to minimize certain effects (homes close to one another, staying on at the same school, keeping the same friends) or maximize them (homes at a distance, annual rotation, changing school, etc.). These are more than minor variations. In the former, the parents accept certain imperatives so that alternating between parents will not affect the child's way of life in a major way, in order to minimize its effect on the parent–child relationship; hence its symmetry with the substitution model. On the durability model, discontinuity of way of life is subordinate to the dangers which any discontinuity of the basic parent–child relationship implies and is in the long run considered to be a stabilizing influence.

In this perspective, parental agreement is highly valued, not as an agreement not to interfere, but as an agreement to co-operate actively.

Although each of these opposed logics represents a coherent conception of the post-divorce situation, in the majority of cases the judges, and in general the professionals involved with the family, cannot be neatly situated in one or other of the alternatives of substitution or durability. Numerous rules tend to lend weight to one or other of the extremes of thought, or rather to alleviate the effects of the dominant logic in each instance.

1 For parents who fall clearly within the substitution perspective, the importance of the relationship of the child to the non-custodial parent is emphasized.

2 In the opposite case, for parents who have opted for change in

line with the durability theory, the child's need for stable benchmarks will be mentioned, not least of which is an uninterrupted education and the unhappiness which would result from further separation from his friends and loved ones.

These attempts to rebalance the situation do not, however, mean that a genuine synthesis is possible, which would permit us to overcome the contradiction between the perception of divorce as a split or as reorganization.

CONCLUSION

Judicial uncertainties reveal the importance of the current social stakes in the post-divorce situation. In the substitution theory, the mother (and, more generally, the woman, if one includes the second spouse) remains the person who is the principal means of ensuring the permanence of the child's relationships. According to the logic of durability, paternal and maternal roles are assumed to be equally important and thus less gender specific.

Thus the present situation which appears to stress and reinforce the most traditional models in the division of parental roles, which seems a sign that there is nothing new under the patriarchal sun, is, in my opinion, actually quite a novel situation. It is no longer the nature of the mother–child relationship but the prevailing definition of the post-divorce family which confines women to their role of the guardian of the hearth. But this definition of the family has become the subject of debates and contradictions, which leave one to ponder on the possibility of an alternative to the dominant model. Is it not disturbing that the feminists leave the initiative on this problem to fathers' organizations?

Chapter Five

BEST INTERESTS AND JUSTICE

Kirsten Sandberg

INTRODUCTION

In Norway a new Children and Parents Act was passed in 1981 and put into force on 1 January 1982. Among other changes, the Act did away with the maternal presumption (the preference given to the mother) in child custody cases. The sole criterion for deciding custody conflicts between the mother and the father after a divorce is now 'the best interest of the child'. In this chapter I want to look into the effects of that rule, both for the children and for the mothers. In the light of these effects I also set out to discuss alternative principles and their basis in legal philosophy. I shall concentrate on young children, since that is where the maternal presumption used to apply.

To give a more complete picture of the rules concerning custody, I should mention that the parent with whom the child does not live normally has visitation rights. If 'ordinary visitation rights' have been stipulated, it means one evening a week, every other weekend, two weeks during summer, and either Christmas or Easter. The visitation rights are, however, intended to be decided in accordance with the circumstances in each individual case. Even though the extent of the visitation rights is important, my focus here will be on the question of with whom the child is to live.

The custody question can be divided into issues of physical custody and of legal custody. Even if one of the parents alone has physical custody of the child (i.e. the child lives with him or her), the parents may have joint legal custody. In that case the decisions concerning the daily care are still left to the parent with whom the child lives, but the major decisions in the child's life (e.g. choice of school) have to be made by the mother and father together. The parent who has physical custody always has legal custody, either alone or jointly with the other parent. Thus physical custody is usually the essential question in cases where both parents want the child. The question of whether or not there will be joint legal custody is of course important as well, but the considerations are somewhat different from those concerning where the child is to live. So the questions may be dealt with separately, and in order not to make the scope too wide, this chapter will only deal with physical custody.

As long as the parents agree, they are free to decide on whatever arrangement they like with regard to physical and legal custody and visitation rights, without having to obtain a formal approval from the authorities.[1] But where the parents do not agree there has to be a formal decision taken in court or by the administrative authority. My concern as regards the 'best interest' criterion which is applied in these cases is whether that criterion is actually in the child's best interest, and whether it does justice to the parents – in particular the parent who has invested most in the daily care of the child. The justice question is not only an individual one; it concerns primary caretakers as a group. Since women are still in most cases the primary caretakers, it may at the same time be viewed as a question of group justice for women.

In order to find out something about how the criterion works in these respects I have examined court decisions from all three court instances – county courts, Courts of Appeal, and the Supreme Court, sixty-three decisions in all. I am not in this chapter going to refer to the decisions, but they serve as background material.

In the second section the best interest criterion will be presented in some more detail. Section three contains a discussion of the problems of that principle. In the last section I shall discuss some alternative approaches for solving custody conflicts.

THE PRESENT LEGAL SITUATION

The removal of the maternal presumption

The best interest of the child was the main criterion in deciding custody conflicts before 1981, but it was combined with a certain presumption in favour of the mother with regard to children below school age (around 7). The presumption was to be applied only when one was not able to tell whether the child would be better off with one or other parent, but in practice the interpretation of the rule and thus the strength of the presumption varied from court to court.

As part of its mandate, the committee which was appointed in 1975 to prepare a new Children and Parents Act was asked to try in general to promote equality between the father's and the mother's relation to the child. The committee published its report in 1977.[2]

With regard to custody disputes the committee wanted the child's best interest to be the guiding principle, and made a proposal to abolish the maternal presumption, which was followed up by parliament. It was argued that the presumption was in conflict both with the principle of the child's best interest and with the principle of the equal position of the parents in relation to the child (*Report*, p. 63). The problem of what is actually to be regarded as an 'equal position' (i.e. according to which criteria) was not touched upon. The irrelevance of traditional sex roles was underlined. It was said to be 'unsatisfactory if a mother should get custody on the grounds that the child is so small that he or she needs a mother's care, since apart from the breast-feeding the care is such that a father is also capable of providing' (p. 64). We can gather from this that at least part of the legislature had a rather idealistic view of the relationship between the sexes within marriage, and of what is possible to obtain by legislation.

The legislators did not want to take into the statute anything more specific about what is in the child's best interest; each case must be decided on its own merits after a consideration of all relevant factors. General rules in this field, it was felt, could easily lead to decisions contrary to the best interests of a particular child. Consequently a completely discretionary rule was favoured. None of the three official reports[3] in the legislative process referred to the counter arguments to such a rule that are also relevant to the child's interests, such as the decision becoming more difficult and thus taking longer to achieve. They underlined the importance to the child of quick decisions, without connecting it to the criteria that the court has to apply.

The 'best interest of the child'

The legislators ultimately gave a few guiding principles as to what is in the child's best interest (stated in the reports, but not in the Act itself). The main one was the importance that should be attached to who has the strongest emotional contact with, and has had the actual care of, the child. The mother would consequently be favoured in most cases concerning a small child, they said, when she has actually been the primary caretaker. The weight attached to these factors should decrease as the child approaches school age (7 years). They presumed that the situation might change as fathers increasingly take part in the daily care of the child from the birth onwards.

In addition there is a list of arguments that the legislators considered relevant in custody cases, based on Supreme Court practice. They are in the following order: the *status quo* argument (the risk that goes with moving the child); the gender and age of the child; the disinclination to split siblings; the possibilities of each parent providing care for the child; the contact between the child and each of the parents; the child's own wishes; the likelihood that the contact with both parents and all siblings will be kept up; and the housing conditions. It was also mentioned that the Supreme Court tends to give great weight to the views of the court appointed expert. The legislators underlined that each case must be decided on its own merits and that the weight of the different factors will vary from case to case.

A wish to have a job outside the home was not to disfavour one or other parent in the custody decision. Another factor which was considered irrelevant by the legislators was the economic advantage of one home over the other. The financial position of the two parents was not supposed to count as long as it is above a certain minimum level. Neither was the question of whose 'fault' the break-up is nor whether the social behaviour of one of them is not blameless, unless it could lead to social adjustment problems for the child. Nor should 'kidnapping' by one of the parents automatically disqualify him or her, since it might not be in the child's interest. Instead a preliminary decision ought to be made quickly so that the 'kidnapper' is not favoured by the *status quo* argument.

The parents' wishes

As long as the wishes of the mother and the father are the same, they are free to decide and the child is subject to their private judgement. When the parents cannot agree, however, their wishes are of little importance. In all the earlier provisions on custody the wishes of the parents were expressly mentioned, as a secondary argument. In 1981 it was removed from the text, on the grounds that parents who disagree presumably have opposing wishes. Still it was stated in one of the legislative documents that, where neither of the solutions is noticeably better than the other, the court can consider which one of the parents is most in need of the child and who will suffer the greatest loss by not getting custody.

So there is an opening for considerations of the parents' interests, which does not follow from the best interest criterion. Behind this may be a sense of justice – the interests of the parents are weighed, and it seems just to 'allocate' the child to the parent with the strongest interests in having him or her. The reason for considering the parents' interests may, however, be a wish to find the solution that maximizes the total welfare. Probably there is a combination of the two. As nothing is said about this in the legislative document, the legislators may well have been unaware of their reasons.

THE PROBLEMS OF THE BEST INTEREST CRITERION

Whilst the interest of the child should have an important place in the considerations of child custody, the parents' interests are not irrelevant. So there are three parties whose interests should be considered in selecting criteria for deciding custody conflicts. As a consequence of the desire to focus on the child, 'the child's best interest' has entered legislation as the criterion for custody decisions. It is easy to believe that this is actually the best criterion for securing the interests of the child. However, several objections may be raised when it comes to using this criterion in individual cases. In addition the present rule is problematic with regard to the interests of the parents.

The lack of predictability

A major disadvantage of the criterion is the lack of predictability which is an effect of the extensive discretion left to the court. The one factor which was particularly emphasized by the legislators with regard to small children, and which would have given greater predictability – the primary caretaker function during the marriage – is hardly used by the courts. Presumably the lack of predictability has an impact on the number of cases that are brought before the courts, since there is a stronger reason to have the case tried when the outcome is uncertain. A lawsuit is undesirable from the child's point of view, because it takes a long time and tends to reinforce the conflict. The lack of predictability may also affect the private arrangements that the parties make, in particular if one looks at the divorce settlement as a whole. The threat of bringing the case to court, with an uncertain outcome, may easily be used as pressure on the other party in order to obtain advantages in the economic settlement. This is more likely to disadvantage mothers, precisely because they are more vulnerable economically than their husbands. It is unfortunate if the parent who gets custody in return accepts a lower maintenance agreement for the children or loses the matrimonial home. The pressure to accept such arrangements is felt particularly by women who have been primary caretakers because their identity is closely linked to the status of motherhood and the bonds with their children.

The length of time

Another considerable problem of the present rule is the length of time it takes to find out what is actually in the best interest of the child. There are innumerable factors to be considered. Consequently the parties need time to prepare the case, the procedure in court is long-winded, and, because the criterion is difficult to apply, writing the judgement may take too long. Among these the crucial problem is the time spent on the preparation of the case.

The ten cases that I have examined from the county courts lasted from six months to one year five months, and this seems to be quite representative of custody cases as a whole. The duration of my twenty-four cases in the Court of Appeal varied from five months to well over a year, starting from the time of the judgement in the county court. Two of them took as long as two years seven months from the summons until the Court of Appeal judgement. In the fourteen cases decided by the Supreme Court from 1982 to 1986, over two years usually passed from the summons to the final decision of the case. The Supreme Court proceedings separately (from the Court of Appeal judgement) took eight months or more.

One of the reasons why the preparation of the case drags on is the fact that the judge often finds his own qualifications inadequate to deal with questions of this kind, and hence he appoints experts. The Children and Parents Act encourages the appointment of independent experts (psychologists, social workers, doctors) where needed. In addition to the difficulties of finding experts who have the time and are willing to do the job, the job itself (examining the parents and children, the home and surroundings, and writing a report) often takes a long time. The strain on the child increases with the duration of the case, because of the continued uncertainty.

Goldstein, Freud, and Solnit (1980, p. 41) have particularly emphasized the importance of considering the child's sense of time, which is different from that of the adult. What seems like a long time even to us, represents an eternity to the child. Even a few months of uncertainty can be a long time of insecurity from the child's point of view.

Indeterminate decisions

The rule does not necessarily lead to materially 'correct' decisions (i.e. decisions that are actually in the best interest of the children). There is great uncertainty attached to the decisions. A main reason for this is the fact that they have to be based on predictions for the future, since the criterion invokes what *will be* in the best interest of the child. The courts are not very well equipped to make this kind of evaluation as legal training is primarily aimed at applying the law to facts established in the past.

Another reason why the decisions are indeterminate is that they are based on value judgements. The legislation says little about the values on which the choice between the parents should be based. That is hardly surprising since it would be almost impossible. Who can say anything in general as to whether a child is better off in a safe but perhaps somewhat dull home, or in a less stable but maybe more challenging one? The plurality of society is better taken care of by the legislation refraining from setting up such general priorities. But in that way the choice of values is left to the judge. This is not an unusual precedent, but the best interest criterion facilitates this difficulty to a particularly great extent, being so dependent as it is on value judgements. Incidentally the judge not only has to choose from among competing values, but also from amongst different theories on the development of children. The views of psychologists not only change over time – there is also disagreement at any time over how the different factors influence the development of the child (e.g. the importance of the *status quo*).

A third reason for indeterminacy is the variation in the descriptions of the facts of the case. For example, the majority in a particular Court of Appeal decision that I studied stated that a period of four years was 'not a very long time'. There were two children of just under 6 and 8, and the court was considering for how long the mother would be able to take care of them full-time. If the court had seen the case from the children's point of view, four years would have appeared to be a very long time. The tendency for 'facts' to be construed in such a way as to obtain the desired result is not unknown in the law in general; but it is possible that a criterion which implies an evaluation of the parents as persons makes the courts more inclined to hide their real considerations behind the representation of the facts.

The parents' acceptance of the decision

It is important that the parents should accept the decision of the court; otherwise they are likely to appeal, and the uncertainty and disquiet is then prolonged. Even if the decision is not appealed, discontentment with the decision may lead to continued disquiet. Many people will, of course, have difficulty accepting a decision in these cases whatever criterion is used because it means so much to them personally and it concerns something that is not easily left behind. But probably the risk of the 'losing party' being discontented is greater with the present criterion than with a criterion based on facts that are more easily established. The present rule to a great extent implies an evaluation and comparison of the parties as parents and thus as persons. They may not recognize the facts as described by the court, or they may consider that the decision takes too little account of their interests for other reasons. It can be difficult to keep up a natural relationship with the child under such circumstances. In the debate in Norway little attention has been paid to this fact. At least there seems to be little awareness that the problems of accepting the decision may have something to do with the basic criterion for the decision.

This is not to say that the attitudes of the parents are mainly a responsibility of the law – the parents themselves are primarily responsible. But the law can make it more or less easy for the parents to reconcile themselves to the arrangements provided. Even if compulsory counselling is introduced, as has been suggested, one must assume that some cases will end up in court. Thus there has to be a criterion in the law, on which the court decision will be based and which will affect the willingness of the losing party to accept his or her situation.

It should be pointed out that the criterion in the law is not only of interest when a court has to decide the case. The criterion also influences the possibility of obtaining an agreement between the parties (e.g. as a result of counselling) and thus of preventing the case from being brought to court at all. If the criterion gives little predictability, the parent who does not get custody by an out-of-court agreement may feel that a case before the court is still worth a try. The rule thus becomes a lever for what the parents are willing to accept in a counselling situation.

The parents' interests

In the previous paragraph I discussed the parents' interests indirectly, connecting them with the interests of the child. I maintained that a decision which takes due regard of the parents' interests provides the best possibility for co-operation in divorce situations. The interests of the parents should, however, be considered on their own account, as long as they do not disadvantage the child. The parents are also persons with thoughts and feelings, having to live with the custody decision. Their interests should at least have a place in the considerations of the legislators. But it is less clear that the interests of the parents should be considered in each individual case, because of the risks of promoting more conflict which this might imply.

The maternal presumption was abolished partly because it was found to be in conflict with the principle of equality. Consequently the legislators must have considered that the present principle does in fact promote equality. However, one may ask according to which criteria this equality is measured. A purely formal equality would be undesirable in that it does not take the facts into consideration – in this case the general practice of child care. (On *de jure* and *de facto* equality, see Dahl, 1987, pp. 48–51.) The equality established by the best interest principle is not totally formal, since it neither 'splits' the child between the parents nor gives them equal chances as in a lottery. But even if it does in fact take reality into consideration, this is only part of the reality. The principle looks only to the future, not to the past.

It might be argued that the past is implicitly included since you cannot judge the future without looking to the past. But the past then enters the decision in a very indirect way. From an examination of the court decisions in Norway, it turns out that the arguments relating to the past (i.e. the primary caretaker function and the emotional attachment) are not as central as one would like to think. Who has been the primary caretaker during the marriage does not seem to be taken into account, even when only a few months have passed since the break-up. The emotional attachment between the child and each of the parents is more frequently taken into consideration. Yet in several decisions this was not expressly dealt with, no doubt because it is a factor which can be very hard to judge. So with regard to the past, the principle puts the parents on a formally equal level, more or less. What each of the parents have invested in their relationship with the child is paid little attention. In consequence, the result of treating people equally when their situation is in fact different is a *de facto* inequality. Fathers have, because of the new legislation, obtained a stronger position in child custody cases than their efforts in the caretaking of children should fairly allow.

The question of justice

We have here entered into a discussion of justice. Whether the reason for wanting to promote equality between the parents was a wish to obtain justice for the parents, or whether it was for the sake of welfare for the child (or children in general) is unclear. Whatever these reasons may have been, it is hard to overlook the question of justice for parties who are so directly involved. A sense of justice is often present when a decision is made – consciously or subconsciously. There is an intuitive feeling of whether a decision is just or not, and this is closely linked to the criterion for the decision.

There are different criteria for what is just, and here I have mentioned one possible criterion – the effort laid down in the caretaking during marriage, which I regard as central. I shall discuss other possibilities and give the reasons for my choice in the next section. Here I shall keep to the caretaking function.

The best interest principle does not necessarily create unjust solutions (i.e. unjust with regard to the effort made in the process of caring) in every case decided by the courts. In some cases, of course, the result coincides with who has been the primary caretaker, but in other cases the result may be unfair in that it does not. It may not, however, primarily be the result which is the problem in the individual case, but the lack of a guarantee that the primary caretaker argument will be considered at all.

There is also an important group aspect to the question of justice. As mentioned above, the present rule has given fathers in general a stronger position than they 'deserve' according to their general investment in their children. Mothers accordingly occupy a weaker position. The reason why they should have a stronger position than the present rule gives them is their function as primary caretakers. Today this function is still, in most marriages, carried out by the mother, and so the argument is easily seen as a gender argument. But it also favours the few men who are the primary caretakers of their children. In any case, justice for primary caretakers, whether women or men, is not well served by the best interest principle.

ALTERNATIVE APPROACHES

General remarks

It appears from the foregoing that the best interest of the child criterion is not necessarily the best one to secure the child's interests in a custody case. The lack of predictability and the long time the cases take are clearly to the disadvantage of the child. The other arguments show that the decision that is finally made according to the rule is not necessarily the best one for the child.

That is particularly true for the arguments of indeterminacy and dependence on the individual judge. This does not mean that the decision is never the best one, but possibly one could reach decisions that would be just as good for the child by a rule that was more easily applicable.

The interest of the primary caretaker – today mostly the mother – is not properly served by the present rule. This is a problem in itself, since it concerns a group of people who have a weaker position in society in general. Had the criterion been an ideal one from the point of view of the child, one might have had to accept the disadvantages to women (or primary caretakers). But since there are objections on behalf of the child as well, it must be legitimate to ask whether there might exist another criterion which is more favourable to mothers, while at the same time serving the child's interest at least to the same extent as the present one. To come up with a flawless criterion is presumably impossible. I shall, however, discuss three alternatives to see if any of them would be preferable.

The maternal presumption

A priority to one of the parents on the grounds of gender has advantages as compared to the best interest principle with regard to some of the objections mentioned above. It implies greater predictability, and lawsuits should take less time. It may be argued that the decisions that such a presumption leads to are not as good for the individual child, but this is debatable since the best interest principle does not guarantee the decisions being actually the best ones for the child either. Besides, one could regard the advantages to the great majority of children in relation to predictability and time as outweighing the possible disadvantages to a few. The presumption would, in that case, have to be in favour of the mother. By far the greatest number of parents who agree on the custody question give custody to the mother, and so a presumption to the contrary would probably increase the number of conflicts. The fact that the parties themselves normally choose the mother should also be an indication that they consider her to be more fit to have custody, in addition to her being more willing. So this would be a better solution for most children than a paternal presumption. A paternal presumption would also be unfair to women as a group, since they are still the ones doing most of the child care work.

Unfairness, however, poses an objection to the maternal presumption as well. It cannot be said to be unfair to men as a group but to some men in individual cases, where they have invested more in the children. It is questionable whether this consideration, together with the interests of the children of those men, is stronger than the counter arguments. In any case the maternal presumption was removed from the law in 1981, and presumably it would not be politically possible to reintroduce it. Consequently it is not a solution to our present problems.

Coin tossing

A more unusual idea, raised by the philosopher Jon Elster, is to toss a coin (Elster, 1987, p. 40). He gives two main arguments for this solution. First, the procedure is simple and automatic, thus sparing the child the pain of custody litigation. The case will be decided as soon as the judge finds that neither parent is unfit, which should be done according to simple, robust criteria – physical neglect, physical abuse, mental disorders. Second, flipping a coin is fair to the parents, since they are treated equally and are given equal opportunities.

The first argument is easy to agree with. One would avoid one of the main problems of the best interest criterion, which is the long time required for litigation. It is true that the lack of predictability would be total, but it might not be much greater than today, and so the number of cases would hardly increase. Should there be an increase, the cases would still not be any particular strain on the child.

But there are counter arguments based on the interests of the child, arguments concerning the contents of the decisions. Introducing a coin tossing rule would mean giving up the attempts to make a decision which would be better for the child than the opposite one. Even though 'the best interest of the child' used as a criterion leads to uncertain decisions, the chances of making the right choice must after all be greater than by the flipping of a coin. Still, admittedly it is questionable whether they would be so much better as to outweigh the pain to the child of litigation.

To his other argument, however, strong objections may be raised. A system of coin tossing would imply formal equality, but not *de facto* equality. The latter is not obtained until reality is taken into consideration. As long as the mothers still do the bulk of child care work during the marriage, it would not seem fair to let the fathers have the children in 50 per cent of the cases after a divorce, which would be the result of coin flipping. The injustice would affect mothers as a group as well as the individual caretaking woman losing the coin tossing (and the individual men – fewer than the women – who were in the same position).

A more fundamental objection to coin flipping as a decision method for the courts is the disclaiming of responsibility to provide decisions for which grounds can be given. It is true that the decisions are uncertain and difficult, but that is hardly sufficient reason to leave them completely to chance. After all there are certain things to go by in considering what is good for a child. One should rather try to transform that information into guidelines that are more easily applicable than the best interests of the child, instead of giving up any possibility of influencing the decisions, which the flipping of a coin would mean. As opposed to other situations where coin tossing is used as a decision method, the 'object' of the decision in this case is a subject with its own interests in the outcome.

The primary caretaker

The interests of the child

The first objection to the best interest rule discussed above was the lack of predictability. In the great majority of cases where there has actually been a primary caretaker the parents themselves will know who it is. Consequently the predictability would be far better if the caretaking function was considered a main factor in deciding with whom the child is to live after the break-up. That should result in fewer cases brought before the court, to the benefit of those children who would then not be made the objects of litigation. Besides, there would not be the same point in using the possibility of litigation as a threat in order to obtain advantages in the economic settlement.

The time aspect ought also to be different if the case was then litigated, because the theme of discretion would be so much simpler. There would be one matter to concentrate on in the production of evidence. Experts would not be needed in as many cases as today, since the decision would be based on an evaluation of facts in the past, which the courts can more easily deal with on their own. The pain to the child would be reduced considerably with a more speedy decision.

Whether the decision would be better for the child under a primary caretaker criterion than under the best interest criterion is hard to say. But if there is to be a presumption, this must be the one which serves the child's interests best. It should only exceptionally result in a worse solution than if the other parent was chosen; the primary caretaker should have a good foundation for continuing the caretaking function. That parent has demonstrated a willingness to take care of the child and has practice in doing the job. There is also reason to believe that the child is emotionally more attached to her or him. Besides, during the marriage the parties after all set up the caretaker arrangement together, and would hardly have done this while thinking that the actual primary caretaker was less fit than the other parent.

The argument that there is a connection between the best interest of the child and the caretaking function, or at least that they are not contradictory, is probably more relevant for smaller children. When the child has reached school age (7 years) there are other points of attachment – to people and places – that can become so important that they ought to count. There may also be other things about the parents that have a greater impact on the relationship to the child than the caretaking function. Chambers (1984), who gives some support to a primary caretaker preference, would only let the presumption apply to small children, i.e. up to about 5 years of age. In West Virginia, USA, where the presumption is actually in use (see below), they make a distinction at 6. The presumption applies above that age as well, but can then be rebutted by the child's own preference. In the following the primary caretaker principle is intended to be applied mainly as a criterion for young children.

A primary caretaker rule would lead to more certain decisions, in the sense that it is easier to check that the criterion is satisfied. This is a consequence of the narrower scope of the evidence to be produced, of the scrutiny of the past instead of the future, and that the choice of values is not left to the judge – the same factors that imply greater predictability and quicker decisions.

The parents should be able to accept a decision based on the caretaking more easily than a decision stating what is in the best interest of the child. This is due partly to my assumption that such a criterion will presumably be perceived as more fair, and partly to the fact that the parents will not have to go through a comparison as parents and persons. It should be easier to bear a loss of custody based on relatively neutral facts in the past than a loss grounded in an evaluation of future fitness as a parent. And as stated above, the parents' attitude is not unimportant to the child.

I have discussed the primary caretaker principle in relation to the interests of the child in the light of the four objections to the present rule raised above. At the two points – predictability and time – concerning the costs of litigation (i.e. the pain to the child of a protracted case) a primary caretaker criterion should give better results than the present one. The same applies to the parents' acceptance of the outcome. As regards the contents of the decision, the proposed criterion would hardly lead to worse decisions than 'the best interest of the child', considering all the uncertainty it implies.

The interests of the parents

What is just with regard to the parents' situation is not obvious. The arguments may concern the consequences for each of them of a decision in one direction or the other, i.e. each parent's need to have custody. These are arguments concerning the future. Alternatively the arguments may be rights-based and thus concerned with the past.

Probably parents' interests lie in both directions. It is possible that future needs are their basic concern. That does not mean, however, that their needs should be used as a criterion for decision, since the underlying reason for a rule or a criterion is not the same thing as the rule itself. Besides I have a strong impression that many people also want to see the decision relate to what has already taken place, and this should influence the choice of criterion. Where there has been a relationship of longer or shorter duration, both between the parents and with the child, it is hard for this to be disregarded in the custody decision. A rule which only looks ahead discounts an important part of the reality on which the parents base their sense of justice.

Another significant disadvantage of basing a decision on the future welfare of the parents is the uncertainty of that argument. The general uncertainty of predictions applies here too. Even more important in this instance is perhaps the problem of evidence – there is little guarantee that parents will not exaggerate their needs. Their statements about future needs are strategically manipulable and not easily verifiable (Elster, 1987, p. 19). The problems of evidence are much greater here than with regard to past behaviour.

Consequently the parents' interests might possibly be better served by a rights-based rule. But there are a variety of rights-based arguments, and not all of them would be as suitable in choosing which parent to give priority to in custody cases.

One question is whether status or behaviour should be used as the criterion. The maternal presumption was a right based on status; it was sufficient to be mother of the child. The presumption consequently was a right for women as a group. You may ask if priority should still be given to the women as a compensation for their vulnerable position as a group in society in general and after a divorce in particular. It is important to try to improve the position of disadvantaged groups by improving their legal position. But it is hard to disregard completely the interest of the child even if I am now discussing the interests of the parents. If mothers should have a right as a group in this respect, it must be based on their relationship with the child and not exist independently of that. Since the mothers are still primary caretakers in the majority of cases, that might still be the basis of a group right. But then the right might just as well be directly connected with the caretaking function, i.e. the behaviour itself. That would in the present-day situation in most cases give the same results as the maternal presumption, and thus favour mothers as a group. But the mother would not have custody of the child in the cases where the father has made the greatest effort in taking care of the child.

Rights based on past behaviour are sex-neutral, and as such perhaps preferable to rights based on status. But it does not follow that any type of sex-neutral criteria are preferable. The best interest principle is sex-neutral, but it represents a false kind of equality since it does not take sufficient account of what has happened in the past, which is an important part of the reality of child care. A status rule like the maternal presumption may consequently render the same degree of *de facto* equality as a welfare-based rule, if the choice of status is based on the facts of life – in this case a consideration of behaviour and needs.

Assuming, however, that among the rights-based arguments past behaviour should be preferred to status, the question becomes which past behaviour to focus on. The two options would be the caretaking function and the matter of 'guilt' toward the other party. A break-up may in some cases quite clearly be the fault of one party, and in that case a pure consideration of fairness might indicate that custody be given to the other. Normally, however, the question of guilt is so complex that it can hardly give rise to any kind of rights in a conflict between the parties. This is just one of the reasons why it is considered unacceptable to bring the question of guilt into custody cases, the most important reason being that it is totally irrelevant from the point of view of the child and thus should not give rise to rights in these cases.

The effort made in child care work is, on the other hand, not irrelevant in considering the interests of the child. It should also be much easier to assess than the degree of guilt of each of the parents. At least that would be the case if the effort was measured in terms of the time spent in caring.

I have argued that a rights-based rule may serve the parents' interests better than a welfare-based rule. But since the welfare is probably central to the parents, a rights-based rule cannot be chosen without regard to whether it will also cater for the parents' needs. In this connection it is the need to be with the children which should be considered – not any other need which might be satisfied by having custody, such as a desire for revenge.

Among the possible rights-based criteria for deciding the custody question, the primary caretaker function is probably the one which, to the largest extent, takes account of the parents' needs. It is at least an indication of ongoing needs, since the parent who has been the primary caretaker until the break-up is presumably in most cases the one who will suffer the greater loss by not getting custody.

The primary caretaker rule in practice

Using the caretaking during marriage as a criterion is not just a theoretical idea. In the state of West Virginia in the USA the 'primary caretaker parent rule' has been enacted, and the principle has been warmly recommended by Chief Justice Richard Neely (Neely, 1984). His main arguments for this, as compared to the best interest principle, are the drastic reduction of the need for a protracted, damaging investigation into family life and the fitness of the parents, and the limited possibility of using the children as bargaining factors in the economic settlement – child support, alimony, and division of property. He is concerned with protecting women from having to accept anything in order to keep the children. At the same time the rule is gender neutral and does not exclude the father from the possibility of getting custody.

It is a condition for using the caretaking function as a factor in a custody case that there has actually been a primary caretaker. In West Virginia the primary caretaker parent is defined as the parent who:

1 prepares the meals;

2 changes the diapers and dresses and bathes the child;

3 chauffeurs the child to school, church, friends' homes, and the like;

4 provides medical attention, monitors the child's health, and is responsible for taking the child to the doctor;

5 interacts with the child's friends, school authorities, and other parents engaged in activities that involve the child.

The formulation of a primary caretaker rule must be discussed in more detail, but it is possible that the practical tasks listed above can be an acceptable starting point for the evaluation of the effort of each of the parents. In the Norwegian situation one parent alone may not have taken responsibility for every item mentioned above. It is gradually becoming more common in this country for the father to some extent to take part in the household work, if only because more married women work outside the home than they used to.[4] But still many women work part-time, and many stay at home for long periods after the birth of each child. Where the woman works full-time, she often has more clearly defined working hours than the man, with less overtime, meetings, and so forth. Yet even if they both work the same hours, the mother tends to do more of the practical caretaking work (e.g. it is often she who stays home with a sick child).

In Norway, an objection to the primary caretaker principle might be based on the possible difficulty of deciding who has been the primary caretaker. I do not consider this to be a valid argument, at least not at present. Even where there has been some sharing, the mother has still, in most cases, had the undefined overall responsibility, taking care of the necessary little details which would otherwise have been overlooked. It will probably take time before an equal sharing of work and responsibility becomes common, if ever. In the meantime a primary caretaker preference would be workable. It does not deny men the possibility of having the custody of children, since if a father has been the primary caretaker, he will benefit from the rule.

The strength of the presumption

In a conflict between the parents the question may arise of whether the child would be better off with the other parent than the primary caretaker. Then the strength of the presumption becomes important, i.e. how much must weigh in favour of the other parent in order that the presumption be set aside.

There are at least three possibilities with regard to the strength of a primary caretaker preference (Chambers, 1984, p. 562). The strongest version would mean that the primary caretaker received custody unless demonstrated to be unfit. The next would be where the other parent received custody upon producing 'clear and convincing evidence' that he or she would be more fit to have custody. In its weakest form, the presumption would only be applied if, after the production of evidence, there was still an absolute uncertainty as to what was in the best interest of the child, or if the parents were then considered to be equal. That is, the preference would be set aside if the balance tipped just slightly in favour of the non-caretaker parent. In this version the presumption would not have many of the advantages which were intended by its introduction. One would risk a full trial with a substantial calling of evidence, and the predictability would not be much greater than today.

The preference in its strongest version would give the greatest advantages at the points on which the present rule is criticized. That is the version applied in West Virginia for children under the age of 6. For children from 6 to 14 the judge may in addition consult the child and give discretionary weight to the answer (Neely, 1984, p. 182). I would argue that the presumption is more suitable for children below school age (7 years), but for that group, too, it is debatable whether it is right to use a presumption which is only rebuttable upon unfitness of the parent. It is possible, as Chambers maintains (1984, p. 562), that it is not because it is too strong that it should be rejected, since the strength will in practice depend on the courts' evaluation of the evidence. The reason why he rejects this version of the presumption is the fact that it invites a concentration on the wrong question – the fitness of one parent in the form of moral or other qualities – and not on the parent–child relationship. He may be right, unless the concept of unfitness is made as narrow as Elster suggests, including only physical abuse, physical neglect, and mental disorders. Such assertions will presumably only rarely be made, but on the other hand it would hardly be desirable to require that much for the presumption to be rebutted. The most acceptable solution would probably be the intermediate presumption, in the sense that it only loses its effect if the other parent is clearly preferable, but is not so strong as to push the question of fitness to extremes. The risk is that it may become less effective with regard to preventing litigation. Yet it would provide a rather strong indication to the parties.

More about time

I have argued that the primary caretaker preference is probably more appropriate in relation to young children than to older ones. Another important reservation has to be made; the custody question must be decided soon after the break-up. The substantive value of the primary caretaker argument decreases as time passes, especially if the child for some reason remains with the other parent. But primarily it is for the child's sake that the case should be decided quickly. Persons with knowledge of psychology underline the significance of a swift clarification, so that the tension and the uncertainty do not last for a long time (Næss and Undersrud, 1987, p. 101).

If the case is to be decided quickly, it must as soon as possible be brought before a body which can either bring about an agreement or make a decision. It should be in both parents' interests to have the case resolved, and preferably before they separate. If there is no clarification before the break-up, the responsibility to bring the case before the body in question will rest in particular on the parent who wants the child moved. Subsequently that body must see to it that a solution is found rapidly. It should *inter alia* be possible to instruct the courts to render a decision within a certain time after the case has come before the court, a month at most. The preparation of the case need not take long if by and large one could manage without experts. Innumerable writs back and forth are unnecessary; what the parties might need some time for is producing information concerning the primary caretaker question. More than a few days for writing the judgement should not be necessary.

Time should also be an issue in the ongoing debate about counselling in connection with a divorce.[5] A time limit for the counselling to come to a conclusion, in the form of agreement on the custody question, may be difficult to set, because the time needed to work out the conflict is variable. On the other hand, for the sake of the children this part of the process should not drag on. Næss and Undersrud (1987) argue that lawyers and the court system ought not to be brought in until the emotional divorce, and thus the custody conflict, has been clarified. That seems, in principle, like a good argument and one which might be supported happily by lawyers. But it is unrealistic to think that it is possible to come to agreement in all cases through counselling. In the remaining cases the court must still be brought in to make a decision. Then a rather easily applicable criterion is needed, as argued above, and the primary caretaker is one such. But the use of that criterion depends on the decision being made soon after the break-up. Besides, for the child a counselling process of long duration is unacceptable, especially if the case still has to be taken to court afterwards. In order to avoid the pressure on the woman to accept her husband's claims in the counselling process, which might be increased by a time limit, one could state that resistance to the counselled remedy should not disadvantage her in a following trial.

So there is reason to set a limit of perhaps one or two months for the parties to spend on trying to come to an agreement. If they have not come to terms in that time the case should be left to the court for a quick decision. Even though it is important that the parents get the opportunity to work things out, this should not result in a long-lasting uncertainty for the child. It must be better to have a decision relatively quickly – without the counter accusations against each other which the best interest principle easily leads to – and then to continue working out the conflict with the counsellor, within the framework provided. There could be visitation rights from the start, even if their extent might have to be fixed later in co-operation with the counsellor. For the child the most important thing must be to know quite soon where she or he is going to live.

CONCLUSION

I have argued that a primary caretaker preference would be better for the child than the present best interest principle, and have outlined my reasons. I have also claimed that the proposed presumption would do more justice to the parents, in that it takes the past, and thus a greater part of reality, into consideration while at the same time taking account of the parents' needs. In the context of this book there is a need for me to sum up my argument with particular regard to the position of women.

There are the arguments of individual justice and that of group justice. At the individual level it is important that the effort put into child care is appreciated; there is a sense of fairness in taking that into consideration when it comes to deciding where the child is to live. The work of child care is not highly valued in our society; it may be praised in words but it gives none of the benefits that paid work does, in the form of pension rights and so on. The unfairness of this is reinforced if the child care work is not even to be considered in a decision which concerns the relationship with the child, namely the custody decision. Since the primary caretakers are still mainly women, this unfairness particularly affects many women.

Not only with regard to the past, but also to the future, the woman's interests would be better taken care of by a primary caretaker preference than by the best interest principle. If she has been the primary caretaker her identity is usually closely connected with caring for the children, and losing custody is felt to be a deprivation. The presumption would regularly result in her retaining custody. As a consequence her bargaining position in the divorce situation would be improved. Her husband could not so easily have her accede to his claims by threatening to bring the custody case to court, since she would have better chances of winning. This applies not only to his claims for custody but also to the other parts of the divorce settlement, for example the division of property and maintenance.

With greater predictability the wife might not have to go through a court hearing, which is not only a strain on the child but on the parents as well. Should there be a hearing, it could hopefully be limited to the issue of who has been the primary caretaker instead of the strenuous uncovering of their private lives and evaluation of their personalities to which the best interest principle almost invariably leads.

During the marriage such a criterion might give her a greater feeling of safety – at least that is if she ever considers what would happen in a divorce situation. She would not have to worry whether her efforts in child care were worthwhile. More important, perhaps, there would be less chance that the fear of losing the children would prevent her from leaving an unhappy marriage. There may of course be other reasons for her to stay, but her freedom of choice would be greater.

A counter argument could be the risk that such a rule would contribute to keeping up the traditional sex roles in the home. But I do not believe that a rule regarding custody after divorce has much effect on the roles within the marriage. If it had, it might just as well encourage men to take a greater part in the child care work. And to the extent that there has actually been a division of labour within the marriage, for whatever reasons, we should not ignore it but rather respond to the consequences of it.

I have described the situation with regard to women, though on an individual basis it applies to a few men as well. From the point of view of group justice, however, it concerns women's position. The arguments used at the individual level are just as valid at group level; actually they become even stronger considering the fact that they regularly affect one gender – women. The injustice of the present rule becomes more apparent in that light. Women, and in particular those who take care of children, are still a vulnerable group in society. By the removal of the maternal presumption this group was deprived of the one privilege which still has good cause. We could make up for this injustice by introducing a primary caretaker preference.

NOTES

1   The system of the law is one parent having custody and the other having visitation rights. But since the parents have the freedom to decide, they may agree on joint physical custody instead (i.e. the child spends 50 per cent of his or her time with each parent). There is no prohibition against that in the law. The authorities do not, however, impose such an arrangement. If the parents cannot agree on the custody question and bring the case before the court, they are not considered to be able to co-operate to the extent necessary for having joint physical custody.

2   The Children Act Committee (Barnelovutvalget). The mandate is referred to in their report, NOU 1977: 35, pp. 10–11.

   The demand for equality was also a part of the feminist strategy at that time. But one can hardly talk about one common strategy, and different feminist groups interpreted the concept of equality differently. One may say that there were two main directions – one direction primarily demanding access to the men's world, and the other wanting to give greater worth to the particular activities of women. There was a general wish to involve men more in the child care work, but I think most feminists – at least those of the second category – were opposed to doing that by way of giving fathers equal rights in the divorce situation. That would mean starting at the wrong end. The demand for equality was a demand to improve the position of women, having been oppressed for so long. If men's position with regard to custody was to be improved, they must first do something to deserve it.

3   The Committee's Report NOU 1977: 35; the Report from the Ministry of Justice to Parliament, Ot. prp. nr. 62 (1979–80); and the Report from the internal Parliamentary Committee, Innst. O. nr. 30 (1980–81).

4   Fathers of young children (below 7 years) in 1981 spent 3.1 hours a day on household work (including child care) on average, which was 0.6 hours more than in 1972 (Social Survey, 1983, p. 107; there are no more recent figures available). With regard to women's employment outside the home, the figures of different surveys are somewhat varied but they all show an increase in the employment of mothers of young children. According to one survey there was an increase from 44 per cent employed in 1981 to 50 per cent in 1985, temporary absences not included. Another one, concerning married women only, shows an increase from 53 per cent in 1981 to 62 per cent in 1985 (Gulbrandsen and Hoel, 1986, p. 10 and English summary p. 50).

5   The scepticism towards counselling which is known from other countries is not seen to the same extent in Norway, probably because the situation is somewhat different. The counter arguments seem mainly to have to do with the pressure to accept joint physical custody. Since in Norway there is no general agreement that joint

custody is a good solution for the child, and the courts do not impose it, I do not think the pressure on the women to accept their husbands' claims would be so strong. However, we should not be so naive as to overlook the possibility that the parent who has resisted the counselled remedy may be seen as an 'unfriendly' parent by the court.

Chapter Six

FROM GENDER SPECIFICITY TO GENDER NEUTRALITY? IDEOLOGIES IN CANADIAN CHILD CUSTODY LAW

SUSAN B. BOYD

There have been various factors, perhaps including statistics, indicating that mothers usually obtain custody of their children (Statistics Canada, 1983), which have led feminists to exclude child custody from critical analysis. During the 1970s, a prolific period of family law reform in Canada, the focus was upon the elimination of gender specific legislation which incorporated stereotypical assumptions about the dependent status of women and the nurturing roles of mothers. Gender neutral child custody provisions which affirmed the ability of both fathers and mothers to care for children by allowing either parent to obtain child custody seemed to be progressive. To submit to feminist analysis an area of the law which is intended to enhance the best interests of children appears to border on the single-minded and to subordinate the interests of children to those of one of their parents, their mothers. Given the troublesome public perception that feminists intend to send all mothers into the workforce, destroy the family, and are therefore responsible for problems suffered by children today, to examine child custody from a feminist perspective is an easily misunderstood task.

Despite these causes for hesitation, various developments have prompted recent feminist attention to child custody. In the United States, identification of the reasons why women lose custody (Polikoff, 1982) and legislative efforts to make joint custody an option, a presumption, or a mandatory consideration (Ryan, 1986; Schulmann and Pitt, 1982) alerted women's groups to the implications of the new philosophy underlying child custody. In Canada, similar concerns as well as the recent use by fathers of the Charter of Rights and Freedoms in custody disputes have stimulated feminist analysis. Feminists have also become concerned with the connection between 'clean break' approaches, which increasingly deny women financial support from their spouses, and the increasingly invisible reality of still overwhelming female responsibility for child care before and after relationships between parents dissolve (Mossman and Maclean, 1986; Rogerson, 1988).

This chapter examines some implications for women of child custody law in Canada from a feminist perspective which uses concepts of gender and ideology to explore underlying assumptions of cases and legislation on child custody, both historically and more currently. In particular, I examine how judicial and legislative treatment of child custody issues have created problems for women, in different ways, at different historical moments. The problems associated with this area of the law highlight the difficulties and limits of seeking both meaningful acknowledgement within the legal system of 'traditional' women's work such as child care, and progressive advances towards a breakdown of the sexual division of labour characteristic of capitalist societies.

FEMINIST THEORIES OF LAW AND IDEOLOGY

The strength of socialist feminist theory in analysing the position of women within the family is its ability to examine the roles of both productive and reproductive forces in structuring women's existence, so that gender is introduced into the traditional Marxian calculation of the reciprocal relationship between productive relations and societal structures. The changing configuration of the family may be seen as influenced by, and having an influence on, not only the nature of productive relations, but also the ability of society to reproduce (procreate, socialize, and maintain) its population. Many aspects of family, labour, and welfare legislation can be understood in terms of the mediation, co-ordination, and balancing of productive and reproductive relations in society (Ursel, 1986).

A multidimensional understanding of the relationship between gender relations, capitalist society, and law is further enhanced by recent work on ideology from a perspective which identifies diverse ideological formations based in various social practices and movements. While law, like other social institutions, may be shaped and restricted by an overarching ideological field based on capitalist relations of production, this does not prevent ideologies grounded in other social practices from influencing various struggles and outcomes within state and law (Sumner, 1979). For feminists, this complex understanding of ideology as something other than a coherent world view or false consciousness presents an opportunity to examine and challenge particular ideologies springing from gender relations, while not losing sight of the potential constraints stemming from the overarching ideology inherent in individualistic bourgeois social relations, and possibly inherent in the very structure of bourgeois law (Pashukanis, 1979).

An understanding of ideology which attends to the variety and complexity of various ideologies and the interplay between them may permit a more subtle and complex analysis of the role of belief systems, and the embodiment of such beliefs in people's consciousnesses, than more instrumentalist uses of ideology to explain all manifestations of patriarchy. To explain all aspects of the oppression of women through a uniform concept of patriarchy or patriarchal ideology makes it difficult to understand such contradictory evidence as women's resistance to patriarchal relations and sometimes even legal enhancement of such resistance (Gavigan, 1986a, 1986b). A diversified concept of ideology permits an understanding of the role of law as neither always uniformly oppressing certain groups nor always benefiting others. It is also important to attend to the connections between the ideological functions of the legal system and those of other social institutions, whether they be economic, political, or cultural. Where the legal system avoids overt references to gender by adopting gender neutral legislation, the reproduction of gender relations may nevertheless be enhanced by another social institution, such as the judiciary or the family.

This chapter advances the view that there is an important connection between the disadvantaged position of women in society and their position within the family. This type of inquiry into gender relations is potentially more capable of comprehending and explaining contradiction and resistance than a straightforward equation of male oppression of women, through law or otherwise (Smart, 1984; Gavigan, 1988). The relationship between family and women's status arises in part because the roles of women in the family affect the expectations of women and their ability to perform various functions outside the family, such as participate in the labour force. Given that the current structure of access to economic resources lies primarily within the public workforce, women may be handicapped in economic competition with men as long as they are primarily responsible for child rearing (Polatnik, 1984, p. 26). To the extent that law plays a role in structuring familial relationships, investigation of areas of family law which concern the gendered division of labour within the family is worthwhile. It is also important to determine the potential for influencing the development of family law in a manner which ameliorates the condition of women both within and outside the family. While undoubtedly reinforcing gendered familial roles which reproduce public and private relationships often oppressive to women, law may also provide opportunities for women's resistance to such oppressive conditions.

Changes in the law of child custody over the last two centuries represent a microcosm of a more general transition, from a period when the impact of gender on law was obvious to the current period when gender neutral legislation and formal legal equality are the norm. These changes are also instructive to the fact that ideological constructs of gender roles within the family do not remain static, but rather adapt according to changing material conditions. The concept of ideology may be of particular use to feminists in periods when, in many areas, law does not appear to be a direct instrument of patriarchy (Gavigan, 1988) and may instruct us as to the need to continue to engage with law. We must go beyond an analysis which argues that the law is a straightforward agent or symbol of male authority to an analysis which investigates the complex interplay of ideologies bearing on particular issues such as child custody (Olsen, 1984b).

GENDER-BASED CHILD CUSTODY LAW

The history of child custody law provides a rich field for investigation of ideologies based on gender difference which were (and are) reflected and reproduced by legislation and judge-made law. Gender-based ideologies such as the ideology of motherhood have played an important role in constructing women's lives, by identifying a special responsibility in women for the rearing of children within the context of a particular familial form (Wearing, 1984). However, the precise specification of the ideal of motherhood has changed over time, as is demonstrated by changes in custody law through history. Insight into changing ideologies may assist in understanding the elastic capacity of the legal system to incorporate amendments and reforms without necessarily contributing to the substantive amelioration of the oppression of women (Smart, 1984).

Pre-twentieth century child custody law

Before the nineteenth century trend in England, the United States, and Canada towards recognition of a juridical personality of women separate from that of their husbands, the legal subordination of women was such that mothers were legally entitled to 'no power but only reverence and respect' (Backhouse, 1981, p. 215, quoting Blackstone).[1] English common law, which was relevant in those Canadian provinces which received English law before the enactment of Lord Talfourd's Act, 1839 (McBean, 1987), acknowledged predominantly paternal rights to the custody and guardianship of legitimate children, including infants at their mothers' breasts (Backhouse, 1981, p. 216; McBean, 1987).[2]

In Canadian common law provinces throughout the nineteenth century, child custody law moved away from 'pure patriarchy' and towards the granting of more responsibility to the mother, with judges lagging behind the legislatures in this transition (Backhouse, 1981, see pp. 214–15 for a description of Quebec law). Those provinces which were created after 1839 received the law under the English Lord Talfourd's Act, which gave the Court of Chancery the right to give a mother access to her child, and even physical custody until the child reached the age of 7. Both rights were contingent on the mother not committing adultery. Most Canadian provinces which enacted their own statutes on child custody modelled them to some extent on Lord Talfourd's Act.

Feminist research on child custody has penetrated below the surface of these developments and understood them as representing more than benevolent changes in the law towards a recognition of mothers' rights as parents. Increased maternal rights can be traced to the increasing split between home and workplace linked to industrialization and urbanization, the emergence of the middle class, and the growing tendency to view childhood and adolescence as distinct developmental periods which required time, nourishment, and 'moulding' by mothers (Backhouse, 1981, p. 213). These developments in turn can be linked to the prevailing relations of production and reproduction. Custody laws which diminished the power of fathers reflected a weakening of familial patriarchal relations, which were replaced in part by 'social patriarchal relations'. One outcome of new legislation representing 'social patriarchy' was that the costs of reproduction remained a private burden. This arose from the enhancement of men's familial responsibilities whilst allowing women to assume responsibilities for children if necessary, in the absence of a functioning male breadwinner (Ursel, 1986, p. 177).[3] The liberalization of family law and the emergence of women's and children's rights did not mark the end of patriarchal relations, but rather represented the growth of social patriarchy showing that 'the "bottom line" of patriarchy is *not* male privilege *per se* but control of reproduction through control of women ... traditional male privileges were dispensed with when they got in the way of controlling reproduction' (Ursel, 1986, pp. 158, 176-7). Furthermore, the law arguably granted to women obligations rather than rights, 'as the economic role of children in the family changed from a benefit to a cost' (Brown, 1981, p. 246).

Shifting ideologies during the nineteenth century enhanced an acceptance of the erosion of exclusive paternal legal responsibility for children and the increase of maternal responsibility. As the rise of industrial capitalism enhanced the value of personal life and encouraged the lengthening and elevation of childhood, the ideology of women's separate but now more equal role as wife and mother in the 'private' sphere began to appear. This increasing recognition of maternal responsibility was by no means uniformly beneficial for women. Paternal authority still took precedence, and was justified by the notion that women were inferior because God or nature made men superior (Olsen, 1984b, p. 10). Recognition of maternal rights (e.g. equal guardianship rights) was linked to the increasing 'cult of domesticity' surrounding middle- and upper-class women. With fathers in these households becoming increasingly involved in the public sphere of business and commerce, women became the 'divinely appointed guardians of the family' (Backhouse, 1981, p. 239). In spite of this 'cult of domesticity' it was still only in fairly exceptional circumstances that courts exercised their increasing discretionary authority to award custody of children to mothers (Backhouse, 1981). Ontario legislation, for instance, only considered awarding custody to mothers where the children were under 12 and where there was no suspicion of adultery on the part of the mothers. These restrictions encouraged an assumption that mothering was connected, first, with young children and was less necessary to older children (especially boys) who were closer to entering a (public) world where their fathers had more authority,[4] and second, with a sexual purity expected of mothers but not necessarily of fathers.

Judicial pronouncements of the period clearly differentiated the gendered roles and statuses of mothers and fathers. The increasing rights of mothers to custody were limited to instances where the father had a serious defect of character (Backhouse, 1981, p. 212). Moreover, mothers who failed to satisfy judges that they had an excuse for leaving their husband's home or their duties as wives often failed to obtain custody, and judges felt free to exhort women to return to their marriages despite alleged cruelty of husbands (Backhouse, 1981, pp. 220-6). Only in the most exceptional instances were mothers accorded rights over their children, for instance where a mother was subjected to repeated ill treatment from her husband who indulged in 'strong drink', and who had once thrown her and her sixteen-month-old infant out of the house. This mother had taken refuge with her brother, which meant that she was under 'male protection', a factor significant to the success of mothers claiming custody in this period (Backhouse, 1981, pp. 221-4).

In order to obtain custody of their children, then, mothers in these nineteenth-century cases normally had to demonstrate conduct which accorded with the expectations of female decency and chasteness. These expectations were linked to the 'cult of domesticity' which saw women as confined to the private sphere, subordinate in normal circumstances to the will of her husband. While mothers did gain more rights (or responsibilities) under the law concerning their children, the terms under which such rights were accorded spoke volumes about, and reinforced, constraints upon female behaviour of the period.

The rise of the tender years doctrine

It was not until the twentieth century that an actual preference for maternal custody of young children became firmly entrenched in the form of the 'tender years doctrine' (Abella, 1981, pp. 13–14).[5] Under this doctrine, a mother was preferred as the custodial parent of young children, all other things being 'equal', including the 'fitness' of each parent. The fitness criterion permitted the consideration of gendered role expectations, with their attendant ideological implications. Although little research details the rise of the tender years doctrine in Canada, American research shows that it built on nineteenth-century precedents which had moved slowly in the direction of a maternal preference (Olsen, 1984b, p. 13) and upon new psychological theories of bonding between the 'psychological parent' and the child (Sheppard, 1983).

The ideology attached to the tender years principle had conflicting implications for women (Olsen, 1984b). On the positive side, it arguably empowered women by allowing them to leave abusive husbands without forfeiting their children, and to play the role of head of a family unit. In addition, it may have increased women's bargaining power within marriage and during divorce or separation. While usually lacking the economic clout of their husbands, mothers could play upon the emotional incentive which men had to keep their marriage intact, lest they lose their children (Olsen, 1984b, pp. 14–15). On the negative side, the ideological aspects of the tender years doctrine which strengthened women's position in custody disputes rendered them ill-suited for public life. That is, the ideology underlying the tender years doctrine was one of inequality in that it enhanced the view of women as wives and mothers within the private sphere of the home. Consider, for example, the feminine expectations inherent in Roach JA's comment in *Bell* v. *Bell* (1955):

> No father, no matter how well-intentioned or how solicitous for the welfare of such a child, can take the full place of the mother. Instinctively, a little child, particularly a little girl, turns to her mother in her troubles, her doubts, and her fears. In that respect, nature seems to assert itself. The feminine touch means so much to a little girl; the frills and flounces and the ribbons in the matter of dress; the whispered consultations and confidences on matters which to the child's mind should only be discussed with

133

> Mother; the tender care, the soothing voice; all these things have a tremendous effect on the emotions of the child. This is nothing new; it is as old as human nature. (*Bell* v. *Bell* [1955] Ontario Weekly Notes 341, p. 344)

Although this view of mothers places women on a pedestal as parents, they were considered only as mothers rather than complete human beings. In turn, any deviation from the 'ideal' vision of motherhood such as leaving a child in the care of another person, working outside the home, or engaging in an adulterous relationship could defeat the maternal preference (McBean, 1987). This phenomenon became increasingly likely in the latter part of the twentieth century when more women entered the public labour market (Armstrong and Armstrong, 1984, p. 55).

A review of recent Canadian custody cases involving employed mothers who lose custody of their children,[6] confirms this analysis. The lifestyles of employed mothers are often found to be less adaptable to spending time with children than those of employed fathers, or as more unstable and unplanned (Boyd, 1987). Judges often fail to counterpose this 'instability' with the stability of the mother–child link where the mother had been primary caregiver. When the review was extended to include cases involving employed mothers who were awarded custody, it was found that those mothers who agree to withdraw from the workforce for a period of time, or who are engaged in part-time work, are more favourably evaluated by judges (Boyd, forthcoming). Their behaviour is more closely in accord with the 'acceptable' model of mothering.

Moreover, judicial discretion to deny custody to unfit mothers enhances the subservience which women were, and possibly are, thought to owe, if not to their husbands (Olsen, 1984b, pp. 13–16), at least to particular feminine roles in the family. A study of fairly recent Canadian custody cases involving lesbian mothers shows that 'the state valued and sanctified mothering, but mothering of a very particular form – within a heterosexual nuclear family structure' (Arnup, 1984, p. 36). Maternal custody, while preferred, is conditioned on conformity to this particular feminine model. A dilemma thus confronts judges who are influenced by the maternal preference, yet are faced with mothers who do not conform to the ideal feminine model, such as lesbian mothers who have detached themselves from the heterosexual nuclear family structure. However, while most lesbians have refused to service the needs of a husband, thus failing to comply with one component of the nuclear family model, they nevertheless might service some needs of capitalism by socializing children in accordance with the dominant values of society. In such cases, when a 'stable facimile [sic] of a nuclear family' (Arnup, 1984, p. 39) is created by a lesbian mother, she might be permitted to retain custody in limited circumstances, especially if the father is undesirable in some respect. Thus, while paternal legal authority within the individual family decreased in the twentieth century, partly due to the tender years doctrine, particular models or ideologies of gendered roles within the family which privatized the costs of child rearing and socialization of children were and are nevertheless enhanced by judicial interpretation.

During the nineteenth century and much of the twentieth, then, ideologies of gender difference have been reproduced at times by legislation and at other times by judicial decisions on child custody which reinforce patriarchal relations both within the family and outside it. In accord with these ideologies, mothers are expected to assume primary responsibility for child rearing and domestic tasks. Although blurred, this basic differentiation of gender roles in both private and public spheres persists even when today a majority (57 per cent) of women with children are in paid work (Statistics Canada, 1985, Table 19 at p. 18 and Table 18 at p. 17). As long as women are allocated primary responsibility for child rearing and housework, even when employed (Statistics Canada, 1985, p. 5), they tend to take employment which allows them to reconcile paid work with household and child rearing responsibilities. Such work is normally undervalued in terms of prestige and pay, is often part time, and tends to be 'dead-end', leading to few promotions (Statistics Canada, 1985, pp. 41-6; Armstrong and Armstrong, 1984, Ch. 2). Pay and prestige differentials between male and female dominated jobs in turn lead to a tendency for mothers to withdraw from the labour force to care for young children, rather than fathers with better salaries and perhaps greater psychological investment in their employment (Barrett and McIntosh, 1982, p. 78). The 'traditional' sexual division of labour is thus maintained in spite of significant changes to women's pattern of involvement in the labour market.

GENDER 'NEUTRAL' LAW? EQUALITY AND THE INVISIBILITY OF WOMEN'S WORK

The ideologies of gender difference outlined above retain considerable influence in child custody decisions (Boyd, 1987) and in current social relations (Baker, 1985). However, it would be misleading to say that the legal system in the 1980s generates only traditional familial ideologies, given the increased participation of women in the public sphere and increasing acceptance, or at least rhetoric, that the public and private roles of women and men need not be assigned by sex. Recent developments in the law of child custody illustrate a tension, and yet a connection, between gender based ideologies described in the previous section and supposedly gender neutral ideologies promoted by the principle of equality, which render invisible to the legal eye social and economic differences between the sexes. Mothers seeking custody in the current period arguably fall, to their detriment, between the two sets of ideologies. This analysis may enhance an understanding of the often sterile debate around the 'best interests' of the child and the desirability of joint custody.

Former legal equality and the Charter of Rights and Freedoms

Canadian society has moved in recent years towards recognition of the formal legal equality of women and men in documents ranging from constitutional provisions 'guaranteeing' the equality of women and men, to gender neutral family law statutory provisions on issues such as support and child custody. The enthusiasm for formal equality surrounding the introduction of the Charter of Rights and Freedoms into the Canadian constitutional framework in 1982 may, however, have obscured fundamental inequalities remaining between the sexes in Canada. Furthermore, the application of formal equality to the 'private' sphere, such as family law, may be more troublesome than its application to some areas of the public sphere (Smart, 1986a, p. 420). The ideologies flowing from Charter equality guarantees may therefore have important implications for modern child custody cases, especially as they interrelate with gender based ideologies.

As part of the Canadian constitution, any law inconsistent with the Charter of Rights and Freedoms (1982) is, to the extent of the inconsistency, of no force or effect.[7] Sections 15 and 28 of the Charter relate directly to equality rights for women, although other sections have the potential either to enhance or conflict with equality interests. Section 15(1) provides that 'every individual is equal before and under the law and has the right to equal protection and equal benefit of the law without discrimination and, in particular, without discrimination based on race, national or ethnic origin, colour, religion, sex, age or mental or physical disability'. Section 15(2) specifies that affirmative action programmes will not contravene the above guarantees. Section 28 provides that '[n]otwithstanding anything in this Charter, the rights and freedoms referred to in it are guaranteed equally to male and female persons'.

The wording in section 15 was intended to go beyond the 'equality before the law' and 'protection of the law' provisions of the earlier Bill of Rights to permit arguments for substantive equality (Day, 1985, pp. 30-1). However, despite innovative feminist arguments for a broad interpretation of the equality provisions (e.g. Bankier, 1985) and the establishment of a group which brings equality cases concerning women to court,[8] serious problems arise in attempts to apply equality rights to women. These problems are illustrated by the 'compliance process' under section 15 of the Charter, which did not come into force until 17 April 1985. The intention was to give federal and provincial governments three years to bring existing legislation into compliance with the equality provisions in the Charter. Among other problems, those involved in the 'compliance process' often made false presuppositions about the actual status of the average woman, including false assumptions of economic equality of women and men (Shrofel, 1985, p. 113). The concept of equality, as it has developed in western liberal democracies, tends to assume that the subjects being compared in equality arguments have similar qualities. Under this model, important differences between women and men, whether biological or social, may be rendered invisible, so that women may be offered an equality model based on a male lifestyle (O'Donovan, 1984, pp. 79-80). In addition, this notion can accommodate only a limited understanding of substantive inequalities of bargaining power caused by class or gender position of the individual.

In the family law context, the gender neutral principle of

equality promoted by Charter equality provisions may obscure the social and economic implications of gender roles within the nuclear family structure prioritized by the legal and social institution of marriage. Thus, the 'traditional division of labour within the family is assumed to be a personally accepted private exchange of services' (Klein, 1985, p. 118), thereby masking and reinforcing the gendered nature and disparate impact of the division of domestic responsibilities. In contemporary society, women's continuing primary responsibility for child rearing, promoted by ideologies of gender difference external to law, is camouflaged as a private decision made between adults presumed to be in equal bargaining positions in the privacy of their family lives: 'individuals are, in theory, expected to bear the costs of the effects of their choices' (Klein, 1985, p. 118). Thus, the liberal juridical approach to equality typically renders irrelevant substantive differences between individuals related to gender, including the sexual division of labour within and outside the family.

The principle of equality and child custody cases

A misplaced application of 'equality' can arguably be traced in the recent development of child custody law in Canada, where any remaining legal preferences for granting custody of young children to mothers have given way to emphasis on the 'best interests' of the child. This principle gives the appearance of a neutral principle and also introduces much scope for the exercise of judicial discretion.[9] Increasingly, the starting point for judges in custody cases is a supposedly gender neutral assumption that women and men are equally situated and thus equally able to assume domestic responsibilities such as child care. The difficulty for judges in the current conjuncture is in applying this gender neutral assumption to an area of social relations which is not yet gender neutral, and where ideologies of male and female behaviour still prevail. The fact that 43 per cent of women with children are not employed (Statistics Canada, 1985, Table 19, at p. 18) and that women 'continue to bear the primary burden of family and home care' even if employed (Statistics Canada, 1985, p. 5) may not be appropriately acknowledged when judges apply gender neutral standards.

We can expect that some judges will continue to exercise their discretion in accordance with the gendered expectations discussed above, although since the *Talsky* case (1976), the tender years doctrine is usually referred to as a rule of common sense rather than a rule of law, meaning that it has less force. As late as 1981, Houlden JA held in the *Macdonald* case (1981) that the trial judge had erred in failing 'to give adequate weight to the common sense rule that a little girl of tender years is better cared for by her mother' (p. 331). Ironically, even in decisions granting custody to fathers, judges often pay tribute to the tender years doctrine, especially when young girls are involved (e.g. *Hurley* v. *Hurley* (1982); see Boyd, 1987). Thus, expectations of female behaviour associated with the tender years doctrine discussed above, which can limit women's options and choices, continue to be reinforced. Furthermore, mothers may continue to lose custody when not conforming to these expectations.

This chapter has highlighted the implications which the ideology of motherhood has had for women. However, a recognition of the influence of ideologies of gender difference concerning both male and female behaviour promotes an understanding of why similar behaviour of fathers and mothers can induce differing assessment from judges in custody decisions (Girdner, 1986). This understanding is particularly significant as the tender years doctrine diminishes in importance. Since societal expectations of active paternal participation in child care are not high, fathers are often applauded when they do as much as any 'normal' father, or especially if they do somewhat more (*R.* v. *R.* (1983)). The expectations held of mothers regarding child care are higher, so that behaviour on their part similar to that of a 'normal' father is often assessed as deviating from the norm of motherhood and frowned upon (Girdner, 1986, p. 174). Furthermore, if a mother performs other roles such as employee or friend, she appears to detract from her role as mother. Other roles performed by fathers, on the other hand, appear to be neutral or even supportive of their fatherly role (Girdner, 1986, p. 175; also Polikoff, 1982, p. 239).

A preconceived assumption that mothers are more naturally adapted to the task of parenting permits legal decision makers to query whether a particular mother has put her 'natural' capacities to the best use (Girdner, 1986, p. 177). If she has not, judicial eyes may turn to the father as a preferred parent, particularly under an 'individual-based ideology', which holds that a 'person is responsible for his or her own actions and has considerable control over his or her own life' (Girdner, 1986, p. 176). In child custody decisions, this ideology, closely connected to liberal approaches to equality in its cornerstones of equality and achievement, is translated into the notion that a father can parent equally well as a mother if he puts his mind to it. Many feminists would agree with this proposition, but it is problematic as an approach to child custody if it encourages the judiciary to underestimate the effort mothers have devoted to child care in the past and the difficulty which fathers may have in assuming a primary child care role if they have not done so in the past. The proposition that men can parent as well as women can be translated into an assumption that it is easy to learn the role of a primary caregiver of children or that it can be done overnight. Such an assumption, whilst perpetuating the invisibility and undervaluation of women's work, also overlooks some of the ways in which employed women have coped with their primary responsibility for child care, such as by taking part-time work or work which does not require overtime or socializing with colleagues after hours.

Recent Canadian cases involving employed mothers illustrate that the gender-neutral principle of equality and its closely related 'individual-based ideology' can be applied in such a way as to undervalue primary caregiving (Boyd, forthcoming). Some women who have been adequate primary caregivers of children lose custody, first, as a result of the favourable comparison of their ex-partner's economic security and lifestyle to their own, and second, as a result of unfounded assumptions that fathers have contributed a great deal to child care.

The first point is that it may be mistakenly assumed that women have equal opportunities to achieve comfortable income levels and the flexible time associated with the status of a professional. That women who are separated or divorced are more likely than their male counterparts to be re-entering, or entering for the first time, the public labour force is often not taken into account, nor is the fact that women tend to occupy less prestigious and more poorly paid jobs than men (Statistics Canada, 1985, pp. 41–62; Armstrong and Armstrong, 1984, Ch. 2). Most fathers who are already employed need not spend time re-educating themselves or searching for work, nor need they move to take positions in other geographical locations. These factors, which are not entirely the result of personal choice but rather of structural constraints on gender roles (Luxton and Rosenberg, 1986, p. 11), are characterized as individual problems of mothers and may be held against them.

For instance in *Yablonski* v. *Yablonski* (1986), the Saskatchewan Court of Appeal confirmed an order of custody to a father who had a farm and a housekeeper to care for the 5-year-old son, rather than to a mother who had fewer material assets, went from job to job, and was sometimes on social assistance. The dissenting judge argued that excessive weight had been given to the father's economic advantage 'which is almost the sole advantage possessed by the father over the mother', and found that the mother could give better emotional support to the child. In other cases, successful fathers offered the stability of their own parents' home, and the presence of a grandmother to assist in primary care.[10] Another phenomenon appearing in these cases is the readiness of some judges to favour fathers who can offer a 'surrogate' mother in the form of a new female partner,[11] or an aunt,[12] or an older daughter.[13] The father has thereby created a family unit containing adults who are willing to perform the traditional gender-based roles associated with breadwinning and parenting (see Boyd, forthcoming).

These lifestyle factors taken into account by courts illustrate the ways in which gender-based and gender neutral ideologies operate together to disadvantage employed women in custody cases. These mothers conform neither to the traditional expectations of stay-at-home motherhood nor to the male model of secure employment and lifestyle arguably expected under the ideology of equality. In addition, fathers are more likely to be able to offer a 'substitute' nuclear family model than mothers who are employed or re-entering educational institutions. Even when mothers offer a 'surrogate' father, the traditional nuclear family model is less likely to be achieved since the mother has already deviated from the expected norm of stay-at-home mother.[14]

The second point is that mistaken assumptions of equality encourage judges to jump to the conclusion that mothers and fathers have shared parenting more or less equally if there is evidence that fathers have engaged in child care to any extent more than the standard model of paternal conduct. Especially where mothers have been employed outside the home, it is often erroneously assumed that domestic work and child care are shared equally between parents, an assumption which devalues the double burden of work carried by most employed mothers (Boyd, forthcoming). For instance, in the *Elbaz* case (1980), a mother whose work required her to travel 'would wash the children's clothing, clean the house and make sure that things were available for the family when she was away' (p. 343). Nevertheless, the judge praised the husband's performance of household and child care duties while his wife was away and did not comment upon his absence from Canada several weeks annually due to scholarly activities. Judges often cavalierly assume that fathers are able to attend to a child's needs throughout the day, especially if they are self-employed, for instance on a farm (*R. v. R.* (1983)). Some judges are also too ready to assume that fathers who have engaged in at least minimal child care can easily adopt the role of primary caregiver of children, while minimizing the value of primary care-giving performed by mothers in the past.

In addition, emotional nurturing by mothers is often devalued in contrast to the sometimes disciplinarian approach of fathers, especially where older or gifted or problematic children are concerned. In *Mes* v. *Mes* (1981), the father 'a highly controlled, undemonstrative, disciplined, intellectual and solitary person' was given custody instead of the mother, a primary caretaker who was 'warm, demonstrative, gregarious and rather immature' (p. 261). In the *Alexander* case (1986), the British Columbia Court of Appeal confirmed a lower court award of custody to a father who had had physical care of the child for only one out of twelve years of the child's life. The child had spent his other eleven years with the mother. This decision was made despite an earlier separation agreement leaving custody with the mother, despite the fact that separation agreements are supposedly rarely disturbed by courts, and despite the child's desire to stay with his mother. There was some indication from a psychologist that the boy, a gifted child, might increasingly benefit from a male parent's influence and that staying with his father would benefit his scholastic success. The mother's eventual request for joint custody was refused.

It is not surprising, then, that in some jurisdictions fathers who genuinely challenge mothers for custody are often successful (Chesler, 1986; Weitzman, 1985). This phenomenon is attributable in part to the ability of fathers to act as individuals without such acts being construed as in conflict with their children's interests. As long as women are primarily responsible for child care, their interests as individuals rather than as mothers will appear as antagonistic to those of their children (Currie, forthcoming). While obscured by assumptions connected to the principle of equality, this assessment continues to ring true. In addition, primary caretaking by women seems to be devalued by judicial application of the principle of equality, while 'male' values such as rationality and minimizing of emotion seem to be elevated.

Fathers' rights, joint custody, and mediation

A misplaced application of equality is also evident in legislative and judicial trends towards recognizing fathers' rights in child custody, including joint custody. Fathers' rights groups have been effective in arguing the importance of 'equal' fatherly input into children's lives, especially at the decision making level (Lamb, 1987). This success arguably obscures the importance of seemingly more 'mundane' input by mothers who tend to be responsible for day-to-day physical and emotional nurturing. The emphasis upon retention of an active and full role for both parents in making decisions concerning the child, potentially impeding the exercise of discretion by parents with physical care of children, is illustrated by recent legislative trends and judicial decisions. It is particularly relevant to a feminist critique because of studies showing that mothers still most often assume physical care and control of children after separation or divorce, even where joint custody is encouraged (Weitzman, 1985).

For instance, the 'friendly parent' rule in section 16(10) of the Divorce Act 1985 directs courts to 'give effect to the principle that a child of the marriage should have as much contact with each spouse as is consistent with the best interests of the child and, for that purpose, [to] take into consideration the willingness of the person for whom custody is sought to facilitate such contact'. This provision has aptly been called 'the silencer', since 'women who seek to have access by the father blocked because of a past history of physical or sexual abuse, risk being labelled as "uncooperative" and stand to lose custody of their children' (Lamb, 1987, p. 22). The negative evaluation of a mother which may occur under the 'friendly parent rule' if she resists a joint custody arrangement is illustrated by James G. McLeod's comment in an annotation to the *Parsons* case (1985): 'The fact that a spouse refuses to cooperate in the plan that best meets the needs of the children is evidence that the parent in question may be putting his/her own interests ahead of those of the children' (pp. 84–5).

A variation on this theme of preserving parental contact almost at any cost appears in the *Tyndale* case (1985), where a mother who evidently had been the primary caretaker during marriage lost custody to a father on the ground that if custody were granted to her, the father was likely to lose interest in the children. This decision was made despite the fact that the father's evidence was not regarded as reliable by the court. Armstrong J added that the father 'talks a good act but there is little evidence of performance' and that he 'only really became a father to the boys after the separation' (pp. 428–9). The mother was seen as 'sufficiently strong in her own right to handle the situation even though she does not have custody of the children and will continue to be a mother to the children' (p. 429).

In other courts the emphasis on participation of both parents in decision making concerning children has meant casting aside the earlier caution of the courts in the *Baker* (1979) and *Kruger* (1979) cases, and ordering joint custody despite one or both parents' unwillingness to try joint custody. As Twaddle JA said in *Abbott v. Taylor* (1986): 'To say otherwise would encourage one parent to avoid the participation of the other in deciding questions as to their child's future by a mere statement that he or she was unwilling to share the responsibility' (p. 171). In the *Parsons* (1985) case, where the parents felt that a mediated joint custody agreement had not worked, the Newfoundland Supreme Court nevertheless ordered joint legal and physical custody, partly because the children wished it to continue. The judge hinted at almost a presumption in favour of joint custody when stating that the 'parties have not satisfied me that ... joint custody has been a failure' (p. 92). Some of these cases may confirm Girdner's observation that joint custody may often be a compromise solution which allows decision makers such as judges and mediators to avoid confronting difficult decisions and power imbalances between parents (Girdner, 1986, p. 181).

Other recent cases demonstrate a tendency to place great

emphasis on retaining decision making power of fathers, even if joint custody is not explicitly ordered, for instance through the mechanism of joint guardianship. In *Charlton v. Charlton* (1980), after hearing a father's request for variance of an earlier custody order to a mother, the British Columbia Supreme Court firmed up the access provisions and ordered joint guardianship to the father and mother, which had much the same practical effect as a joint legal custody order. The mother retained 'day to day responsibility for their guidance and upbringing' (p. 224), while the father acquired a right to be consulted 'in planning the religious upbringing, educational programs, athletic and recreational activities, health care (excluding emergency health care) as well as significant changes in the social environment of the said children' (p. 224).[15] While this court recognized the potential difficulties of such consultation and advised that the 'power and authority hereby granted shall not be exercised by either of the parties so as to frustrate or unduly affect the life of the other', the ability of the mother to order her family's life would necessarily be impeded. Once a joint legal custody type of relationship is in place regarding decision making, it becomes difficult for parents with primary physical custody to exercise discretion concerning the children.[16] Indeed, they may forfeit their ability to move to another location if they are viewed as putting their interests before those of their children.[17] Undoubtedly parenting involves the making of personal sacrifices for children, but this type of restriction may have a differential impact upon mothers since they are more likely to be seeking new employment or retraining than fathers, and may need to move in order to obtain it.

Another recent trend is the refusal by courts to make explicit custody orders, resulting in *de facto* orders resembling joint custody. In *Abbot v. Taylor* (1986), the father did not oppose sole custody to the mother, but asserted an interest in being involved in the child's upbringing. He asked that the mother's sole custody be subject to his 'right of decision in matters concerning the child's education and elective medicine, and subject to liberal access' (p. 166). In response, the trial court avoided the terms 'custody' and 'access', instead delineating particular times when the child would live with the father, and giving the mother 'prime' responsibility for making major decisions. The Manitoba Court of Appeal affirmed this arrangement despite the mother's complaint, amending the order only by granting her 'ultimate' rather than 'prime' responsibility for major decisions. Twaddle JA noted that recently amended Manitoba legislation emphasized the contribution of each parent to the development of children, and then expansively interpreted a provision (increasingly appearing in custody legislation) guaranteeing to non-custodial parents the right to receive school, medical, psychological, dental, and other reports affecting the child. He said that the provision recognized 'the right of the non-custodial parent to participate in the process of making important decisions involving his or her child. The legislation stops short of making the responsibility to decide questions of importance to the child's upbringing joint, but it does anticipate consultation' (p. 169).

The Charter of Rights and Freedoms may have implications for joint custody if fathers argue, as in *Keyes* v. *Gordon* (1985), that the Charter guarantees both parents and children the right to an order of joint custody. The court did not accept the father's argument in this case, finding that the mother had 'shouldered practically the entire burden financially and otherwise of bringing up the children'. However, the father's arguments provided a vivid example of the ways in which Charter equality rights may be argued to grant formalistic rights not reflecting the substantive realities underpinning legal claims.[18] The father argued in the alternative that if he did not obtain joint custody, it would be contrary to his constitutional rights to pay support for children 'banished' from him despite his willingness and ability to care for them. Although this argument was also rejected by the court in *Keyes* v. *Gordon*, in the *Wilton* (1982) case maintenance was denied to the custodial mother on similar grounds: 'the husband is willing and anxious to have custody of the children and to bring them up himself ... she has sufficient moneys to care for herself and for the two children so long as she *insists* on keeping custody of them' (emphasis added, p. 175).

Finally, the fact that the vast majority of custody cases are settled out of court, increasingly after some form of mediation or conciliation, has important implications for analyses of child custody. In addition, courts increasingly order that should disputes arise in the future, for instance under joint custody orders, they should be taken to mediation before returning to court.[19] The ideologies discussed in this chapter, enunciated in legislation and court decisions, are important also in mediated settlements which are conducted in the shadow of the law (Bottomley, 1984). Given the problems for women inherent in the contract model (Klein, 1985), and given the emphasis in mediation upon the satisfaction for parties of arranging their own contractual solutions to domestic issues such as custody, the arena of mediation deserves immediate attention, not least because joint custody is most often agreed upon in the 'privacy' of the mediation room. In its emphasis upon parents putting aside their own interests for those of their children (Irving and Benjamin, 1987), mediation may obscure the differential impact which this approach might have upon women. As seen above, it is more frequently the interests of mothers as individuals than fathers which are seen to be antagonistic to those of their children, due to the self-sacrificing ideology of motherhood. It may be correspondingly easier for fathers to agree in mediation to put aside their personal interests and to appear more willing than mothers to do so, which will in turn assist them under the philosophy of the 'friendly parent' rule. Furthermore, in mediated custody arrangements, a financially disadvantaged mother may be persuaded through a form of economic duress to see the attractiveness of agreeing to custody of the other parent, or at the very least to joint custody, with a corresponding undermining of her non-economic contributions to parenting.

Legal efforts to preserve parent–child relationships and the equal participation of parents in decisions concerning their children might be desirable in a world where shared parenting was a reality and social support for parenting was more generous. In the present social and economic context, however, these efforts can be blind to the realities of the lives of parents (usually women) with primary physical care of children. Unless the parents agree to such an arrangement, in which case it may be the best possible solution to a difficult situation, it is probable that 'equity cannot be achieved by granting equal participation after divorce, to parents who have not shared equally in parenting during marriage' (Lamb, 1987, p. 20). There is a danger that as paternal rights increase, maternal responsibilities grow heavier (or at least remain the same) while women's rights and autonomy are hampered by the increased paternal intervention in decision making (Brown, 1981). Even parenting which is genuinely shared between individual mothers and fathers 'cannot in itself overturn the power and status of men in wider economic, political and cultural spheres' (Segal, 1987, p. 157), at least not until it results in pressure for meaningful recognition of reproductive as well as productive labour and for changes in the public sphere of labour. Because in the context of current socioeconomic conditions, custody of children constitutes a 'power-resource' (Sevenhuijsen, 1986, p. 337), and because mothers may have more psychological investment in parenting than fathers, the application of a principle of equality to child custody is misplaced for the time being at least. Legal provisions which presume a norm of shared parenting before it has become a social reality may reinforce unequal power relations between men and women rather than encourage their demise.

Thus, in modern child custody decisions, women may fall between gender-based and gender neutral sets of ideologies. While the tender years doctrine went too far in emphasizing emotional involvement with children by presuming it to be present because of the mother–child biological relationship, current judicial trends arguably have delivered 'equality with a vengeance' by assuming equal economic opportunities for men and women, undervaluing primary caretaking, and yet still expecting a significant degree of conformity to the ideology of motherhood. Since many mothers are given physical care and control of children under joint custody arrangements, with legal decision making power shared with the father, expectations of the ideology of motherhood may still apply. The ideology of equality obscures economic inequalities and unequal contributions of men and women to parenting, and arguably renders it easier for judges and mediators, and indeed women themselves, to ignore the extra social and economic burden which arrangements such as joint custody may place on mothers.

TOWARDS A VALUING OF PRIMARY CAREGIVING?

The history of child custody shows that women's work as child caregivers in the 'private' sphere is devalued in comparison with that of male or 'public' labour. The manner of this devaluation has changed in the current period, and is heightened by the ideology of equality, which too readily assumes equal contribution or talent of both men and women in every sphere, without sufficient factual inquiry. One method of combating this devaluation may be to stress the value of primary caregiving to children still performed predominantly by women.

The primary caregiver presumption

In West Virginia, USA, a new means of legally recognizing women's child caring responsibilities has arisen through judicial development of a 'primary caretaker presumption'.[20] In *Garska* v. *McCoy* (1981), the West Virginia Supreme Court of Appeals developed the primary caregiver presumption when considering the interaction between new custody legislation which eliminated any gender-based presumption, and a previously binding custody case which established a strong maternal presumption. A lower court had awarded custody to a father based on his better education, greater intelligence, ability to offer a better social and economic environment, and his better command of the English language. The appellate court found that as there was no evidence that the mother as primary caregiver had been an unfit parent, the lower court was not justified in removing custody from her and vesting 'it in a parent who had had no previous emotional interaction with the child' (p. 360). The court's enunciation of a primary caregiver presumption may eliminate some problematic aspects of both the 'tender years doctrine' and more modern legislation based on the 'best interests of the child' which, as we have seen, takes insufficient account of gender.

The *Garska* v. *McCoy* case rightly stressed the terrifying spectre to primary caregiver parents, usually mothers but sometimes fathers, of losing their children. Also recognized was the link between custody and financial issues such as support, and the tendency for non-primary caregiver parents, normally in the superior financial position, to trade custody for lower alimony and child support payments in negotiation or mediation. In the court's view, the private ordering of family affairs currently encouraged by the legal system, for instance through mediation, has not been accompanied by a reliable legal framework within which to bargain intelligently. In order to protect each spouse during out-of-court bargaining, in particular the primary caregiver parent who suffers most from uncertainty because of her/his willingness to sacrifice everything in order to retain the children, the court held that there was a presumption in favour of the primary caregiver parent obtaining custody if a minimum objective standard of fit parenting was met. Primary parenting was defined as including many activities often overlooked by courts:

1 preparing and planning of meals;
2 bathing, grooming, and dressing;
3 purchasing, cleaning, and care of clothes;
4 medical care, including nursing and trips to physicians;
5 arranging for social interaction among peers after school;
6 arranging alternative care such as day-care;
7 putting child to bed at night, attending to child in middle of the night, waking the child in the morning;
8 disciplining, such as teaching manners and toilet training;
9 educating in religious, cultural, and social spheres;
10 teaching elementary skills such as reading (p. 363).

If these tasks were shared entirely equally, no presumption would arise and a court would have to inquire into relative degrees of parental competence. But if one parent were clearly the primary caregiver, then if fit, she or he should be given custody if the child were of tender years (under 6 years). Older children would be given the opportunity to give their own opinions as to which parent they would prefer to stay with. In West Virginia court-ordered joint custody is not encouraged, although parents can agree to it voluntarily (Neely, 1984, p. 184).

Pitfalls and potential of the primary caregiver presumption

An impediment to achieving legal recognition of primary caregiving done by parents in the past is that many Canadian judges tend to read modern child custody statutes, which prohibit consideration of past spousal conduct such as adultery unless relevant to parenting, as licence to ignore past track records of input into child care by each parent unless it is a question of tracing a mother's departure from the ideal model of motherhood. As we have seen, judges tend to emphasize current and future participation in child care, often with an overly generous evaluation of any fatherly participation in parenting and good intentions for the future, and an overly punitive evaluation of any motherly deviation from full-time mothering, including those in the past. A few Canadian judges have, however, begun to emphasize primary caregiving without going so far as to create a presumption in favour of the primary caregiver parent. These judges seem to have had no problem overcoming the tendency in child custody determinations to look to the future rather than the past.[21] Indeed, a more accurate reading of the statutes which permit consideration of past conduct if relevant to parenting ability is surely that past demonstrated parenting ability should weigh heavily in assessing the genuineness of current offers to parent in the future.

Efforts by Canadian feminists to 'socialize' the judiciary into an appreciation of the significance of primary caregiving, and an awareness of the pitfalls for women of the equality principle and the ideology of equality accompanying it, have been instructive of the difficulties of arguing that social and economic differences between men and women should be taken into account in legal determinations. These efforts have included 'The Socialization of Judges to Equality Issues' Conference held in Banff, Alberta, May 1986 (Martin and Mahoney, 1987) and the panel on Gender Equality in Family Court organized by the Ontario Women's Directorate and presented to the family division judges of the Provincial Court of Ontario in March 1987. One judge's opinion was probably typical and was indicative of the problem; he mistakenly felt that in emphasizing any criteria such as primary caregiving feminists were asking for a favouring of mothers' claims in child custody determinations which discriminated against fathers. A related danger is that if judges are asked to pay further attention to primary caregiving by mothers, they may resuscitate traditional criteria such as maternal chastity, with possible detrimental consequences for women. We do not want to encourage, in gender neutral form, a set of expectations attached to primary caregiving which would operate in a differential fashion depending on whether female or male primary caregiving was being examined.

Neither do we wish to devalue work which some men are putting into caring for children, but only to emphasize that at present, contrary to public opinion, these men constitute only a small minority and the basic sexual division of labour remains intact. The advantage of a primary caregiver presumption, in contrast to a maternal presumption, is its ability to recognize paternal primary care where it exists, and thereby to encourage it. It also gives a fairer basis upon which women (and men) can choose whether to ask for custody or not, with greater certainty as to the likelihood of success. While it does not solve the problems of the adversarial system, the presumption has diminished the volume of litigation over child custody in West Virginia (Neely, 1984, p. 182). This phenomenon may indicate that when fathers are confronted with some legal recognition of the value of primary child care that mothers have given to children, they are less willing to contest publicly for custody. The presumption may thereby grant some autonomy to women who have invested a large portion of their lives in mothering, an activity which when rendered invisible can contribute to the power of men over women even after separation or divorce (Sevenhuijsen, 1986). Perhaps it is only after we succeed in enhancing legal and social recognition of the significance of the caregiving to children which has historically been accomplished by women that we can safely adopt social options which transcend the gendered division of labour within the family, and legal principles which support these social options. Legal rules such as joint custody which lend ideological support to the notion of shared parenting, but which are imposed before the gendered division of labour breaks down, may not promote the interests of women, but rather diminish attention to the social and economic implications of motherhood for women, for instance in the labour force (Brophy, 1985, p. 111). To hope that a legal norm such as joint custody could promote social change without a material basis for such change would be to give too much credit to the ideological power of law.

CONCLUSION

The legal system has moved from an approach which failed to give any legal credit to maternal responsibility for child care, to an approach which gave a considerable degree of such credit but only to mothers who conformed to a particular model of female behaviour, to an approach which attempts to apply gender neutral principles of equality to fathers and mothers in child custody cases. In so doing, the legal system fails to take account of the different positions of women and men within and outside the family, positions which are characterized by unequal power relations. A complex interplay of ideologies based on gender difference (such as the ideology of motherhood) and principles which purport to be gender neutral and even geared towards the equality of women and men has undermined women's resources even within the family, for instance in their relations with children. The couching of the principle of equality in language directed at protecting children, for instance the 'best interests of the child' standard commonly referred to in Canadian custody statutes and cases, further renders invisible women's responsibilities for child care. It also increases the difficulty of making arguments in favour of mothers obtaining custody since these arguments appear to detract from the protection of the welfare of children.

We cannot, however, ignore the potential of law as an arena of struggle for women, especially given its day-to-day impact upon the lives of women and children, as well as its power as a conveyor of ideologies. To the extent that family law provides a link between 'public' and 'private' ideologies concerning the labour of women and men, we must work towards encouraging the valuing of women's child care labour in legal decision making, without reinforcing the ideologies identified in this chapter which have had negative implications for women, for instance in the labour force, such as the ideology of motherhood. In Canada, and elsewhere, we may wish to counteract tendencies in law and society to obscure the value of women's child care labour and connections with children, for instance by developing a primary caregiver presumption. At the same time we must work towards legal and social policies which potentially enhance greater social responsibility for child care and a wider range of choices for women in both 'private' and 'public' spheres.

NOTES

Thanks to the Canadian Research Institute for the Advancement of Women (CRIAW) for funding this research, and to Kathleen Nicholson for assisting in the research.

1 See, however, Martha Minow (1985) '"Forming underneath everything that grows": toward a history of family law', *Wisconsin Law Review*, pp. 819–98, for an illustration of ways in which women resisted their lack of juridical power.

2   Backhouse cites *R. v. De Manneville* (1804) 5 East 221; 102 English Reports 1,054 (KB). No Canadian cases were reported during this period.

3   Ursel later explains that the purpose of welfare legislation appearing in the same period was to step in where privatization failed.

4   For a discussion of implications of the designation of women as primary parents of young children for the reproduction of gender and of sexual inequality, see Nancy Chodorow (1978), *The Reproduction of Mothering: Psychoanalysis and the Sociology of Gender*, Berkeley, University of California Press.

5   Abella reports that mothers and fathers gained equal entitlement to custody in Ontario around 1925. A 1933 Ontario case, *Re Orr* [1933] Ontario Reports 212 (Ontario Court of Appeal), stated that, as a general rule, children under 7 years of age needed their mothers more than their fathers.

6   These cases were taken from the *Reports of Family Law* from 1980 to 1987. This law report series selects cases from across Canada and from various levels of courts. While not a statistically valid 'sample', the cases do indicate trends in judicial decision making. Cases involving employed mothers were chosen because these mothers had departed to some extent from the traditional stereotype of a stay-at-home mother, and thus might prompt judicial comment or reaction. The study was intended to be qualitative rather than quantitative, and to illuminate the attitudes of judges in order to identify ideological influences on the judges and, in turn, the role that the judges played in reinforcing various ideologies.

7   My brief discussion of the Charter draws upon essays in Lynn Smith *et al.* (eds) (1986) *Righting the Balance: Canada's New Equality Rights*, Saskatoon, The Canadian Human Rights Reporter, and in particular William Black's essay 'A walk through the Charter', p. 47. For critical perspectives on the Charter, see *Socialist Studies*, vol. 2 (1984).

8   The Women's Legal Education and Action Fund (LEAF), 344 Bloor St W., Suite 403, Toronto, Ontario, Canada, M5S 1W9.

9   See, for example, subsection 24(1) of the Children's Law Reform Act, Revised Statutes of Ontario 1980, c. 68, amended in Statutes of Ontario 1982, c. 20, s. 1; subsection 16(8) of the Divorce Act, 1985, Statutes of Canada 1985, c. 4.

10   See the *Boehmer* (1985), *Cotton* (1981), *R. v. R.* (1983), and *Ellert* (1982) cases.

11   As in the *Fishback* (1985) case.

12   As in *Despatie* v. *Larouche* (1983).

13   As in *Cain* v. *Cain* (1983). See also *Williams* v. *Williams* (1980).

14   *Hurley* v. *Hurley* (1982); *Cain* v. *Cain* (1983).

15   See also *Hackett* v. *Hackett* (1985).

16 As in *Chauvin* (1987).

17 See *Crawford* (1985) and *Smith* (1987) cases.

18 See also *Harden* v. *Harden* (1987), where the father argued that the tender years doctrine violated the Charter by discriminating against him because of his sex. The Saskatchewan Court of Appeal avoided dealing with this argument and confirmed an award to the mother, emphasizing the primary parenting of the stay-at-home mother. See also *Bendle* v. *Bendle* (1985), where the father did obtain custody after having argued the Charter but the judge did not base his decision on the Charter.

19 As in *Charlton* v. *Charlton* (1980).

20 For many women who care for children, in Canada at least, the term 'caregiver' might be more acceptable than 'caretaker'.

21 For an example of the tendency to look to the future, see *Adams* v. *Adams* (1987), at p. 303. Two cases where judges looked to primary parenting in the past are *Grills* (1982) and *Burgmaier* (1986).

CASES

Abbott v. *Taylor* (1986) 2 Reports of Family Law 3d 163 (Manitoba Court of Appeal).

Adams v. *Adams* (1987) 6 Reports of Family Law 3d 299 (Nova Scotia Supreme Court).

Alexander v. *Alexander* (1986) 3 Reports of Family Law 3d 409 (British Columbia Court of Appeal).

Baker v. *Baker* (1979) 8 Reports of Family Law 2d 236 (Ontario Court of Appeal).

Bell v. *Bell* (1955) Ontario Weekly Notes 341 (Ontario Court of Appeal).

Bendle v. *Bendle* (1985) 48 Reports of Family Law 2d 120 (Ontario Provincial Court).

Boehmer v. *Boehmer* (1985) 45 Reports of Family Law 2d 433 (Manitoba Court of Appeal).

Burgmaier v. *Burgmaier* (1986) 50 Reports of Family Law 2d 1 (Saskatchewan Court of Appeal).

Cain v. *Cain* (1983) 33 Reports of Family Law 2d 353 (Saskatchewan Queen's Bench).

Charlton v. *Charlton* (1980) 15 Reports of Family Law 2d 220 (British Columbia Supreme Court).

Chauvin v. *Chauvin* (1987) 6 Reports of Family Law 3d 403 (Ontario District Court).

Cotton v. *Cotton* (1981) 23 Reports of Family Law 2d 141 (Manitoba Court of Appeal).

Crawford v. *Crawford* (1985) 46 Reports of Family Law 2d 331 (Prince Edward Island Supreme Court).

Davis v. *Davis* (1986) 3 Reports of Family Law 3d 30 (Manitoba Queen's Bench).

Despatie v. *Larouche* (1983) 36 Reports of Family Law 2d 30 (Quebec Supreme Court).

Dussault v. *Ladouceur* (1986) 3 Reports of Family Law 3d 65 (Quebec Supreme Court).

Elbaz v. *Elbaz* (1980) 16 Reports of Family Law 2d 336 (Ontario Supreme Court).

Ellert v. *Ellert* (1982) 30 Reports of Family Law 2d 257 (Saskatchewan Queen's Bench).

Fishback v. *Fishback* (1985) 46 Reports of Family Law 2d 44 (Ontario District Court).

Garska v. *McCoy* (1981) W.Va. 278 S.E. 2d 357 (West Virginia Supreme Court of Appeal).

Grills v. *Grills* (1982) 30 Reports of Family Law 2d 390 (Alberta Provincial Court).

Hackett v. *Hackett* (1985) 43 Reports of Family Law 2d 5 (British Columbia Supreme Court).

Harden v. *Harden* (1987) 6 Reports of Family Law 3d 147 (Saskatchewan Court of Appeal).

Hurley v. *Hurley* (1982) 29 Reports of Family Law 2d 144 (Newfoundland Supreme Court).

Keyes v. *Gordon* (1985) 45 Reports of Family Law 2d 177 (Nova Scotia Court of Appeal).

Kruger v. *Kruger* (1979) 11 Reports of Family Law 2d 52 (Ontario Court of Appeal).

Macdonald v. *Macdonald* (1981) 24 Reports of Family Law 2d 327 (Ontario Court of Appeal).

Mes v. *Mes* (1981) 24 Reports of Family Law 2d 257 (Ontario Supreme Court).

Parsons v. *Parsons* (1985) 48 Reports of Family Law 2d 83 (Newfoundland Supreme Court).

R. v. *R.* (1983) 34 Reports of Family Law 2d 277 (Alberta Court of Appeal).

Smith v. *Smith* (1987) 7 Reports of Family Law 3d 206 (Nova Scotia Family Court).

Talsky v. *Talsky* (1976) 2 Supreme Court Reports 292 (Supreme Court of Canada).

Tyndale v. *Tyndale and Foster* (1985) 48 Reports of Family Law 2d 426 (Saskatchewan Queen's Bench).

Williams v. *Williams* (1980) 15 Reports of Family Law 2d 378 (Ontario District Court).

Wilton v. *Wilton* (1982) 30 Reports of Family Law 2d 170 (Manitoba Queen's Bench).

Yablonski v. *Yablonski* (1986) 5 Reports of Family Law 3d 140 (Saskatchewan Court of Appeal).

STATUTES CITED

Canadian Charter of Rights and Freedoms, Constitution Act, 1982 (enacted by the Canada Act 1982 (UK) ch. 11, Sched. B), ss. 1–34.

Children's Law Reform Act. Revised Statutes of Ontario 1980, c. 68, amended in Statutes of Ontario 1982, c. 20.

Divorce Act, 1985. Statutes of Canada 1986, c. 4.

Family Maintenance Act. Statutes of Manitoba 1978, c. 25; as amended in Statutes of Manitoba 1982–83–84, c. 54, s. 19.

Chapter Seven

EQUAL RIGHTS *VERSUS* FATHERS' RIGHTS: THE CHILD CUSTODY DEBATE IN AUSTRALIA

REGINA GRAYCAR

INTRODUCTION

Throughout the 1970s and 1980s the rhetoric of equal rights for women has gained considerable currency in Australia. It manifests itself in a plethora of law reform measures, such as laws proscribing discrimination on the grounds of sex and marital status, and affirmative action programmes at the federal level and in some of the Australian states, designed to secure equal employment opportunity for women in the workplace (Ronalds, 1987). These laws address the 'public' world of the workplace and the market, but leave unregulated the 'private' sphere of home and family. During this same period, Australia's national family law has been transformed from a fault-based to a no-fault divorce regime. Major debates have taken place about issues such as the basis for allocating matrimonial property on divorce (e.g. Women's Electoral Lobby, 1981, 1985; and Australian Law Reform Commission (ALRC), 1987b), and about the appropriate mix of public and private support which should be accorded to the children living in one parent families (Cabinet Sub-Committee on Maintenance, 1986). Some of the arguments that have been employed in these family law debates have proceeded from the same assumptions about the need to secure formal legal equality between women and men as have informed the debates in the 'public' sphere.

More recently, the issue of child custody has been placed on the public agenda by a variety of different and contradictory interest groups. In particular, the advantages of joint custody have been increasingly extolled in Australia, presumably as a response to moves in that direction in other jurisdictions, most notably in the USA. Much of the enthusiasm for joint custody appears to be grounded in rhetorical arguments about equality between women and men, in this case between mothers and fathers. Perceived as one of the few areas where historically the law has 'favoured' mothers, joint custody is now mooted as a 'script for equality' (Lehmann, 1983, p. 66).

This chapter will canvass the nascent debate about joint custody in Australia and examine its origins against the background of current laws relating to guardianship, custody, and access to children. The arguments of the proponents will be scrutinized with a view to discerning themes within this debate. In particular, the growing band of fathers' rights groups and their support for joint custody will be examined and it will be suggested that their use of 'equality' rhetoric and their resort to charges of 'discrimination' against them by the Family Court of Australia in custody cases represents a backlash against what these groups perceive to be advances made by women through, amongst other things, the enactment of anti-discrimination laws.

In fact, for all of these 'reforms', women in Australia have not been particularly well served by their achievement of 'equality' when one considers matters such as women's and men's relative wage rates and the increasing trend towards the 'feminization of poverty', as evident in Australia as it is in the US and elsewhere. In addition, at an ideological level, single parents (i.e. custodial mothers) have become the new 'undeserving poor',[1] as recent reforms to the social security system and the collection of child maintenance demonstrate.

I will start with a brief discussion of the Australian family law system. Current custody law, some of the reported decisions, and the (sparse) empirical data on custodial dispositions will then be canvassed. Next, the chapter will examine the arguments made in favour of 'joint custody', pointing out the range of disparate meanings attributable to this concept. It will be suggested that in the context of current Australian custody laws, 'joint custody' is a vague term, easy to invoke in rhetorical debate but difficult to define. It will be demonstrated that proponents use the concept in varying, and at times contradictory, ways, thereby rendering proper debate, analysis, and assessment difficult. Finally, a brief account of the 'poverty of equality' for women in Australia is followed by discussion of some of the possible implications were joint custody to become the preferred custodial disposition in Australia.

It will be argued that debates about custody now taking place in Australia fail to locate this issue in the much broader context of women's economic and social disadvantage. By discussing the issue in isolation from the material situation of women and men, particularly the economic consequences of divorce, the debate has taken place largely in rhetorical terms only. This can be contrasted with the way other family law issues, such as matrimonial property law, have been approached in Australia. Unless and until the debate is broadened, and realistic account is taken both of women's financial position relative to men, and the unequal distribution of child care responsibilities, 'joint custody' will continue to develop particular ideological purchase in securing (or restoring) authority in the guise of 'equality' for men. In addition to providing a 'script for equality', 'joint custody' may also serve a further ideological function by constructing and reinforcing a notion of the 'eternal biological family' (Sevenhuijsen, 1986, p. 336) as the legitimate organizing structure of society. This operates with total disregard of significant changes in the way people choose to live their lives in the 1980s.

THE AUSTRALIAN FAMILY LAW CONTEXT

Under the Australian constitution, the national, or federal, parliament has only limited law making powers over family law, extending to laws about marriage and divorce, and laws which deal with the children of those marriages (Jessep and Chisholm, 1985). Issues involving family relationships not formalized by marriage, and those concerning ex-nuptial children, are left to the six states and two territories to regulate. This situation changed in 1988 after lengthy negotiations between the Commonwealth and state governments finally led a majority of the states to refer some of their powers over family matters to the Commonwealth (Guthrie and Kingshott, 1987). However, this unified system is only recently established and the case law referred to in this chapter was generated under the previous separate systems of federal and state family law.

The single most significant reforming event in Australian

family law was the enactment of the Family Law Act 1975 (Commonwealth) which overhauled laws governing divorce, maintenance of spouses and children, matrimonial property and custody, guardianship, and access to children. Under the Family Law Act, the single ground for divorce is irretrievable breakdown of marriage, evidenced by twelve months' separation (s.48). The Act's underlying philosophy is that marriage breakdown is an inevitable, if regrettable, fact of life, the consequences of which should be dealt with as painlessly as possible, without attribution of fault. To implement this, a national specialist court, the Family Court of Australia, was established. The legislative scheme is gender neutral. Women and men have equal access to divorce, maintenance is available equally to women and men, based on the criteria of need on the one hand and capacity to pay on the other, and an attempt has been made, in the provisions dealing with matrimonial property, to deal fairly with the different financial and non-financial contributions made by women and men to the acquisition of matrimonial assets (see, generally, Finlay, 1983; and Dickey, 1985). In this chapter, unless explicitly stated, the cases and statutory provisions discussed arise under the national family law system. It is, however, noteworthy that the reforms of the 1970s which replaced the previous and acrimonious fault-based system under the old Matrimonial Causes Act have to some extent filtered through to the states, at least in relation to issues of guardianship, custody, and access to ex-nuptial children (Guthrie and Kingshott, 1987).

Australian custody law and practice

The Family Law Act provides that, subject to any contrary orders, both parents are guardians of any child of the marriage and have joint custody (s. 63F(1)). Guardianship refers to the responsibility for the child's long-term welfare and gives a parent all the common law rights, powers, and duties, other than those involving daily care and control (s. 63E). It is the latter aspect which is encompassed by the notion of custody (sometimes called 'physical custody' in other jurisdictions and, prior to amendments to the Family Law Act in 1983, referred to in Australia as 'care and control').

Despite the clear statement in the Act that, in the absence of a contrary order, both parents are guardians and have joint custody, the Family Court has not interpreted this as giving rise to any presumption in favour of joint guardianship or joint custody where disputed cases are taken to the court, and such orders are rarely made (Horwill and Bordow, 1983; Nygh, 1985; Family Law Council, 1987). Instead, in disputed cases of guardianship, custody, or access, the court is given broad powers to make orders, all of which are subject to the statutory requirement that 'the court shall regard the welfare of the child as the paramount consideration' (s. 6OD).

In 1979 the High Court,[2] in a rare consideration of child custody principles, firmly rejected any official endorsement of the 'mother principle' or the 'tender years' doctrine as a determinant in custody cases, stating that a preference for mothers, especially in cases involving young female children

> is not, and never has been, a rule of law. It is, or was, a canon of common sense founded on human experience.... In earlier days, when there was no role for a father in the upbringing of children and in the running of the household, the care and the upbringing of children was left almost entirely to the mother who was able to devote the whole of her time and attention to that responsibility and to household affairs.

But the court went on to state, without citing any evidence for this, that

> there has come a radical change in the division of responsibilities between parents and in the ability of the mother to devote the whole of her time and attention to the household and to the family. As frequently as not, the mother works, thereby reducing the time which she can devote to her children. A corresponding development has been that the father gives more of his time to the household and to the family. (*Gronow* v. *Gronow*, 1979, p. 528, *per* Mason and Wilson JJ)

However, only three years earlier, a New South Wales Supreme Court judge had stated:

> I am directed by authority to apply the common knowledge possessed by all citizens of the ordinary human nature of mothers.... That knowledge includes an understanding of the

162

strong natural bond which exists between mother and child. It includes an awareness that young children are best off with both parents, but if the parents have separated, they are better off with their mother. The bond between a child and a good mother...expresses itself in an unrelenting and self-sacrificing fondness which is greatly to the child's advantage. Fathers and stepmothers may seek to emulate it and on occasions do so with tolerable success. But the mother's attachment is biologically determined by deep genetic forces which can never apply to them. (*Epperson* v. *Dampney*, 1976, p. 241 *per* Glass JA)

This attitude, though not formally part of the legal framework of custody law, may well reflect community practices, as two recent research reports indicate. In 1983 the Australian Institute of Family Studies (AIFS) was commissioned to conduct a major empirical study of the economic consequences of marriage breakdown. This research included custodial outcomes in recognition of the financial implications for both parents, particularly the custodial parent (Australian Institute of Family Studies, 1986, p. 269). Although the Institute reported 'a relatively high percentage of younger men who had care and control of one or both of their children' (13 per cent continuously; 17 per cent after a change of parenting), it was still overwhelmingly women who looked after their children on a full-time basis (p. 268). They concluded:

> Despite the increasing emphasis in research and media reports on the growing participation of fathers in the parenting process, it is still unusual for fathers to have the custody of their children. It appears that society at large still sees the nurturing of children as being the primary responsibility of women. (p. 268)

The only other Australian study on the outcome of custody cases (Horwill and Bordow, 1983) found that fathers had a greater likelihood of being awarded custody in defended than in undefended cases. In that study, which looked at all orders made in 1980 in the Melbourne registry of the Family Court, 79 per cent of orders, including consent orders, vested sole custody (care and control) in the mother. Defended cases accounted for only 10 per cent of the total; of these, fathers obtained sole custody in 31 per cent of cases. Added to this were 'split' decisions involving either separating children, or awarding joint custody; after these were taken into account, care and control (now 'custody') of at least one child of the family was awarded to the father in 44 per cent of cases (Horwill and Bordow, 1983, p. 30; see also Nygh, 1985). It should be noted that this study was expressly undertaken to respond to claims by fathers' rights groups (specifically, The Army of Men) that the court discriminated against them and in favour of women. They had claimed that men had a less than 2 per cent chance of gaining custody (Horwill and Bordow, 1983, p. 1).

A Family Court judge has suggested that the outcome of the 1983 study demonstrates

> that the mother preference is still alive and well in the general community, the fathers generally not contesting custody. The fact that fathers do appreciably better in contested cases does not mean, of course, that if only more fathers were encouraged to stand up for their rights, more would gain custody. The figures do not suggest how many successful fathers will personally undertake the caring responsibility and how many delegate that responsibility to relatives, *de factos*, new spouses or hired help. (Nygh, 1985, pp. 67–8)

While the mother preference may be 'alive and well', it would be misleading to assume that all mothers are similarly favoured. Lesbian mothers, for example, received short shrift from the Family Court in a number of early cases (see Anon, 1980; Harrison, 1980; Rights of Women Lesbian Custody Group, 1986, Chapter 16). While the current position of the Family Court is that lesbianism *per se* will not disentitle a woman from custody, in several cases a number of conditions have been placed on these mothers' custody awards (compare, e.g., *PC and PR*, 1979, and *In the Marriage of L*, 1983).

A woman's involvement in the paid workforce can sometimes raise questions about her fitness as a parent and lead to the father being awarded custody even though the father will delegate the children's day-to-day care to other women. In one such case (*Mathiesen and Mathiesen*, 1977) three older children were living with their father, while the youngest, a daughter aged 6, was with the mother and her *de facto* husband. The mother worked full time, and the child was cared for after school in another woman's house until the mother returned from work. The judge awarded custody to the father. Amongst the other reasons for this, he expressed the view that this case was 'an illustration of role reversals in our community.... The husband...has tailored his life so as to act as mother and father to the three older children, running the home efficiently and well with assistance from the older daughter and his mother and sister' (p. 76, 221 *per* Fogarty J). In another recent state court decision concerning an ex-nuptial child the judge made clear his disapproval of the mother's

> tendency to allow herself to be so absorbed by her personal ambitions as to show a lack of maternal feeling towards the children and to be unconscious of and unsympathetic to their emotional needs (p. 297).... The defendant was and still is a working mother. Prior to and at the time of the previous hearing she was enthusiastically pursuing a career which placed a strain upon her ability to cope with the demands of her domestic life and her children. (*Harrington* v. *Hynes*, 1982, p. 302 *per* Holland J)[3]

In both of these two cases, the judges expressly suggested that the parties were equally situated as full-time workers who would need to accommodate their time to the care of the children. In both cases also, the judges referred extensively to the women who would care for the children if the fathers obtained custody (in the first the older daughter, the mother, and the sister, and in the second the new wife), yet in neither case did that detract from the judges' notion the parties were under 'equal handicaps' in their ability to care for their children. When the relative re-partnering rates of men and women are taken into account (Australian Institute for Family Studies, 1986, pp. 58–9), it becomes clear that a full-time male worker is much more likely than his female counterpart to have a 'mother substitute' to care for the children, a matter that at least one Family Court judge has expressly acknowledged (Nygh, 1985, p. 68). In this way the 'equal handicap' of participation in the workforce may well result in men being awarded custody where there is little else to choose between the parents.

One particularly egregious example of this phenomenon received some public notoriety in 1987 when questions were raised about the case in Federal Parliament (see Australian Senate, 1987).

Two professional parents (both were medical practitioners) were in dispute over custody of their children (*Ward* v. *Ward*, 1987). The judge awarded the wife custody on a conditional basis; on 6 August she agreed to the wife having custody if, but only if, she resigned her job and was pregnant by her new husband by 7 October. In her judgment on 6 August, Murray J had stated 'The major question mark hanging over the wife...is whether she would be prepared to sacrifice her career for the sake of the children.' The wife had told the court that she wished to complete her specialist qualifying examinations and continue to work part-time. She had also stated that she planned to have another child with her new husband. The judge decided that the wife would not give up her job – 'she wants her cake and eat it too – unremarkable in these days of equality of opportunity' (p. 19). When they came back to the court on 7 October, and the wife had not become pregnant, she awarded custody to the father, despite the fact that she had earlier commented that the father, at 57, was more like a grandfather to the children, two young girls. There was, of course, no suggestion that the father give up his job in order to qualify as a suitable full-time parent, and it was made clear in the judgment that his new wife would undertake the day-to-day care of the children.[4]

It would be misleading to suggest that these cases described are clear evidence of a trend against working mothers and demonstrate the courts' favouring of fathers as custodial parents. The AIFS study and the Family Court's research (Horwill and Bordow, 1983) mentioned earlier demonstrate that disputes about custody are infrequently litigated, with most arrangements being made by agreement of the parties. Clear trends are not readily discernible from adjudicated cases and, far less, from the small number reported. And, as noted, in the absence of a court order, both parents remain guardians and have joint custody under the Family Law Act.

Reported case law does, however, demonstrate the Family Court's early position that joint custody (guardianship) orders were to be made only in exceptional cases. This has since been rejected by the Full Family Court (see *In the Marriage of Chapman and Palmer*, 1978; *In the Marriage of Cullen*, 1981). If any common theme emerges from the reported cases, it is that the Court is most likely to order joint guardianship where it believes that the parties will be able to co-operate in matters concerning the child's welfare (Chisholm, 1987, p. 1,313).

Available Australian data indicates that joint guardianship orders are made in 21 per cent of defended disputes (Horwill and Bordow, 1983, p. 31). However, joint physical custody is rarely, if ever, awarded by the Court. The Family Court's study further demonstrated that there was no significant difference between the recipients of care and control under joint or sole custody (guardianship) orders. But as more overseas jurisdictions amend legislation to require some form of joint custody, and as more advocates, particularly from influential bodies like the Australian Institute of Family Studies (Edgar, 1986) and the Family Law Council (1987), propose changes to custody laws in Australia, it is quite likely that their arguments for reform will gain significant support. Accordingly, it becomes necessary to scrutinize what 'joint custody', as a reform proposal, signifies.

THE POLITICS OF REFORM: THE MOVE TOWARDS JOINT CUSTODY

Elsewhere, a number of commentators have pointed out that 'joint custody' has a range of disparate meanings covering a variety of situations. Accordingly, there is no guarantee that a court order of joint legal custody will have any real effect on the day-to-day caretaking practices of parents. Schulman and Pitt (1982) note that most of the statutory joint custody regimes in the US, as well as the majority of court orders, expressly provide for joint legal custody independently of the day-to-day care and residence arrangements (p. 543), and they conclude that many advocates of joint custody are concerned more with legal rights than with physical custody, 'which is not even envisioned as part of the concept'. Fineman (1987) has also suggested that 'joint custody dispositions, in practice, continue to resemble sole maternal custody and father visitation' (p. 3).

The increasing popularity of the rhetorical notion of joint custody has a number of contradictory origins. Feminist concerns to transcend the stereotype of women's place as homemaker and child carer (e.g. Brophy, 1985; Fineman, 1987; cf. Bartlett and Stack, 1986) have combined in uneasy association with the ideology of equality to prompt moves in a number of overseas jurisdictions throughout the 1970s and 1980s to enact 'joint custody' laws. Some proponents argue that with men and women now enjoying 'equal status', they should have 'equal rights' to their children after divorce. After all, haven't women complained that men have not taken sufficient responsibility for their children? Another argument for joint custody states that while divorce may separate the adults, there is no basis for ending the children's association with both their parents. Such an ongoing relationship with both parents is said to be in the children's best interests (e.g. Edgar, 1986; Mark, 1987). The social work literature has become saturated with articles with titles like 'Joint custody: affirming that parents and families are forever' (Elkin, 1987). Joint custody, like motherhood, is hard to argue against. However, before attempting to look more critically at the concept, some of the recent Australian manifestations of this world trend will be examined.

Who supports joint custody in Australia?

In Australia, there has been considerable agitation in recent times for the establishment of a 'joint custody' norm to be applied by the Family Court. However, just as Schulman and Pitt (1982), amongst others, have demonstrated the variety of possible legal and practical meanings of 'joint custody' in the US, the Australian debate has taken place in similarly loose fashion. It is accordingly difficult to discern the extent to which the proponents discussed here seek merely formal legal 'rights' (in the nature of the Family Law Act's notion of guardianship) or intend to alter day-to-day caretaking practices, i.e. they seek a presumption in favour of joint custody, akin to shared care and control. Despite the fact that it was earlier feminists who most clearly argued that men should share the care of their children, most of the recent agitation about custody in Australia has come from men. Some of it derives from reputable institutional sources such as the Institute of Family Studies (see Edgar, 1986) and the Family Law Council (1987), which in its recent report on access has also expressed a preference for a move towards joint custody, although it has done so without indicating precisely what is envisaged by this proposal.

In 1986 the Australian Law Reform Commission (ALRC) conducted public hearings as part of its work on the law of contempt.[5] These gave fathers' rights groups an unprecedented forum in which to air their grievances about the current family law system. The majority of those who gave evidence did so in response to the contempt and family law aspect, though this was only one part of the total project. Of the seventy-one oral submissions made, forty-six were from fathers' rights groups such as Lone Fathers' Association, Men's Confraternity, Families Against Unnecessary Legal Trauma (in Divorce) (FAULT), Family Law Action Group, Parents Without Rights, Family Law Reform Association, Divorce Law Reform Association, Fathers Against Discrimination in Custody, or from individuals sympathetic to their position. These groups also made seven written submissions (see Australia Law Reform Commission, 1987a, pp. 605–9). By contrast to the disproportionate representation of these groups, single custodial mothers, or organizations representing them, were notably absent, even though their interests were directly affected since they are potentially subject to contempt action by the Family Court for defying access orders.[6]

Although it was made clear early in the course of the hearings that custody was clearly outside the terms of reference (Australian Law Reform Commission, 1986, p. 11), many of the men who gave evidence expressed their view that the law should require joint custody. California was cited as the example to follow, where, it was submitted, it was 'working fantastic' (Barry Williams, Lone Fathers' Association, Australian Law Reform Commission, 1986, p. 11; see also Mr Weeden, Lone Fathers', p. 198; Mr Seare, p. 209; Mr Romeyko, p. 667).

These men's arguments in support of what they call joint custody are threefold. First they believe themselves to be the victims of discrimination by the Family Court, which is run, in their view, by 'radical feminists'. Thus, it was submitted, that '95% of cases [in the Family Court] are resolved in favour of mothers', indicating that 'Justice Evatt [the Chief Judge of the Family Court from 1976–88] and her fellow judges have decided that in 95% of Australian homes, the female of the species is the better parent' (Mr Foster, p. 547). It should be reiterated here that earlier similar claims by the Army of Men were taken up and refuted by the Family Court's research section in 1983 (see Horwill and Bordow, 1983, p. 1). Yet to read the transcripts of the 1986 public hearings, one would think that men were never awarded either sole or joint custody of their children.

A prolific campaigner for joint custody has been former legal academic Geoffrey Lehmann, who has pursued the 'discrimination' theme.

If men can have their children confiscated from them irrespective of their own moral worth and effort, then they will be obliged to avoid marriage, vasectomize themselves, become narcissistic and use women as sexual objects. (Lehmann, 1983, p. 62)

Sole custody is an anachronistic survival from fault divorce and an era when there was, in effect, a legal presumption against men to balance the discrimination against women elsewhere in society.

Joint custody would appear to benefit children and parents. It is a script for equality. We are proud of our anti-discrimination laws, yet continue to discriminate against non-custodial mothers and fathers. We harass the latter for maintenance payments for children but deny them a normal parental relationship. (Lehmann, 1983, p. 66).

The second argument is that while divorce can end relationships between adult parties, the child–parent relationship is eternal and should not be broken. The Family Law Council's support for 'joint custody or joint parenting' on divorce flows from its view that 'it encourages people to consider more carefully their joint responsibilities towards their children which continue after divorce' (1987, para. 6.13). However, the Council qualified its proposal by acknowledging, realistically, that 'in practice, communication between the parents on a rational level is essential if the joint custody arrangements are to be successful' (para. 6.14).

Family Court judge Peter Nygh is more cautious in his advocacy, acknowledging Carol Smart's arguments that joint custody (guardianship) has the potential to preserve the authority of fathers over families, without their undertaking any of the disadvantages involved in actually caring for children (Nygh, 1985, p. 71, citing Smart, 1984, p. 139). Nevertheless, for him, 'this is not a reason for ceasing to pursue it' (Nygh, 1985, p. 72).

The third related, and at times overlapping argument, is based around the 'welfare of the child', which, it is suggested, is best served by an ongoing relationship with both mother and father. This notoriously loose concept (see Chapter 4) has considerable rhetorical purchase, in Australia as elsewhere. However, it can readily be subsumed within the parents' own interests. Many of the men's groups who advocated joint custody, in reliance on the welfare of the child principle, appeared to do so in response to their dissatisfaction with access arrangements rather than because of perceived benefits to the child.

Despite the fact that maintenance and access are formally not related in the Family Law Act, the men who gave evidence to the ALRC overwhelmingly submitted that they were not willing to support their children financially without their access demands being met (see Australian Law Reform Commission, 1986, e.g. Mr Aitken, p. 309; Mr Stewart, p. 317; and, for a contrary view, Mr Bender, p. 573). In fact, recent Australian data indicates that less than 30 per cent of non-custodial parents pay periodic child maintenance (Cabinet Sub-Committee on Maintenance, 1986, p. 11).

Joint custody: some feminist concerns

As the material documented above demonstrates, joint custody, at least as a rhetorical notion, has been placed squarely on the Australian agenda and has become much more frequently discussed in the family law and social work literature, though critical consideration of the issue in Australia has been scarce. By contrast, overseas writers, particularly feminist writers in jurisdictions where joint custody has been enacted by legislatures, have increasingly questioned these developments. Although this experience in other jurisdictions may not be readily translatable to Australia, it is salutary to consider it, if only because of the reliance placed by Australian joint custody advocates on overseas developments, in particular those in California.

It has been suggested that advocacy of joint custody is associated with a backlash against the apparent successes of the women's movement through the 1970s and 1980s (see, e.g., Smart, 1986b; Sevenhuijsen, 1986). While it is certainly true that the law has shifted away from the nineteenth-century notion that fathers have 'absolute rights' over their (legitimate) children, as Brophy has pointed out, the backlash against women is misdirected. The law has not shifted so as to favour women; rather, the shift away from fathers' absolute rights has been associated with an increase in the powers of courts who now have a broad discretion under the rubric of the 'welfare', or 'best interests of the child' principle (Brophy, 1985, p. 113). None the less, the ideology of equality has provided fuel for, in particular, fathers' rights groups, who argue that the shift away from their 'rights' must be redressed. For them, the issue is clear; if they do not 'win' a custody 'battle', there is discrimination and inequality.

In Australia, groups like the Men's Confraternity[7] have been established in response to concern

> about discrimination against men in pensions, law, welfare and education. Concerned about continual attacks on men, led by men-hating feminists, who have entrenched themselves in positions of power and influence, in government, media and education.
>
> Their aim is not to obtain equality but total domination of men at all levels.... We are concerned also at the continual attacks by feminists at the family unit, which have created a society of single parent families, made motherhood a dirty word, and also put the job of housewife as the lowest form of human endeavour, and put *de facto* relationships on the same level as married couples.... It is time for the majority of people, both male and female to take on the radical feminists and re-introduce sanity to our society. (Men's Confraternity, n.d.; *Sydney Morning Herald,* 16 October, 1987)[8]

Litigation instigated in various overseas jurisdictions aimed at establishing that custody awards to women are unlawful sex discrimination is consistent with these arguments[9] (Boyd, forthcoming; De Hondt and Holtrust, 1986b). Feminist critics have responded to the use of equality rhetoric in child custody debates by suggesting that there is a need to look beyond the rhetoric of equality which in this context has become, MacKinnon has suggested, 'equality with a vengeance' (MacKinnon, 1987, p. 72), to the reality of day-to-day caretaking practices (see Fineman, 1983, 1987; De Hondt and Holtrust, 1986b; Schulman and Pitt, 1982; Polikoff, 1982 and 1983; Uviller, 1978; Smart, 1986b). Whether we like it or not, it is still predominantly mothers who care for their children in our societies. But that reality, so clearly understood by feminists, is often ignored by legislators, courts, and policy makers in their zeal to implement 'equality'.

This commitment to the notion that formal legal equality has actually changed the way people live their lives has also led to what Polikoff has described as 'a corollary misconception' which applies to employed mothers, viz. 'that if both parents work outside the home, then the care of the children is evenly divided' (1983, p. 188). This was the view expressed by the Australian High Court in its leading custody decision (*Gronow*, 1979), described above. In another context,[10] an Australian state Supreme Court judge stated:

> Those incidentally who care to dabble in jurimetrics might care to consider what is to be made of this: of the seven wives of the seven judges of the Court of Appeal, three are in full-time professions or occupations, two are in part-time professions or occupations, one was in full-time employment before marriage, and the remaining one in part-time employment before marriage. I would think therefore that all of us have experience of what might be regarded as a more modern way of life, in which household tasks are shared. (Samuels, 1982, p. 311)

In fact, this rosy picture of domestic life, where housework and child care are shared, does not accord with any of the empirical evidence. Women who work outside the home carry a double burden as they are also primarily responsible for housework and child care (e.g. **Game and Pringle, 1984; Russell, 1983; Bryson, 1985**), but this reality can be easily ignored by courts if they eschew concern with hard data (Davis, 1987).

Feminist theorists have pointed out that the ideology of equality is based squarely within the liberal political tradition, the fundamental premise of which is that society is composed of (male) individual autonomous actors (e.g. **Pateman, 1983; O'Donovan, 1985; Sevenhuijsen, 1986; Boyd, forthcoming**). This has a number of important consequences for the debate. Translated into legal discourse, liberal ideas of equality in the 1980s have resulted in the widespread use of gender neutral language, despite the persistence of a highly gender specific world. And the most common way in which equality claims are channelled into legal discourse is through the language of 'rights'. Both the artifice of gender neutrality in the search for equality (e.g. Boyle, 1985; Olsen, 1986) and the relevance of 'rights' discourse as a strategy for women's claims (Olsen, 1984a; Kingdom, 1985; but cf. Schneider, 1986) have been subjected to important feminist critiques which point out the problems in adapting these traditional legal labels and tools to deal with claims on behalf of women, a group historically oppressed by law.

Aside from its tendency to ignore the reality of child care responsibilities in the 1980s, gender neutrality can also be used to judge the fitness of mothers. A disturbing trend noted in the US, though not (yet) apparent in reported cases in Australia, is to take into account the relative economic positions of the parents, in order to assess what is in the child's best interests (see Chesler, 1986; Woods, Been, and Schulman, 1983; Polikoff, 1982; MacKinnon, 1987; New York Task Force on Women in the Courts, 1987). The slightest attention to wage rate statistics, and the disproportionately high percentage of single mothers whose only source of livelihood (at least in Australia) is welfare support, would make it only too clear that, were such a 'gender neutral' criterion to be given weight, women would lose their children almost as a matter of routine. MacKinnon (1987) has suggested that gender neutral rules like level of income make men look like 'better parents', because men both make more money and are more likely to 'initiate the building of family units', i.e. are more likely to re-partner.

> In effect, they get preferred because society advantages them before they get into court, and law is prohibited from taking that preference into account because that would mean taking gender into account. . . . So the fact that women will live their lives, as individuals, as members of the group women, with women's chances in a sex-discriminatory society, may not count, or else it is sex discrimination. (MacKinnon, 1987, p. 35)

Olsen argues (1984b) that a consequence of the shift to gender neutrality in custody laws has been to diffuse the political content of decisions over custody, turning them instead into individual disputes between individual men and women. In her analysis of the rise and fall of the 'tender years' doctrine, she demonstrates that its demise has had contradictory effects. It can be viewed as constituting both victories and defeats for women, at both practical and ideological levels. It becomes an ideological defeat in the sense that when women lose custody of their children, this is seen as a private, individual matter, thereby overlooking the fact

174

that 'custody decisions also reflect and shape society's attitudes towards women and motherhood'. She adds:

> Within this privatized perspective, women lose their group identity. Women no longer have a political definition as women, and the custody of children ceases to be an issue of gender politics. The fall of the tender years doctrine thus depoliticizes the issue of custody and deprives individual mothers of their children, one at a time. (Olsen, 1984b, p. 17)

At a more specific level, it has been widely noted that an increased use of joint custody has the very real potential to expand the control of men over not only their children, but also over their former wives. According to Polikoff (1983, p. 192), 'overwhelmingly, children live with their mothers when there is joint legal custody, with the result that fathers get equal rights without incurring equal responsibility' (see also Smart, 1984; Brophy, 1985). Even though, as a number of commentators have noted, such arrangements in fact closely resemble sole maternal custody, with access to the father, there is arguably a significant difference. As a matter of law, disputes in either case would be determined by the court on the basis of the 'best interests', or 'welfare of the child', irrespective of the actual subsisting order. However, as a matter of practice, since such disputes rarely reach the courts, the symbolic force of a legal 'right' to custody, and therefore to decision making powers over a child, may give the father, already most likely to be the economically and physically stronger parent, a tactical advantage in a dispute between parties of unequal bargaining power. So, while not having the responsibility for the day-to-day care and nurture of children, fathers may none the less maintain the power to make decisions, often important decisions, and, in doing so, revive the very disagreements between the adult parties that led to the marriage breaking down. In particular, this is a problem in cases where the relationship was characterized by violence (see Schulman and Pitt, 1982; and Germane, Johnson, and Lemon, 1985).

Sevenhuijsen (1986) has pointed out that while feminist theories on motherhood have been concerned to unravel the threads of biology from notions of social relations, the concept of 'fatherhood', by contrast, still carries a monolithic unitary sense (see also Fineman and Opie, 1987, p. 155). In this way, it can be garnered by fathers' rights activists and others, asserting 'rights' over their children based solely on biology without any need to justify those claims with evidence of actual involvement with their children or a social rather than biological relationship. This leads to her conclusion that the current notion of fatherhood, as a legal institution of rights over women and children, 'shows a remarkable continuity with 19th century patriarchal law' (Sevenhuijsen, 1986, p. 338).

Feminists in Australia have recently begun to express concerns about 'fatherhood' and 'masculinity'. Early in 1987, the 'Coming Out Show' (a weekly national radio programme produced by the Australian Women's Broadcasting Co-operative) ran a disturbing programme entitled 'Men as Fathers: Care or Control?' (Earle and Jacobs, 1987) in which they interviewed Phyllis Chesler about her work on custody in the US. They also interviewed Graeme Russell, author of *The Changing Role of Fathers* (1983), whose study demonstrated that while a small number of 'new-look dads' are sharing the caring, the vast majority were not actively involved in day-to-day child care. His research found that most men spend only about one hour per week alone with their children. Russell also pointed out that the failure of non-custodial parents to pay maintenance demonstrates the disjunction between their perception of themselves as primarily breadwinners during marriage, and their perceived role after divorce. The programme documented the rising profile of fathers' rights groups in Australia, and described the disturbing advertising campaigns run on television by Fathers Against Discrimination in Custody (FADIC) ('Sometimes the best mothers are fathers'), and in newspapers by Fathers of Australia ('Victim fathers: fight for rights', *Sydney Morning Herald*, 6 November 1986).[11]

Feminist historian Judith Allen has drawn a link between the resurgence of positive images about fatherhood, and the increase in family-based violence. She argues that the 'feminist "discovery" of domestic violence has stimulated many mainstream professional responses, often in the attempt to re-locate analysis of the problem in a gender neutral perspective without reference to the context of societal male supremacy' (Allen, 1985, p. 132). She draws a parallel between this trend and the shift in the early 1970s to no-fault divorce, and continues:

If the feminist contribution to defining 'the family' as a dangerous place had initially favourable effects for women seeking child custody under the Family Law Act (1975) the honeymoon soon was over. While detailed work on the first ten years remains to be published, impressions abound. The negative picture of masculinity has been challenged in cultural production. A process of 'sentimentalising' the father–child bond is a striking feature of the last decade, nowhere more unctuously portrayed than in films such as *Kramer versus Kramer*, *Ordinary People*, and *Author, Author*, and in the plots of popular television soap operas. A more chilling note has been struck more recently in organised and violent masculinist attacks on the Family Law Court and its judges and their relatives. Meanwhile, although my information is verbal, welfare workers are reporting a disquieting tendency of judges to grant custody or else extraordinarily generous access conditions to violent husbands, even to those proven to have raped daughters – since these attacks on the Family Court. (Allen, 1985, p. 132)

No discussion of family law in Australia would be complete without a reference to the terrorist violence directed against the Family Court (see Green and Gurr, 1987). In 1980, a Family Court judge was shot dead on his front doorstep. Throughout 1983 and 1984 there were numerous bombings or bomb scares at both Family Court buildings and judges' homes and, in one related case, a church hall. These culminated in the bombing murder of Family Court counsellor (and wife of a Family Court judge) Pearl Watson in July 1984. A 1986 inquest into her death has not resulted in the laying of any charges.[12]

Not all the violence has been directed at the court itself. Bates (1986, p. 17) notes that, at least for 1985, 'Instead of terrorist attacks on judges of the Family Court of Australia and on legal practitioners, dissatisfied parties – invariably, thus far, fathers involved in custody disputes – have responded by killing the children in dispute and themselves.'[13] It is noteworthy that references to the pattern of violence, specifically to violence directed at the Family Court, are chillingly scattered throughout the transcripts of the Law Reform Commission's public hearings on contempt (Australian Law Reform Commission, 1986). While none of the men who gave evidence expressly condoned these killings, there are frequent statements of understanding towards the perpetrator(s), and predictions that more violence will follow 'until discrimination against men' is ended (see, e.g., Mr Findon, p. 114A; Mr Spanger, p. 293; Mr Aitken, p. 300; Mr Stewart, p. 317; Mr Lee, pp. 327, 328; Mr Foster, p. 547; Mr Romeyko, p. 675; cf. Ms Egg, p. 427).[14]

WOMEN'S POVERTY: THE POVERTY OF 'EQUALITY' IN AUSTRALIA

Having demonstrated the way in which notions of equality have been relied upon by the proponents of joint custody in Australia, it is salutary to step back briefly from the ideological arena and consider to what extent, if any, 'equality' has been materially achieved by women in Australia. As noted earlier, this broader context has rarely, if ever, been acknowledged as relevant to the debate about child custody. In fact, while the guiding principle remains 'the welfare of the child', it is argued here that the economic position of single mothers is an essential matter to consider.

It is by now well documented that Australia has the most highly gender segmented workforce of any OECD country, with women's work falling within a narrow range of occupational types (see Ronalds, 1987, pp. 3–6). The woeful level of government support for child care (currently under increasing pressure) makes it structurally impossible for many women to work. As to wages, while the infamous *Harvester* decision (1907) which established the Australian version of a 'family wage' for a man, wife, and three dependent children is no longer formally a part of the industrial framework for wage setting, its ideology lives on, and women continue to earn considerably less than their male counterparts. Recently, the Conciliation and Arbitration Commission (the national wage-fixing body) refused to extend the equal pay ruling of the 1970s to equal pay for work of equal value, i.e. rejected the principle of comparable worth (Innes, 1986; Burton, 1987; Burton, Hag, and Thompson, 1987; O'Donnell and Golder, 1986; Johnson and Wajcman, 1986).

Laws such as anti-discrimination legislation, which create a limited right to formal legal equality (Ronalds, 1987), do not

178

touch relations within the family. There is no law which compels people to share their income within the household, or to share domestic work and child care responsibilities. While the Family Law Act spouse maintenance obligation (s. 72) technically applies both during marriage and after marriage breakdown, in practice orders are sought only after the marriage has broken down.

Social Security's 'cohabitation' rule, by which women who live in *de facto* marital relationships with men are denied state benefits altogether in the case of widow's pension[15] or supporting parent's benefit,[16] or, where they are eligible for other forms of assistance, are paid a rate which takes into account their *de jure* or *de facto* spouse's income, is clearly based on the assumption that women (both married women and those living in *de facto* relationships) are or should be supported by the men with whom they live (see Bryson, 1983; Shaver, 1983; Graycar, 1987a). In both cases, the state constructs these women as dependants, whether or not they actually are (see also Montague and Stephens, 1985).

In a country with particularly low labour force participation by single mothers (see Raymond, 1987), any move towards financial independence for women can only be achieved by specific government interventions, such as increasing child care spending and establishing training programmes to help women re-enter, or enter, the workforce. Yet concern about the poverty of women and children has increasingly moved governments to seek private solutions, for example, cracking down on recalcitrant non-custodial fathers, rather than formulating public policies around women's employment, child care, and related services. The choices remain only twofold: dependence on men or dependence on the state. This preference for private, rather than public, solutions resonates with the ideological position that issues relating to 'the family' are outside the purview of state responsibility. Feminists have directed considerable energy towards deconstructing this 'public:private' split (e.g. Pateman, 1983; O'Donovan, 1985) but it resurfaces constantly, as the recent debates about joint custody and child support (see below) demonstrate.

JOINT CUSTODY AND EQUALITY

Given this context, it remains to be seen what specific conse-quences for Australian women might follow a move towards a new legal regime requiring courts to make orders of joint guardianship or, possibly, joint custody. A change in current custody laws and practices may well prove to be inconsistent with, and undermine, other recent reform moves.

The child support scheme: a private solution for a public problem

The federal government has recently introduced legislation which established a Child Support Agency in 1988, responsible for collecting child maintenance from non-custodial parents, through the taxation system. The central purpose of the scheme is to diminish the 'burden on the taxpayer' for the support of single parent families, though the government at the same time has stated its concern about the increasing poverty of those families (Cabinet Sub-Committee on Maintenance, 1986). Extremely stringent means tests will apply for social security pensions and benefits, greatly diminishing any potential benefit for recipients. This maintenance income test, which includes provision for imputing certain transfers of property to income, will be separate from the more generous work income test which operates for single parent recipients of state income support, where the 'free area' is more than double that for maintenance income. This is significant, since very few women on state benefits are in the labour force (Raymond, 1987).

Feminist groups have raised a number of concerns about this plan (Feminist Legal Issues Group, 1986; Earle and Graycar, 1987; Heron, 1987; Graycar, 1987b; Cox, 1987). One of these, of particular relevance here, is the extent to which the scheme will prompt demands for custody or access from non-custodial parents whose dormant interest in their children is revived by resort to the hip pocket nerve. After all, a father who successfully pursues a sole or joint custody order cannot be described as a non-custodial parent and will therefore not be subjected to the scheme. The effect of joint guardianship is unclear. The government is not unmindful of these concerns, and has strenuously stated, in response to the 'no access – no maintenance' lobby, which emerged so clearly at the contempt public hearings described above, that maintenance and access are not related and will remain that way (Howe, 1987, p. 1,370). This guarantee, whilst reassuring, seems hollow in the light of the evidence collected by the ALRC from the fathers' rights groups in its 1986 public hearings on contempt. In its report, the ALRC concluded:

> if the arguments put to it in submissions and at public hearings truly represent the feelings of a large proportion of access parents in Australia, the strengthening of maintenance enforcement by government collection schemes will provoke considerable resentment unless *either* access enforcement is strengthened at the same time...*or* access denial is treated as a mitigating factor in maintenance enforcement, *or* both. (Australian Law Reform Commission, 1987a, para. 739)

Matrimonial property

The recent debate in Australia about matrimonial property demonstrates the difficulty of basing reform arguments around the concept of 'equality'. Some feminists in Australia have argued strenuously in favour of 'equal rights to marital assets' – specifically, the establishment of a community property regime (e.g. Women's Electoral Lobby, 1981, 1985; Scutt, 1983; Scutt and Graham, 1984). 'Equality' was the central plank of these reform proposals. It was argued that this could only be achieved by a full community of property regime that divided all marital assets on a 50:50 basis. Others, however, argued that a non-discretionary system of formal equal sharing of matrimonial property may rebound against women (see, for example, Cox, 1983 and 1985; O'Keefe, 1983; Shiff and MacIllhatton, 1985). Detailed empirical work in the US, where community property is increasingly the norm, has shown that this form of equality is 'illusive' (e.g. Fineman, 1983 and 1986; and Minow, 1986). Lenore Weitzman's work on the economic consequences of divorce for women and children in the US (1985), paralleled by recent research conducted by the Australian Institute of Family Studies (1986), indicates all too clearly that 'equal sharing' of marital assets can leave women, with their more limited access to the workforce and the disadvantages accrued through years of child bearing and rearing, much worse off financially than men. After divorce 78 per cent of women who had not re-partnered were significantly worse off than before their divorce and 35 per cent were living below the poverty line, according to the Australian study (see Australian Institute of

Family Studies, 1986, pp. 115–23, 311–12; Australian Law Reform Commission, 1987b, paras 163–7). Significantly, this research demonstrates that under the present discretionary system women overall (particularly those who are custodial parents) received a greater share of what the AIFS referred to as 'basic marital assets' (Australian Institute of Family Studies, 1986, Chapter 9; Australian Law Reform Commission, 1987b, paras 177–80). This led the ALRC in its 1987 report on matrimonial property, established in part to respond to some of this controversy, to eschew the rhetoric of equality in favour of a more realistic way of attempting to spread the economic disadvantages of divorce. The Commission concluded that a regime of equal sharing would leave women worse off than they already are (Australian Law Commission, 1987b, para. 273). It favoured 'practical, rather than formal equality', a distribution that would take account of and compensate women for their impaired capacity to achieve a reasonable standard of living and for the responsibility for the children, still overwhelmingly looked after in Australia by women (para. 350). In a society where men and women are not equal, the ALRC correctly recognized that 'equal sharing' could disadvantage women.

Empirical work undertaken by both the AIFS and the ALRC, including surveys of Family Court judges and registrars, demonstrated the significant effect of women's greater custodial responsibilities on the skewing of awards in their favour. Automatic joint guardianship orders, particularly if day-to-day custody is left to the parties to organize (and, therefore, overwhelmingly to the woman), might well lead courts in future to decide that there is no basis for taking women's custodial responsibilities into account in determining property distribution. If this were to happen, it would undermine the very careful approach of the ALRC in looking towards 'practical, rather than formal equality' (para. 273).

State support for single parents: possible implications for joint custody

Another matter of concern is in the area of statutory income support. Under the current legislative framework widow's pension and supporting parent's benefit can only be awarded to a parent who has 'custody, care and control' which involves, for social security purposes, 'the right to have, and to make decisions concerning the daily care and control of the child' (Social Security Act 1947 (Commonwealth), s.3(2)). A recent case raises a disturbing possibility. There the unmarried parents were awarded joint custody of their only child by a state court. The father applied for and obtained a supporting parent's benefit. The mother subsequently applied for it and was rejected. She appealed to the Social Security Appeals Tribunal,[17] which concluded that the benefit could not be split and, since the father got in first, there was no basis upon which they could say that he was not entitled to it (Social Security Appeals Tribunal: NSW, Appeal no. 12,347/1987). Certainly, there is no statutory provision for splitting the benefit and such an exercise would be pointless as its purpose is to provide income support (rudimentary as that may be). However, it suggests a disturbing possibility for future cases if joint custody becomes a routine arrangement. This is especially problematic as the language of custody, care, and control in the Social Security Act is not consistent with the terminology used in the Family Law Act.

'EQUAL RIGHTS FOR PARENTS'

In spite of these very practical concerns, the current political climate appears to favour 'equal rights for parents'. Single parents in Australia (overwhelmingly mothers) are the new 'undeserving poor'.[18] By contrast, fathers' rights groups have achieved remarkable political acceptance – for example, the spokesperson for the Lone Fathers' Association (an organization with exclusively male membership, and 'associate member' status for women – see Australian Law Reform Commission, 1986, p. 4) has been made a member of the National Consultative Committee on Child Maintenance. Fineman has documented the extent to which fathers' rights groups in Wisconsin achieved disproportionate political legitimacy, while their far more numerous female counterparts remain unorganized and accordingly unheard (Fineman, 1986). The fathers' claims to custody, their refusal to pay maintenance without custody of, or access to, their children, and their deeply misogynist complaints about their ex-wives being favoured by the courts and supported by the government, all demonstrate a concern that their control over their family, even after its dissolution, has been undermined. For these groups, patriarchal control should continue even after divorce, and perceived diminutions in that power have prompted loud and long complaints. Dissolution of their marriages has not stopped them from pursuing and asserting the existence of the 'eternal biological family'. Children have become pawns in this broad political battle and, to the extent that mothers' custody has been characterized as their acquisition of some modicum of power, it is likely that it will continue to be resisted. Related to this, the child support proposals, under which women dependent on social security will be required to seek maintenance orders or risk losing their income support, constitute a clear undermining of women's ability to get on with their lives and those of their children after divorce, unimpeded by unwanted, continuing dealings with reluctant, and possibly violent, non-custodial parents. They also demonstrate a clear rejection of women's 'right to choose' single parenthood (at least to the extent that women rely upon the state for income support). The focus upon private maintenance, as a pre-condition to public support, also asserts the primacy of the 'eternal biological family'.

AN AGENDA FOR A DEBATE?

This chapter has argued that the Australian debate about 'joint custody' has effectively occurred in a vacuum, with no clarity as to what is actually sought by the proponents, and little, if any, consideration of the impact such reforms may have on women or on related matters of family law and state policy. Elsewhere, feminist commentators have made alternative suggestions about the future direction of custody reforms. One commonly expressed concern is that responses to shifts away from preferring women as the automatic custodial parent should not facilitate any resuscitation of biologistic notions of the innateness of 'motherhood' which would reinforce outmoded views of women's rightful sphere – something feminists have struggled long and hard to destroy. A frequently proposed alternative for evaluating the ubiquitous 'welfare of the child' principle has been to focus attention on the caretaking practices during the subsisting marriage (e.g. Boyd, 1987, forthcoming; Polikoff, 1982; Fineman,

1987). A presumption in favour of awarding custodial 'rights' to the primary caretaker, while *prima facie* a gender neutral criterion, would hopefully not routinely serve to disadvantage women, unlike the purportedly gender neutral practice developing in the US of considering the relative economic positions of the parties.

But it is not the purpose of this chapter to construct an ideal custody law. My concern rather is with the terms of the debate to date and the failure not only of the fathers' rights groups, but also of the more reputable policy bodies such as the Family Law Council, both to specify what they are proposing and to think through the implications of their attraction to the ideal of 'joint custody'. It has been suggested that the arguments canvassed here rely heavily on the ideology of equality at the same time as they ignore the realities of matters such as the day-to-day caretaking practices of divorced mothers and fathers and the relative economic situations of women and men in Australia. Moreover, at a time when single mothers have become increasingly subjected to community opprobrium, the 'eternal biological family' has reasserted itself with considerable vigour.

Law reformers and policy makers must stand back from the heat of the current political attacks on single mothers. Just as the ALRC eschewed the rhetoric of equality in its carefully argued and extensively researched work on matrimonial property and sought instead to look at the underlying realities of women's post-divorce experiences, so also we can hope that law reformers who attempt to rethink current policies on custody might do likewise.

NOTES

A number of people have made extremely valuable contributions to this chapter. I should like to thank Sheila Begg, Sophy Bordow, Michael Chesterman, Richard Chisholm, Hester Eisenstein, Owen Jessep, Maureen Kingshott, Genevieve Lloyd, Deena Shiff, and Carol Smart. I am especially indebted to Annette Hasche and Jenny Morgan.

1 On 4 September 1987, paediatrician Dr David Fraser was named father of the year in the state of Queensland. In his acceptance speech he urged the government to stop channelling resources into supporting single parent families. He suggested that, instead, children in families

without fathers should be adopted out, presumably into 'real families'. Taking up his call, the then Queensland Welfare Minister, Mrs Chapman, suggested that there should be compulsory sterilization for women on welfare, after the first child (ABC Radio News, 4 September 1987 and *Courier Mail*, 5 September 1987).

2 The High Court is the apex of the judicial system in Australia, somewhat comparable to the House of Lords in Britain.

3 The state supreme courts, not being specialist family courts are more likely to make explicitly stereotyped comments on their perception of the parents than the Family Court, a specialist court with a developed body of doctrine around the concept of the 'welfare of the child' which at least in theory commits them to reject some of the more traditional assumptions about motherhood. That does not mean that Family Court judges may not share those assumptions, but simply that they are less likely to state them explicitly in their reasons for decisions. Arguably, this is one of the significant effects of having specialist family courts.

4 An expedited appeal against this decision was allowed by the Full Family Court in December 1987 (Appeal no. 221 of 1987) and the matter was settled prior to rehearing by the Family Court *Swaney* v. *Ward*, 1988.

5 The Commission had been asked by the federal government to review the law of contempt, both civil and criminal. It had published extensive research and discussion papers on a wide array of topics, including civil contempt, contempt and the media, and contempt and family law, before embarking upon public hearings around Australia as part of the consultation process.

6 Fineman, 1986, p. 788 has documented a similar phenomenon in Wisconsin. In Australia, the absence of women's groups at the ALRC contempt hearings was noted by a number of the fathers' groups; the convenor of Men's Confraternity stated: 'You do not see any female groups here tonight because they are quite happy and contented with the Family Court situation because it is going their way and they know it' (Australian Law Reform Commission, 1986, p. 378).

7 In his evidence to the ALRC contempt inquiry, the group's Mike Ward stated: 'the Family Court situation is organised by radical feminists. They control the welfare section, they control the counselling section. So when a man goes in the Family Court he is guilty until proven otherwise' (Australian Law Reform Commission, 1986, p. 378). He went on to suggest: 'Misogynist is, you know, a hater of women if you like. There is no such word in the English language for a hater of men. We call it Ryanism for obvious reasons' (p. 380). (Senator Susan Ryan was the federal minister responsible for women's affairs from 1983–8.)

8 This backlash against 'women's equality' is not solely confined to the custody area, as the following three items published in just one day in

a Sydney newspaper indicate. A group of male school teachers has been formed to fight against a government Equal Employment Opportunity programme which they say discriminates against men ('Male teachers rally to the flag on eve of battle of the sexes', *Sydney Morning Herald*, 24 October 1987). Meanwhile, advertising industry executives have described the announcement of a government study to be held into the portrayal of women in advertising as a 'sop to the Minister's mates in the feminist movement' and the 'Hawke Ministry pandering to the bleatings of the unrepresentative old feminist lobby' ('Sexism study "a sop to Minister's mates"', *Sydney Morning Herald*, 24 October 1987, p. 15). Finally, the editorial for that day repeats criticisms made by the Bar Association to proposals for changes in criminal law procedures in cases of violence and sexual assault against women and children. The editorial writer is not so persuaded as are the lawyers that these will necessarily reduce the protections available to the accused. S/he concludes:

> One criticism by lawyers of the proposed changes is that they have emanated from a women's lobby in the Premier's Department. But again, the profession will have to come up with stronger arguments than that. Otherwise, it risks the counter-accusation that it is fighting an irrelevant war of the sexes to preserve a male-constructed system at all costs. If there are to be arguments, they must be from reason, not prejudice. ('Law reform and war of the sexes', *Sydney Morning Herald*, editorial, 24 October 1987, p. 30)

9 Despite the resort to 'equality' and 'discrimination', these men's demands appear to go beyond a concern for egalitarianism based on simple equality between women and men. In a submission to the ALRC Inquiry into Matrimonial Property, this group argued that:

> Men should be given first consideration for custody of the children on the basis that they are more caring, better equipped for long term planning and hence able to provide a more stable life for the children. Women on the other hand tend to be emotive, superficial and self-centred. (Men's Confraternity, n.d. (1985?), para. 3.7)

10 This relates to research I undertook on compensation for women accident victims who suffer injuries impairing or destroying their capacity to undertake domestic work. In that context, it became abundantly clear that courts used the rhetoric of equality to assume that if both adults work outside the home, both participate equally at home; therefore the loss to a woman of her capacity to work in the home is less significant than it would be if she were 'a housewife' (Graycar, 1985a and 1985b).

11 The advertisement stated: 'All fathers who have been separated/ divorced or married should join or donate money to help the struggle against sexual bias in Family Law.'

12 Popular media coverage of the Family Law Act and the Family Court

relies heavily on this pattern of violence. But it is not only the popular press who do so. In 1985 then Chief Justice of Australia, Sir Harry Gibbs, drew a nexus between the violence and what he perceived as inadequacies in the law. These unhelpful comments were of course widely reported and added to calls for a return to a fault-based system, more formality, and, in particular, the return of wigs and gowns (see Chisholm and Jessep, 1985; Green and Gurr, 1987).

13 For a recent example, see the reports of a murder-suicide in Western Australia by a recently separated father: *Sydney Morning Herald*, 4 and 5 November 1987.

14 These sentiments were echoed by the Men's Confraternity of Western Australia in a covering letter enclosing a submission to the ALRC Matrimonial Property Inquiry:

> There is a growing awareness in our state, that the men here are being discriminated against to an alarming degree. [A] quite seething rage is developing in our state, among the male populace, the consequences, we believe, will become obvious in the future.... The murders of family court judges over your side of the country, will happen here unless you do. We beg you not to be swayed by the feminist movement which will be making their own submissions. (Letter to ALRC, 17 September 1985, on file with ALRC)

15 The benefit is available only to women. The name is deceptive; the majority of 'widows' are actually divorced or deserted wives (see Department of Social Security, 1987, p. 157).

16 This benefit was introduced as a benefit for single or separated mothers in 1973; in 1977 it was extended to men and the name changed to reflect that change. By far the largest number (nearly 95 per cent) of recipients are women (see Department of Social Security, 1987, p. 159).

17 The Social Security Appeals Tribunal hears appeals against decisions made under the Social Security Act.

18 There is a prevailing and persistent myth in the community that women, and in particular young women, are choosing single parenthood as an easy way to live a 'life of luxury' on the meagre state benefits provided for single parents. So popular is this notion that it leads to periodic suggestions like those by the Queensland Welfare Minister (see note 1) that single parents be compulsorily sterilized or their 'fatherless' children be removed to 'real families'. Early in 1987, a leader writer in one of the national newspapers, referring to single motherhood, suggested that 'this phenomenon is increasing – both amongst unemployed girls and professional women – even though it rarely involves the lesbian "milk run in reverse", by which "anonymous input" is collected from a variety of lap-dog male donors' (Clark, 1987).

CASES

In the Marriage of Chapman and Palmer (1978) Family Law Cases
90-510.

In the Marriage of Cullen (1981) Family Law Cases 90-695.

Epperson v. *Dampney* (1976) 10 Australian Law Reports 227.

Gronow v. *Gronow* (1979) 144 Commonwealth Law Reports 513.

Harrington v. *Hynes* (1982) 8 Family Law Reports 295.

In the Marriage of L (1983) Family Law Cases 91-353.

Mathiesen and Mathiesen (1977) Family Law Cases 90-230.

Ex parte McKay (the Harvester Award) (1907) 2 Commonwealth
Arbitration Reports 1.

PC and PR (1979) Family Law Cases 90-676.

Swaney and Ward (1988) Family Law Cases 91-928.

Ward v. *Ward* No. AD 1039 of 1985, Family Court of Australia at
Adelaide, 6 August, 7 October, 1987.

Chapter Eight

THE CUSTODY OF CHILDREN IN THE REPUBLIC OF IRELAND

DELMA MACDEVITT

INTRODUCTION

The law governing the custody of children in Ireland does not appear, at first sight, to differ greatly from that of other European countries. As in other countries, the development of custody legislation has involved changes in the relative rights of parents and in the way these are balanced against the welfare of the child; as in other countries, women have acquired formal equality and, in practice, by virtue of their role as mothers, greater opportunity for custody than men; and, as in other countries, the trend in statutory and case law has been to give priority to the welfare of the child. In Ireland, however, these developments have come about against the background of the overwhelming influence of Catholic social doctrine on the entire area of family law. This is particularly evident in articles 41 and 42 of the constitution which deal directly with 'The Family'. Since these articles are crucial to an understanding of the development and state, not just of custody, but of all aspects of family law in Ireland, they are worth quoting here:

Article 41 – The Family:
- 1.1　　The State recognises the Family as the natural primary and fundamental unit group of Society and as a moral institution possessing inalienable and imprescriptible rights, antecedent and superior to all positive law.
- 1.2　　The State, therefore, guarantees to protect the Family in its constitution and authority, as the necessary basis of social order and as indispensable to the welfare of the Nation and the State.

2.1 In particular, the State recognises that by her life in the home, woman gives to the State a support without which the common good cannot be achieved.

2.2 The State shall, therefore, endeavour to ensure that mothers shall not be obliged by economic necessity to engage in labour to the neglect of their duties in the home.

3.1 The State pledges itself to guard with special care the institution of Marriage, on which the Family is founded, and to protect it from attack.

3.2 No law shall be enacted providing for the grant of a dissolution of marriage.

3.3 No person whose marriage has been dissolved under the civil law of any other State but is a subsisting marriage for the time being in force within the jurisdiction of the Government and Parliament established by this Constitution shall be capable of contracting a valid marriage within that jurisdiction during the lifetime of the other party to the marriage so dissolved.

Article 42 – Education:

1. The State acknowledges that the primary and natural educator of the child is the Family and guarantees to respect the inalienable right and duty of parents to provide, according to their means, for the religious and moral, intellectual, physical and social education of their children. (Bunreacht na h-Eireann, 1937)

These articles reflect a concept of the family which derives directly from Catholic social teaching. 'The Family' is a monomorphic social and moral institution based on indissoluble marriage between one man and one woman; marriage, the primary purpose of which is the procreation of children, is the only legitimate 'forum' for sexual relations; and parents have certain inalienable rights and obligations to provide, not just for the material well-being of their children but, in the first instance, for their moral and religious upbringing.

This concept of 'The Family' is, of course, prescriptive rather than descriptive. Various types of family are to be found in the country, parents do not always provide for their children, and the prohibition of divorce does not prevent marriages from breaking down. Nevertheless, the status accorded to 'The Family' under the constitution reflects the strength of Catholic ideology and has had direct effects on the development and interpretation of statutory and case law on custody. I have tried in this chapter to identify and describe these effects. Section one provides a brief outline of the development of the custody law. Section two looks at the way these laws were interpreted in the 1940s and 1950s and argues that judicial practice, and particularly, judicial recourse to the provisions of the constitution have had a lasting effect on custody legislation and decisions. The constitutional status of 'The Family', the definition of what 'The Family' is, and the repercussions that these have for the regulation of custody disputes between parents and outsiders, including the state, are the subject of the third section. Many of the cases discussed in this section concern adoption, which must be considered an important area of custody legislation in Ireland. In fact, it was in the context of a dispute about adoption that 'The Family' was defined, and that definition has continued to inform judicial decisions in custody disputes. The section that follows deals with the effects of the behaviour of parents on the outcome of custody disputes, while the fifth and final part of the chapter looks at gender roles in custody. The chapter argues that although the principle of the 'welfare of the child' is regarded by law as primary, it is only by looking at the way in which this principle is interpreted that the content, rather than the form, of custody legislation can be understood. An examination of that content shows that the similarities between Ireland and other European countries are, indeed, only apparent and that issues that are crucial to other contributors, such as fathers' rights, joint custody, and the implications of the new reproductive technology, can, as yet, be of only marginal concern in a country which prohibits divorce and, in effect, recognizes only one form of family, that based on indissoluble marriage.

THE DEVELOPMENT OF CUSTODY LAW

Until the establishment of the Irish Free State in 1922, Irish law was largely, though not completely, the same as that of England, and the custody of children was regulated by the same plurality of potentially conflicting principles.

1 At common law the father was the sole guardian of his legitimate child. His right to custody, though not quite absolute, could be forfeited only in exceptional cases of grave misconduct which might result in physical or moral harm to the child.

2 The custody rights of the father could be overridden by equity which stressed the welfare of the child as the paramount consideration. After the passing of the Judicature Act in 1877, the equitable rule stressing the importance of the child's welfare prevailed in all courts.

3 The unequal position of women was changed in part by the statutory legislation of 1839, 1873, and 1886 which allowed women to apply for the custody of their children under 7, 16, and 21 years, respectively. This did not involve a formal recognition of the equality of men and women *qua* parents but, as a result of the partial erosion of the rights of the father and the application of the equitable principle of the welfare of the child, the tendency was established for the courts to award the custody of particularly very young children to the mother while continuing to recognize the father as the head of the family. The judicial basis for the division of custody into care and control was thus established. This tendency continued to exist in the case law of Ireland after 1922.

4 In cases of divorce and/or legal separation, which were available only on fault grounds, the law of 1886 laid down that the person whose misconduct had led to the decree could be declared to be unfit to have custody. In Ireland after 1922, fault in marital breakdown and/or legal separation could act as a bar to custody (Shatter, 1977, pp. 184–6).

The situation was complicated further after 1937 when the new constitution of the Irish Republic, which included the articles quoted above, came into force and when, to the issues of the rights of the individual parents and the welfare of the child, was added the question of the rights of 'The Family' which the state had undertaken to protect and uphold. As far as custody is concerned, this has proven to be of crucial importance in cases which involve disputes between parents (or a parent) and outsiders. It has also had important indirect effects on disputes between the father and mother of a child or children.

Disputes between parents usually arise on or after the breakdown of the marriage of the parents. Since divorce is expressly forbidden by the constitution, breakdown is dealt with in a variety of ways. The parties may seek a judicial separation (divorce *a mensa et thoro*) or a legal annulment of their marriage; they may contract a separation agreement; they may obtain a foreign (generally speaking, British) divorce;[1] they may seek a church annulment of their marriage;[2] or they may split up and do nothing to obtain either civil or religious recognition of their change of status. Comprehensive and detailed statistics on marriage breakdown in Ireland are not available so it is difficult to establish what proportions opt for these various solutions. The estimates made by the Joint Committee on Marriage Breakdown suggest, however, that the level of formal legal regulation of marital breakdown is very low (*Report of the Joint Committee on Marital Breakdown*, 1985, pp. 132–5). It would seem, moreover, that, in many cases of breakdown, the custody of children does not become a matter of litigation.[3] Arrangements about custody are not at any rate an automatic corollary of the legal regulation of breakdown and, where a dispute exists, proceedings are brought under the Guardianship of Infants Act 1964.

The Guardianship of Infants Act was the first statute regulating custody to be introduced in the history of the Republic. Section 11 of the Act provides a mechanism whereby any person being the guardian of an infant may apply to the court for direction on any question affecting the welfare of the infant and the court can make such order as it thinks fit in the circumstances. This is the procedure which is usually invoked to resolve custody disputes.

The 1964 Act is not innovative. In fact, it merely formalizes and gives statutory recognition to several principles that had already been established in case law. Section 3 lays down that the 'welfare of the child' is to be given priority; s.6 recognizes the equal custody rights of parents; while s.18 (1) reiterates the principle that 'fault' in marital breakdown can constitute a bar to custody. The Guardianship of Infants Act is worded in internationally comparable legal-rational terms of individual rights, but formal provisions in themselves give an inadequate indication of trends in custody law both because of the vagueness of the concept of welfare (and even of its 'definition' in terms taken straight from the constitution, as comprising the 'religious and moral, intellectual, physical and social welfare' of the infant) and because of the latitude that judges have in defining and interpreting the law. An adequate understanding of custody law requires, therefore, an examination of judicial practice in custody disputes.[4]

THE EARLY CASES: MORALITY AND 'MIXED MARRIAGES'

As well as undertaking to protect 'The Family' and 'Marriage', the 1937 constitution also recognized the 'special position' of the Catholic Church as 'the guardian of the faith professed by the great majority of citizens',[5] and the period following the acceptance of the new constitution – the late 1940s and the 1950s – was one of marked integrationism. The idea of a Catholic state for a Catholic people was widely espoused in the political culture and in judicial circles. There were several important and controversial custody cases during this period, the main issue in which was whether the children of 'mixed marriages' (marriages between Catholics and non-Catholics) which had broken down were to be brought up as Catholics or not. It is possible to examine these cases, which have all been reported and described and discussed extensively elsewhere (Shatter, 1977, pp. 187–93; Whyte, 1971, pp. 167–71; O'Reilly, 1977), in terms of a sectarian tug o'war or numbers game between the majority Catholic and the minority Protestant populations and to hypothesize that the dominant, though not uniform, trend was for the courts to use the provisions of the constitution and the conflicting principles in custody law to ensure the victory of the Catholic party to the dispute. This type of sectarian partisanship did, and indeed does, continue to exist (*H. v. H.*, 1976) and it reflects one facet of integrationism which recent events in Ireland – notably the June 1986 referendum on divorce[6] – have shown to have been merely dormant during the apparently more 'liberal' 1970s. Custody disputes involving children of 'mixed marriages' have become relatively rare but the way in which the predominantly Catholic judges in the first integrationist period interpreted and defined the law and the constitution has, in several ways, had lasting effects on custody legislation.

In the first place, the judgements in all these cases made at least some reference to the welfare of the child, and some claimed to be based on that consideration alone. In defining welfare, however, paramount importance was given to religious upbringing, the child's 'most precious inheritance in the eyes of a Christian state' (Gavin Duffy J, in *In re Tilson (Infants)*, 1951, p. 18). Thus, half way through the 'Century of the Child', when the concept of welfare was being expanded and when a movement towards child-centredness was underway in psychology and education as well as in family law, the majority of judges in the High and Supreme Courts persisted in defining welfare in terms of formal religious (preferably Catholic) training and gave little, and sometimes no, consideration even to economic, social, and physical, let alone psychological, factors (Black J in *In re Corcoran (Infants)*, 1950, p. 19). In contemporary cases which involve differences in religion, this is the definition of welfare that prevails, though it may be, and has been, overridden in extreme cases (*B. v. B.*, 1972). The number of such cases is, however, now very small. More important, in numerical terms, is the continued equation of welfare with a proper upbringing, though the emphasis, again in terms of the numbers involved, has shifted from religious training to the pro-vision of a suitably 'moral' atmosphere. Given that 'immorality' in Ireland is perceived almost exclusively in terms of extra-marital sexual activity, this means that 'the welfare of the child' is frequently perceived as a corollary of the sexual behaviour or, more precisely, of the absence of any visible sexual activity on the part of the parent by whom s/he is to be brought up.

Second, in these early cases the 'welfare of the child' was discussed within the context of the status accorded to 'The Family' by the constitution. In fact, both judges and litigants used the provisions of the constitution either to override precedents and/or to forward the claim of an individual parent. The result was that it became an established practice to invoke the constitution in custody disputes (and, indeed, in other areas of family law) and to assert the inviolability of the rights of 'The Family', i.e. of parents in disputes with outsiders including the state apparatus. This practice, together with the way the family was defined in these judicial decisions, has had a continuing effect on custody disputes. It would be difficult to determine the extent to which judicial decisions and the periodic 'official' reassertion of the sanctity of 'The Family' have contributed to the ideological status enjoyed by that institution. It is, however, reasonable to maintain that the unquestioning obeisance accorded to a particular form of family as the natural and primary moral unit of society, even in custody disputes where that unit has patently and by definition broken down, has not been conducive either to a critical examination of the family nor to any radical re-evaluation of the meaning of the concept of the 'welfare of the child'.

Finally, the unquestioning veneration of 'The Family' and the automatic acceptance of a division of labour and of gender roles within it were not affected by the establishment of equal custody rights for women. These rights were first established in the *Tilson* case, in which it was decided that parents had equal rights to custody according to article 41 of the constitution. This equality was, however, established merely as a means of ensuring that the Catholic party, the mother, was awarded custody. There was neither a demand for nor an opposition to sexual equality *per se*; indeed, the entire concept was neither examined nor discussed. Thus, equal custody rights were given to women; they were emphatically not achieved and their establishment was neither preceded nor accompanied by any increased awareness or consciousness of the unequal position of women in the family and in society. The relative position of men and women was not an issue in the *Tilson* case and the unquestioning acceptance of traditional sex roles continues to be a feature of custody decisions.

THE STATUS OF 'THE FAMILY' AND CUSTODY DISPUTES

Article 41 gives constitutional status to 'The Family' but it does not in fact define what 'The Family' is. In article 41.3, the state undertakes to guard the institution of marriage but this is not defined either. The early attempts to define 'The Family' in the courts have been examined elsewhere (Staines, 1976). Suffice it here to mention the leading case, which was decided by the Supreme Court in 1966 – *The State (Nicolau)* v. *An Bord Uchtala* (The Adoption Board). Nicolau, a Greek Orthodox Cypriot, was the father of an illegitimate child who had been placed for adoption by the mother without the father's knowledge and against his wishes. He sought to have the adoption order quashed, and argued, *inter alia*, that the Adoption Act 1952 was unconstitutional in that it involved the alienation of the 'inalienable and impre-scriptible rights' of 'The Family'. The Court decided that the 1952 Act was not unconstitutional and that arts 41 and 42 referred only to families and parenthood based on marriage and that an unmarried father had no constitutional rights in relation to his child. In his judgement, Walsh J stated:

> While it is true that unmarried parents cohabiting together and the children of their union may often be referred to as a family and have many, if not all, the outward appearances of a family and may, indeed, for the purposes of a particular law be regarded as such, nevertheless, as far as Art. 41 is concerned, the guarantees therein contained are confined to families based on marriage. (pp. 643-4)

This restricted view of what constitutes 'The Family' has continued to prevail in the courts and has various implications for custody disputes between parents and outsiders.

Only families based on marriage are 'protected' by the constitution, and the rights and duties of these families are inalienable and imprescriptible. This means that legitimate children cannot, under any circumstances, be adopted, though they can be taken into care.[7] An unmarried mother and her child are not considered to be a family (Staines, 1976) as defined and protected by the constitution. The question of art. 41, however, can and has arisen in custody cases where illegitimate children, who have been placed for adoption or adopted, are subsequently legitimated by the marriage of their biological parents, if the validity of the adoption order is contested or if the process is still incomplete. This has led in some cases (*In re J. (an Infant)* 1966; *McL. v. An Bord Uchtala*, 1976) to adoption orders being declared invalid and the child being returned to the custody of its biological parents. In the case of *McL. v. An Bord Uchtala*, for example, the Supreme Court declared that an adoption order made five years previously was null and void and that, as a consequence, the child in respect of whom the proceedings were brought was legitimated by the marriage of its natural parents. This decision was made without any reference to the welfare of the child (Shatter, 1977, p. 176) and while it is obvious that the judge would have preferred to leave the child with its adoptive parents, he concluded: 'In coming to a just conclusion, however, one must not allow compassion to confuse or permit sympathy to conceal fundamental rights' (O'Higgins J, p. 8).

In a more recent case (*In the Matter of J. H. (Otherwise R.) (an*

Infant), 1985, 1986) a child who had been adopted for three years was removed from her adoptive parents and custody was given to her (now married) biological parents. The High Court had originally left the child with the adopters on the basis that 'pursuant to s.3 of the 1964 Act, the child's welfare was best served by avoiding the potential long term psychological risks in removing her from the custody of the adopting parents' (1986, p. 65). The biological parents appealed and the decision was reversed by the Supreme Court on the grounds that the child, though born illegitimate, had become a member of 'The Family' of her biological parents within the meaning of art. 41 of the constitution.

As far as the welfare of the child was concerned, the Chief Justice pointed out the limits placed by the constitution on basing decisions on this consideration, and quoted from another judgement:

> The word 'paramount' by itself is not by any means an indication of exclusivity; no doubt, if the Oireachtas[8] had intended the welfare of the child to be the only consideration, it would have said so. The use of the word 'paramount' certainly indicates that the welfare of the child is to be the superior or the most important consideration, *in so far as it can be, having regard to the law or the provisions of the Constitution applicable to any given case.* (emphasis supplied) (Walsh J in *In G. v. An Bord Uchtala*, 1980, p. 37)

Referring to another case (*J. v. D.*, 1977) where it had been decided that the welfare of the child was a sufficient reason to refuse custody to the father who was the sole surviving parent of the child, he went on to say:

> Insofar as that judgement may be construed as clearly indicating that, in the case of legitimate children, paramount consideration of their welfare, as defined in the Act of 1964, can be applied as the sole test without regard to the provisions of Articles 41 and 42 of the Constitution, I must, respectfully, refuse to follow it. (Finlay J in *In the Matter of J. H. (Otherwise R.) (an Infant)*, 1985, p. 318)

The problem of reconciling the provisions of arts 41 and 42 with the principle of the welfare of the child was overcome, in this case, as indeed it had been previously (*In re J. (an Infant)*, 1966), by the expedient of equating the welfare of the child with remaining in the custody of her 'Family' as defined by the constitution.

> I would, therefore, accept the contention that in this case, Section 3 of the Act of 1964 must be construed as involving *a constitutional presumption* that the welfare of the child which is defined in terms identical to those contained in art. 42.1 *is to be found within the family* unless the court is satisfied that evidence establishes an exceptional case where parents have failed to provide education for the child or continue to fail to provide education for the child for moral or physical reasons. (Finlay J in *In the Matter of J. H. (Otherwise R.) (an Infant)*, 1985, p. 318) (my emphasis)

In the case in point, in addition to the problem associated with removing the child from one family to another, there were conflicting psychiatric reports as to the psychological stability of the biological mother but neither of these factors was considered as 'compelling reasons' to overlook the constitutional rights of 'The Family'. The court did, however, consider the question of the welfare of the child but was satisfied with 'establishing' that a change in custody would not be detrimental to her well-being in that the biological parents were capable of providing 'a good home' for her. This is, in fact, a negative definition of welfare, in that it is not concerned with actively promoting the best interests of the child but merely with ensuring that these are not seriously impaired. It echoes the judgement in an earlier case:

> I am clearly satisfied that, on the evidence before me, the welfare of this child does not in any sense *overwhelmingly require* that she should remain in the custody of her present custodians and not be returned to the custody of her mother. (Finlay J in *In the Matter of J. H. (Otherwise R.) (an Infant)*, 1985, p. 318) (my emphasis).

It also overturns the positive approach adopted by the High Court which was 'Is there anything really worthwhile to be gained for the child by transferring her from the adopting parents to the parents?' (Lynch J in *In the Matter of J. H. (Otherwise R.) (an Infant)*, 1985, p. 312).

The limits imposed by the constitutional rights of 'The Family' on the definition and application of the principle of the welfare of the child are compounded by judicial acquiescence in the myth of maternity (i.e. by the apparent belief of at least a section of the judiciary in the inherent superiority of maternal care). This is illustrated by a case which involved a dispute between the mother and the maternal grandparents of a 7-year-old girl (*O'N.* v. *O'B. and Others*, 1980). While she was pregnant the mother married the father of the child, an alcoholic, and lived in considerable poverty. She suffered from depression which was compounded by a physical ailment which required an operation and a period of convalescence. Subsequently, she had a major breakdown and had twice attempted suicide. She had first been in psychiatric daycare and was later admitted to a psychiatric hospital. On her discharge, she had her marriage annulled by the Catholic Church and had 'married' (according to the rites of the Catholic Church) another ex-patient. The child had lived with her grandparents from the age of 2 and these were supported in their claim by the father but, despite psychiatric evidence as to the instability of both the mother and her consort and the precariousness of their economic situation, the child was removed from the custody of the grand-parents and returned to her mother.

In another case (*W.* v. *W.*, 1980), however, an aunt retained custody of a child against the claim of a mother who was suffering from a psychiatric illness, on the ground that the daughter's personal constitutional right was best served by the aunt's retaining custody and that there was no constitutional impediment to this. It should be pointed out, however, that neither of these cases involved adoption and that there was no question that the imprescriptible rights of 'The Family' would be violated.

The protection given to 'The Family' by the constitution has led to a certain amount of what could be called 'forum shopping' by non-residents. The case of *Northampton County Council* v. *A. B. F. and M. B. F.* (1983), for example, involved the English father of an English child. The mother had consented to have the child adopted and the court agreed that it would be adopted if it were returned to England. It refused the order for the return of the child to the plaintiffs on the grounds that the protection of 'The Family' extended also to non-citizens/residents. In a similar case (*In the Matter of Article 40 of the Constitution and in the Matter of S. S.*

(an Infant), 1984), which also involved the father of a legitimate child, the child was returned to the English local authority in question as the court held that there was no immediate intention on the part of the local authority or indeed any threat made by them to place the child for adoption against the wishes of his mother and father.

It is clear, therefore, that articles 41 and 42 continue to be crucial in custody disputes between parents and outsiders and that the welfare of the child cannot, in any real sense, be a paramount consideration while these articles stand. It has even been suggested that the provision that requires that priority be given to the child's welfare is, itself, unconstitutional (Henchy J in *In re J. (an Infant)*, 1966, p. 298). The constitutionality of s. 3 of the 1964 Act has not, to my knowledge, been contested in court. Nevertheless, the attempts to reconcile this provision with the constitutional status of 'The Family' can, and in the case of the adoption of legitimated children must, result in a negative, derivative, and restricted concept of the welfare of the child.

The constitutional status of 'The Family' does not *per se* impinge directly on custody disputes between parents but the definition of 'The Family' and of the welfare of the child and the links that are posited between them are very important factors. The definition of 'The Family', which has been laid down mainly in adoption cases, and particularly the exclusion from that definition of all families which are not based on marriage, has been carried over into custody disputes between parents. The 'constitutional presumption' is that the welfare of the child is best served by its living, not just in a family, but in 'The Family' as defined by article 41 and the law. Thus the most important component in 'The Family' is not the presence of two parents nor the quality of their relationship and parenting but the mere fact that they are married. Any family based on a relationship outside marriage is emphatically not 'The Family'. Nor is living in it automatically conducive to the welfare of the child: on the contrary, it is detrimental to her/his moral and religious well-being. This attitude is illustrated by the judgement of Walsh J in a case in which a mother sought to get custody of her children from the father who was living with another woman:

The household in which these children now reside with their

father is not a family in that sense (as defined in the Constitution).... These children would, in my view, be far more of a family unit if they lived with their mother instead of in the mixed menage in which they now find themselves. So far as the physical and educational or intellectual aspects of their welfare are concerned the difference between what their mother can provide for them and what their father can provide is at best marginal. So far as the social, moral and religious aspects are concerned, the present atmosphere in which they are found, in spite of every good intention on the part of their father and the woman he is living with, is one which is a manifest repudiation of the social and religious values with which they should be inculcated at this stage of their lives.... In my view, the welfare of the children requires that they should be returned to their mother to form the natural family unit from which, unfortunately, only the father is missing but in which there is no element alien or hostile to ordinary family life. (*M. B. O'S.* v. *P. O. O'S.*, 1973, p. 61)

This is not to say that in all cases an extra-marital relationship is in itself a bar to custody. In fact, in the case cited above the father retained custody, despite the irregularity of his relationship. But it remains an important factor. In *J. J. W.* v. *B. M. W.* (1971), for example, the court considered it better that the three children involved remain in the custody of their father rather than their mother who was living, in comfortable economic circumstances, with a divorced man in England, despite the fact that two of the three children were being looked after in an institution run by nuns because their father and his aged parents could not look after them.

The relationship between the behaviour of parents and the welfare of the child in custody disputes will be dealt with in the next section. For the present, suffice it to emphasize that it is not family life *per se* but the very fact of living in 'The Family' that is presumed to be conducive to the welfare of the child. By the logic of the constitution and its interpretation, the most stable extra-marital relationship cannot form the basis of a 'Family' and, far from being an asset in a custody dispute, such a relationship is likely to be considered at least a drawback, if not inherently detrimental to the interests of the child. The interpretation given to article 41 in the *Nicolau* case has not been challenged in the courts and it continues, therefore, to have serious implications for custody disputes between parents.

THE BEHAVIOUR OF PARENTS AND THE WELFARE OF THE CHILD

In deciding disputes as to custody and access in regard to children, the courts have consistently stated that an award of custody is not and should not be, a reward for one party's good behaviour in the marriage, but that the function of the court is to decide whether the welfare of a particular child would best be served by being left in the custody of one parent rather than the other. This principle has been applied not only in theory but in practice and in a number of cases the 'innocent' party has been unsuccessful in an application for custody of the children. The Committee noted that applications in relation to custody and access are among the few areas of family law in which the legal principles applied by the courts are such as to generally make it unnecessary for one party to make allegations against the other in an effort to win the case. (*Report of the Joint Committee on Marriage Breakdown*, 1985, p. 59)

This extraordinarily complacent statement by the Joint Committee on Marriage Breakdown deserves some comment. There is no doubt that when the behaviour of either parent (or religious differences or the constitutional status of the family) is not at issue, the welfare of the child, in the broad sense, is the determining factor in custody cases (e.g. *M. K.* v. *P. K.*, 1982). It should also be noted that in many and possibly the majority of cases of marital breakdown, custody does not become a matter of litigation. In cases where a genuine dispute exists, however, the behaviour of parents before and after breakdown is of crucial importance for a number of reasons. First, though it need not necessarily be applied, fault in relation to marital breakdown remains, on the basis of the 1964 Act, as a possible bar to custody. Second, since there is no divorce, the law, and particularly the dominant Catholic ethos, holds that people whose marriage has irrevocably broken down are still married and behaviour after breakdown – in effect the existence of a sexual relationship between a legally or informally separated person and anyone who is not that person's ex-spouse – can have a determining adverse effect on the outcome of a custody dispute. Third, the very fact that custody orders are interlocutory and can be rescinded on the production of new evidence of 'unfitness' is, in itself, conducive to acrimony and allegations in custody disputes. Furthermore, the application of the principle of the welfare of the child is, as we have seen, restricted by the interpretation of arts 41 and 42 of the constitution and is limited by the emphasis on moral and religious welfare. Finally, the way parental behaviour is linked to this definition of the welfare of the child has important implications for judicial decisions in custody disputes. At the same time, the Catholic ethos, though very strong indeed, is not completely monolithic and is itself conditioned by the formulation, application, and operation of legal provisions and procedures. There are, in fact, various discernible tendencies in current case law. These can, perhaps, be best illustrated if we start with an examination of one particular case – that of *E. K.* and *M. K.* (1974).

The case concerned the custody of two children, a boy aged 5½ and a girl aged 3½. The wife took custody proceedings because she feared that the husband might try and take the children from her. Before the oral hearing, the parties agreed to joint custody with care and control being given to the wife. A year later, the husband re-opened proceedings and claimed that 'continued adultery' on his wife's part made her unfit to have custody. The case centred on this allegation of adultery by the husband and the evidence amassed by private detectives he had hired. In the High Court, custody of the children was given to the mother as the judges chose to ignore her personal conduct as the welfare of the children required it. On appeal, the Supreme Court, by a majority of three to two, reversed this decision and awarded custody to the father.

This case illustrates, first of all, the importance of the composition of the courts, the uncertain status of precedents in custody law, and the orientation of individual judges. Only the year before, the Supreme Court had awarded custody to the 'adulterous' father in the *M. B. O'S.* and *P. O. O'S.* case mentioned above. The complete turn about was due, according to O'Reilly (1977), to the different composition of the court, there being three judges in the earlier case and five in *E. K.* and *M. K.* Judges also differ in the way they deal with precedents. Kenny J, in deciding against the father in the High Court hearing of *M. B. O'S.* and *P.*

O. O'S., felt obliged to follow the precedent of the Supreme Court decision in *J. J. W.* v. *B. M. W.* which, in fact, had reversed his own High Court decision in the same case. The Supreme Court in *M. B. O'S.* v. *P. B. O'S.*, however, held that there was no principle that Kenny J was obliged to follow. *J. J. W.* v. *B. M. W.* 'was decided on the facts in that case as indeed must all cases of this unhappy nature' (quoted in Shatter, 1977 p. 201). More importantly, perhaps, judges differ in the way they interpret the law and in the weight they give to parental behaviour in defining the welfare of the child.

Second, the case illustrates the effects of the interlocutory nature of custody orders. The fact that orders can be rescinded and cases re-heard on the production of new evidence and the nature of the evidence which is admissible means that the parent with custody is, potentially, under constant surveillance with regard not only to the quality of the care she/he is providing, but also with regard also to her/his sexual behaviour. In *E. K.* v. *M. K.*, the husband hired a firm of private detectives to watch his wife. In *P. B.* v. *N. B.* (1975) the wife attempted to introduce evidence against the husband's fitness by affidavit, and when the same case came up again before the courts some time later the husband alleged adultery by his wife, used the evidence amassed by a private detective, and admitted that he had persuaded his two eldest children (who were in his custody) to pin a small transmitter to the sheets of their mother's bed while they were visiting and tried to get his youngest child (who was in his mother's custody) to procure incriminating evidence (in the form of a photograph, allegedly of his mother's lover in the nude) against his mother. These cases may, indeed, be in a minority, but the very fact that it is possible to re-open a custody case on the production of evidence of sexual activity on the part of the parent with custody exacerbates the already precarious position in which these people (most usually mothers) find themselves.

Third, despite the fact that the courts do indeed frequently maintain, as the Committee on Marriage Breakdown says, that 'custody is not to be considered a prize for good matrimonial behaviour' (Kenny J in *J. J. W.* v. *B. M. W.*, 1971, p. 47), there is nothing to prevent the courts from so considering it. In fact, in *E. K.* v. *M. K.*, although one judge claimed that doing justice between husband and wife was an extraneous factor and that the welfare of the child was the only consideration (Walsh J in *E. K.* v. *M. K.*, 1974b, p. 10), the Chief Justice in the case was quite unambiguous in regarding the wife's petition not only as one for custody but 'for a licence from this Court to have custody of the children while she carries on an adulterous intercourse with another man' (Fitzgerald CJ in *E. K.* v. *M. K.*, 1974b, p. 1) and added that 'no such allegation has been established against the husband'. We could refer also, in this regard, to the judgement of Parkes J in *H.* v. *H.* (1976). This case concerned a 2½-year-old boy. The mother had left the father, who was proven to be drunken and violent. She had been awarded an interim order for custody and sought custody so that she could take the child out of the jurisdiction to England where she wished to live and, hopefully, eventually marry an Englishman of the Reformed Branch of the Jewish Congregation. She also intended to change her own religion. Parkes J awarded custody to the father and, referring to the mother, stated that 'a parent who has acted immorally is not to be punished by being deprived of a child' (p. 17), and went on to say, 'In general, however, the Courts will not grant custody to a parent who has abandoned the matrimonial home and lives in an adulterous establishment.'[9]

It is clear that the sexual behaviour of parents after breakdown is an important factor in custody disputes, given that all relationships outside marriage are 'adulterous', regardless either of the length of time that has elapsed since breakdown or the stability of the relationship in question. Indeed, it would appear that casual sexual encounters, being less visible, are less 'dangerous' for parents seeking, or seeking to retain, custody than marriage-like 'adulterous' relationships. Judges do, however, take up different positions on this issue. In *MacD.* v. *MacD.* (1979), for example, the 'adulterous' nature of the custodian parent's sexual relationship was ignored for the sake of the best interests of the children. In this case, the Supreme Court, by a majority of three to two, overturned a High Court decision and awarded custody to the adulterous wife on the grounds that the welfare of the children required it and that the mother's relationship was 'already an accomplished fact in the children's lives' (p. 67). In the same judgement, Kenny J went on to say that he reserved 'for future consideration by a full court the questions of whether the decisions of this court in *J. J. W.* v. *B. M. W.* and *E. K.* v. *M. K.* were correct'.

The 'mere fact' of adultery is, however, of crucial importance in other cases and for other judges. The dissenting judges in the Supreme Court hearing of *E. K.* v. *M. K.* would have allowed the mother to keep her children but for the majority in that, and indeed in other cases, an 'adulterous' relationship in itself is a sufficient reason to remove children from the custody of a parent. In fact, some decisions would lead one to the logical inference that life with a violent, drunken (*H.* v. *H.*, 1976) or mentally ill parent (*A. H. S.* v. *M. S.*, 1982) is considered to be more conducive to the welfare of the child than exposure to the moral dangers of living in a stable but 'adulterous' environment. Some judges show a somewhat extreme reluctance to grant custody to an adulterous parent. The case of *M. W.* v. *D. W.* (1972, 1974, 1975), for example, came to court several times before custody was finally awarded to the adulterous father when the children refused to live with their mother who abused them to the extent of banging their heads against a wall. In *M. O'B.* v. *P. M. O'B.* (1971), custody was eventually given to the adulterous mother when the children (one of whom had a speech defect and who, four years after the original custody award, had been removed from the mother to the 'faultless' father) had been moved about from place to place and neglected to such an extent that they ended up in a nursing home to recover. Where there is no question of adultery, the courts are, of course, likely to take account of other aspects of character and behaviour and are unlikely to award custody to a violent or alcoholic parent (*C. O. B.* v. *A. O. B.*, 1984). But, though it may be overridden by some judges and in extreme cases, adultery in itself can and frequently does constitute a bar to custody (*J. C.* v. *O. C.*, 1985) and the fact that a parent, can show that an adulterous association is at an end can increase his/her chances of custody (*Cullen* v. *Cullen*, 1970). One of the clearest examples of the importance of this aspect of parental behaviour is, in fact, the *E. K.* v. *M. K.* case, and the strength of the hold of the Catholic perception and definition of morality on the judiciary is illustrated by the somewhat pathetic spectacle of the mother in that case making a solemn promise before the Court to end her 'adulterous association' in the hope of retaining custody.

In one sense, judges manage to achieve a considerable degree of consistency in simultaneously maintaining that custody is not a reward for good behaviour and that adultery can be a bar to custody. They do this by focusing, not on parental behaviour *per se*, but on the effects that living in the 'moral atmosphere' of an adulterous relationship is presumed to have on the welfare of the child. Thus, one of the judges in the *E. K.* v. *M. K.* case stated:

> The life which is being led by the mother in this case is a manifest repudiation of the social and religious values with which children should be inculcated and which she believes she can teach them while at the same time clearly repudiating them herself in the sight of her own children. (Walsh J in *E. K.* v. *M. K.*, 1974b, p. 12)

In *J. J. W.* v. *B. M. W.* it was, as has already been mentioned, held to be preferable that the children be brought up, effectively, in an institution than by their 'adulterous' mother.

> The fact is that the home she [the mother] has to offer to her children is one in which she continues an adulterous association with a man who has deserted his own wife and children. A more unhealthy abode for three...children would be difficult to imagine. (Fitzgerald CJ in *J. J. W.* v. *B. M. W.*, 1976, p. 52)

Even the fact that the parent has or intends to get a (foreign) divorce does not alter this view.

> She has obtained a *decree nisi* against her husband and has presently the intention of proceeding to have the decree made absolute and then to enter into marriage with L. Even assuming that her intentions in this regard are fulfilled and she is in English law established as L.'s wife, her status in relation to her own children would not appear to be thereby in any way advanced. (Fitzgerald CJ in *J. J. W.* v. *B. M. W.*, 1976, p. 52)

This prohibition does not, however, appear to apply to Catholic Church annulments and 'remarriages'. In *O'N.* v. *O'B.* (1980) for example, the child in question was returned from her grandparents to her mother and stepfather, both of whom were considered psychologically unstable and whose 'marriage' was bigamous in the eyes of the state but, obviously, morally sound in the eyes of the law.[10]

There is, therefore a discernible tendency in custody case law to regard the 'moral and religious' welfare of the child as a factor that outweighs all other considerations. But even 'religious and moral' welfare itself is defined in the narrow terms of the prevailing Catholic ideology. From this perspective, the welfare of the child is seen almost as a corollary of the sexual behaviour of its parents. People who live in an extra-marital situation cannot provide a suitable moral and religious atmosphere and, because this is of primary importance, they are *ipso facto* unfit for custody, though of course there is nothing to stop them having their own (illegitimate) children. Unions which are legally bigamous but are orthodox from a Catholic point of view are not considered extramarital or adulterous. Apart altogether from the integrationism implicit in this point of view and the lack of clear boundaries between church and state that adherence to it indicates, it should be pointed out that it reflects a totally adult-centred definition of welfare. Other aspects, e.g. the child's physical, intellectual, social, and economic welfare, are, at best, secondary, and psychological well-being is often not seriously considered. In one case which involved a change in custody, for example, one judge dismissed the effects of separation as follows:

> It may very well cause some immediate grief to the children to be removed from their present home to be returned to their mother but I think that will be very quickly assuaged by the fact that they will be living with their mother and their grandparents. (Walsh J in *M. B. O'S* v. *P. O. O'S.*, 1973, p. 18)

On the other hand, there are judges who have tried and who continue to try to ignore the obsession with 'adultery' and to base decisions on a more child-centred concept of welfare:

> The main need of children, if they are to be happy, is the sense of security which comes from a feeling of being loved, for their own sake. They are not pieces of furniture to be moved around from house to house. (Kenny J in *E. K.* v. *M. K.*, 1974a, p. 4)

There is no doubt that most, if not all, of the judiciary would accept, at face value, that happiness, feelings of security, and parental love are important considerations in child rearing but the fact is that by no means all decisions in custody dispute are based on this kind of consideration. Indeed, a substantial portion of the judiciary appears to be more concerned with religious and moral upbringing (and with ultimate eternal salvation) than with the more immediate and mundane considerations of physical and psychological welfare. On the other hand, the fact that Caesar has undertaken to look after God's business is hardly surprising in a country whose constitution undertakes to protect 'The Family' as defined by Catholic teaching and whose dominant political culture is distinctly and at times virulently anti-pluralist in matters of social legislation.

GENDER ROLES IN CUSTODY DISPUTES

The extent to which custody decisions in Ireland ascribe, reinforce, or reflect existing patterns in gender roles in child rearing must, like other aspects of custody, be considered within the context of the definitions of welfare that prevail and of the divergences and similarities that exist between the more integrationist and adult-centred sections of the judiciary and their less rigid and more child-centred associates. Attempts to examine the ascription of gender roles in terms of the number of times custody is awarded to the mother or the father are misleading if they do not also take into account the potentially determining factors of religion or 'morality'. At the same time, some patterns are discernible. Judges of both orientations adopt the tender years doctrine and unquestioningly accept traditional gender roles within the family. Take, for example, these quotations from judges who have adopted quite different perspectives on other aspects of custody:

> It is notorious that children of that age are much closer to and dependent on their mother than on their father.... Fathers are ill-qualified to look after children who are five and three. (Kenny J in *E. K.* v. *M. K.*, 1974a, p. 6)

> At the age when their relationship with their mother is a very close one and, if all other things are equal, there could be no question that in a choice between a father and mother, children of this age should be given in custody to their mother. (Walsh J in *E. K.* v. *M. K.*, 1974b, p. 11)

Both favour giving custody of small children to the mother. In this sense, the judiciary can be said merely to reflect cultural patterns. In Ireland, small children are, in fact, generally looked after by their mothers; there are little or no child care facilities and participation of married women in the labour force is very low

211

compared to other European countries. The less integrationist and more child-centred 'school' are, if anything, more fixed in their application of the tender years doctrine. In fact, those who adopt the adult-centred and rigidly moralist perspective can be said to do little more than pay lip-service to the importance of a mother's care since any (sexual) misdemeanour on her part can result in custody being taken from her and given to the father.

This does not mean, of course, that the father is expected actually to look after his small children. It is enough that he can pay someone else to do so. Thus, in *H*. v. *H*. (1976), the fact that the father, who was unemployed himself, paid a 15-year-old girl to look after his 2-year-old son was a factor in his favour. In another case (*H*. v. *H*., 1980), the custody of three small children was given to the father who was obtaining 'domestic help'. In *E*. *K*. v. *M*. *K*., the little girl in the case suffered from a chronic skin disease which required the nightly application of ointment and had been looked after from birth by her mother. In deciding against the mother, Walsh J said:

> So far as the medication or the application of medication is concerned, it appears to me that the husband is sufficiently well-to-do to provide if necessary a properly trained children's nurse to look after his children. (Walsh J in *E*. *K*. v. *M*. *K*., 1974b, p. 15)

Thus an award of custody to a father in no way implies an assumption that he is to care for his children personally.

CONCLUDING REMARKS

The issues in custody in Ireland are therefore somewhat different from those in other countries. These arise, first and foremost, from arts 41 and 42 of the constitution, which are frequently invoked in custody cases and which do not simply express a pious desire to protect 'The Family' but ascribe inalienable and imprescriptible rights to it. 'The Family' is, moreover, defined in the most restrictive way as being based on marriage. In effect, these articles have been used to lend weight to the refusal to recognize any family based on an extra-marital relationship, a refusal which is bolstered by the prohibition of divorce.

There is nothing remarkable about the state's attempting to

support a particular form of family. Smart (1982) argues that this is precisely what, historically, the law has tried to do and that discrimination against women in favour of men, for example, can be seen not necessarily as the result of a deliberately misogynist policy but rather as a corollary of the state's attempt to regulate the family. At the same time, there is no doubt that the rigid anti-pluralism of the Irish situation is unusual in the context of late twentieth-century western Europe. Moreover, the very real commitment by the state to uphold 'The Family' can and does have adverse effects on the development of the rights of children and on the position of both women and men who do not conform to the dominant ethos.

The rights ascribed to 'The Family' are held to pertain to the child, as a member of a particular family. As far as custody is concerned, however, it is difficult to see what the content of such rights are or could be since the 'inalienable and imprescriptible rights' in question are, in practice, parental rights which can over-ride and, in fact, have overridden the principle of the welfare of the child. It is even more difficult to see how the rights of the child are in any way furthered by the expedient of equating its welfare with membership of 'The Family', as defined by the constitution, or by defining its 'welfare' in completely adult-centred terms of the extent to which its parent/s adhere to Catholic notions of monogamy and 'morality'.

In Ireland the state with, it must be said, the majority of the electorate, regards marriage as a life-long commitment, rather than as a contract that can be terminated at the will of the parties concerned. The implication of this, as far as custody is concerned, is not simply that marital breakdown and re-marriage are not legally recognized. What is possibly even more important is that any extra-marital relationship is regarded as 'adulterous' and that the 'immoral atmosphere' that any such relationship creates is seen as inherently detrimental to the welfare of the child. On the other hand, the more progressive, i.e. the less rigid, sections of the judiciary have tried to stress other aspects of welfare, and in so doing have emphasized the importance of the role of the mother. Since custody is, as a general rule, awarded to the mother of young children, it is her behaviour that is likely to come under scrutiny. Thus, the ascription, acceptance, and indeed espousal of traditional gender roles have been used in Ireland to override the rigid moralism of the dominant ideology which considers the commitment to monogamy that marriage entails as binding even when that marriage has patently and irrevocably broken down.

The hegemony of Catholicism in Ireland has had, and continues to have, a determining effect on the development and implementation of custody law. In fact, it is within the framework of this hegemony that other aspects – such as the equal custody rights of fathers and mothers – must be considered. It is for this reason that I have concentrated on the way in which apparently internationally comparable principles, such as that of the equal rights of women and men and that of the welfare of the child, have been interpreted and applied and ignored questions which are of vital importance to other contributors. Important as the issue of joint custody may be on an international level, it is not the main issue in Ireland, if only because it implies the existence of altern- ative lifestyles and methods of child bearing and rearing, and, therefore, of a substantial level of cultural, social, and political pluralism.

NOTES

1 The question of the recognition of foreign divorce is, because of article 41.3.3, still in some dispute. For a discussion of the state of the law in this regard see Buckley and O'Mahoney (1982).

2 Church annulments, because they are easier to obtain, appear to be more common than legal annulments or separation. Custody of children can be an issue in cases of legal separation but in the case of legal annulment the children of the annulled marriage are declared illegitimate and custody is given to the mother. However, a statutory right to apply for custody under section 11 of the Guardianship of Infants Act 1964 is given to the natural father of an illegitimate child, although such a father has no constitutional rights in relation to the child (see below).

3 Indeed, this is suggested by the relatively low number of applications to the courts under the Guardianship of Infants Act 1964 compared with applications for maintenance orders under the Family Law (Maintenance of Spouses and Children) Act 1976, numbers of women in receipt of deserted wives' allowance (and who, by definition, because of the eligibility criteria, have dependent children), the estimated rates of marital breakdown, etc. See *Report of the Joint Committee on Marriage Breakdown*, 1985, pp. 132–4. See also 'Family law – coping with the growth' (editorial) (1983) *Incorporated Law Society of Ireland Gazette*, vol. 77, no. 6, pp. 165–6.

4 Very few of the cases brought under the Guardianship of Infants Act 1964 are reported, and in those that are there is a considerable time lag between the hearing and the reporting of any particular case. The cases quoted in this chapter are not, therefore, representative in a statistical sense, though it is hoped that they give some indication of trends in, and the present state of, custody law.

5 Article 44.1.2. In 1972, following a referendum, articles 44.1.2 and 44.1.3 (which recognized other churches) were deleted from the constitution.

6 An attempt to remove article 41.3.2 from the constitution and, therefore, to open the way for divorce legislation was defeated by referendum in June 1987.

7 In fact only a child who is an orphan, illegitimate, or who has been legitimated by virtue of the Legitimacy Act 1931 but whose birth has not been re-registered under that Act can be adopted. An adoption order is final but can be declared invalid, usually on the grounds of consent or procedure.

8 The Two Houses of Parliament, the Dail and the Seanad.

9 The importance of the religious factor, i.e. the fact that the mother might change the child's religion without the father's consent (though she was not asked not to do so by the court) in this case should be noted.

10 In this case, however, the dispute was not between parents but between a parent and outsiders, in which case the constitutional status of 'The Family' would make it unlikely that considerations of the welfare of the child alone would prevail. For a discussion of the legal problems that arise from the increase in Church annulments and bigamous marriages, see Duncan (1978).

CASES

A. H. S. v. *M. S.* (1982) unreported, High Court Rec. no. 1982/183 Sp.

B. v. *B.* (1972) unreported, High Court Rec. no. 1968/146 Sp.

C. O. B. v. *A. O. B.* (1984) unreported, High Court Rec. no. 1984/659 Sp.

Cullen v. *Cullen* (1970) unreported, Supreme Court Rec. no. 1969/59.

E. K. v. *M. K.* (1974a) unreported, High Court Rec. no. 1973/17 Sp. (1974b) unreported Supreme Court Rec. no. 1975/86.

H. v. *H.* (1976) unreported, High Court Rec. no. 1975/450 Sp.

H. v. *H.* (1980) unreported, High Court Rec. no. 1980/683.

In G. v. *An Bord Uchtala* (1980) Irish Reports, 32.

In re Corcoran (Infants) (1950) 86 Irish Law Times Review, 6.

In re J. (an Infant) (1966) Irish Reports, 295.

In re Tilson (Infants): (1950) 86 Irish Law Times Review, 49; (1951) Irish Reports, 1.

In the Matter of Article 40 of the Constitution and in the Matter of S. S. (an Infant): Kent County Council v. *C. S.* (1984) Irish Law Review Monthly, vol. 4, pp. 292-7.

In the Matter of J. H. (Otherwise R.) (an Infant), K. O, and A. O. v. *An Bord Uchtala (and M. C. and M. C. and An t-Ard Chlaraitheoir, Notice Parties):* (1985) Irish Law Review Monthly, vol. 5, no. 6, pp. 302-19; (1986) Irish Law Review Monthly, vol. 6, no. 2, pp. 65-8.

J. v. *D.* (1977) unreported, Supreme Court Rec. no. 1977/26.

J. C. v. *O. C.* (1985) Irish Law Review Monthly, vol. 5, p. 167.

J. J. W. v. *B. M. W.* (1971) 110 Irish Law Times Review, 45, 49.

MacD. v. *MacD.* (1979) 114 Irish Law Times Review, 66.

McL. v. *An Bord Uchtala and the A. -G.:* (1974) unreported High Court, Rec. no. 1974/1,689P; (1976) unreported Supreme Court, Rec. no. 1974/164.

M. B. O'S. v. *P. O. O'S.* (1973) 110 Irish Law Times Review, 57.

M. K. v. *P. K.* (1982) unreported High Court Rec. no. 1982/417 Sp.

M. O' B. v. *P. M. O'B.* (1971) unreported High Court Rec. no. 1965/207 Sp.

M. W. v. *D. W.* (1972, 1974, 1975) unreported High Court Rec. no. 1971/203 Sp.

Northampton County Council v. *A. B. F. and M. B. F.* (1981) Incorporated Law Society of Ireland Gazette, vol. 77, Jan-Feb. 1983, p. vi.

O' N. v. *O' B. and Others* (1980) Incorporated Law Society of Ireland Gazette, vol. 75, March 1981, pp. v-vi.

P. B. v. *N. B.* (1975) Irish Reports 54.

The State (Nicolau) v. *An Bord Uchtala and the A. -G.* (1966) The Irish Reports 567.

W. v. *W.* (1980) Incorporated Law Society of Ireland Gazette, vol. 74, May 1980, p. viii.

Chapter Nine

CUSTODY LAW, CHILD CARE, AND INEQUALITY IN BRITAIN

JULIA BROPHY

A movement in favour of joint custody of children following divorce became discernible in the United Kingdom in the mid-1970s. It began as a loose coalition, embracing people from a wide range of professional, voluntary, and pressure groups and culminated in a Law Commission[1] review of the custody of children on divorce in 1986. In view of the general support for joint custody it seemed probable that the Law Commission would recommend that existing custody laws be reformed so that joint (legal) custody of all children on the divorce or separation of their parents would become the standard order of the court. Indeed, such was the pressure in favour of this move that joint (legal) custody had already been promoted in an earlier consultative document on legal procedures on divorce in 1983 (Booth, 1983), and it was posited as the preferred outcome when this Committee tabled its Report (Booth, 1985). After some deliberation, however, the Law Commission rejected joint legal custody as a solution to the problems surrounding custody of children. Instead the Commission took a new approach to parenthood on divorce. It argued that the concept of 'time sharing' is an accurate description of child care after divorce, and proposed a new legal framework for courts based on this concept.

In this chapter I shall look at the issues which underscore the appeal of joint custody in Britain. I shall outline and discuss the Law Commission proposals for court orders on the basis of parental 'time sharing'. Finally, I will address some of the problems for feminists of attempting to devise radical policies within a liberal legal framework.

I will argue that it is important to locate this discussion within

217

the broader social and economic framework of Conservative Britain and the specific impact of government policies on the position of women and mothers in particular – both within and outside heterosexual marriage. Discussion must also locate family law within the social structure, and recognize the limitations of family law (i.e. statute law and legal practices) in transforming certain social and economic relationships. Moreover, policy discussions must begin with concrete relationships and gendered legal subjects.

THE APPEAL OF JOINT CUSTODY

In Britain the increase in demand for joint custody is in fact a demand for joint legal custody, as opposed to joint physical custody. The demand is rooted in a number of concerns. Initially, the most vocal group in terms of campaigning for mandatory joint custody of all children was the fathers' rights group Families Need Fathers (FNF). But increasingly academic and practising lawyers (e.g. Maidment, 1982, 1984; Grossbard, 1982; Freeman, 1983; Eekelaar, 1984), psychologists, social work trainers, divorce court welfare officers, and conciliators (e.g. Richards, 1982; Lees, 1972; Parkinson, 1981, 1986, 1988) have articulated a case for joint legal custody.

In promoting joint legal custody, these diverse groups have focused similar criticisms on various aspects of existing law and legal practice. These criticisms fall into four major categories. First, there has been criticism of law arising out of confusion generated by recent case law. Second, these groups are highly critical of the dominant court practice of awarding sole custody to the mother. Third, most are critical of statute law itself because of its complexity. Fourth, and of particular importance in terms of the Law Commission proposals, there is considerable criticism of the supposed impact of law and legal practices on parental behaviour, primarily fathers' behaviour.

Case law and confusion surrounding parental rights

The first aspect of criticism currently levelled at custody law is concerned with the meaning, in practice, of court orders. There is some confusion amongst parents and practitioners as to the precise rights now embodied in post-divorce parental status. Currently the vast majority of orders from the divorce courts are for sole custody, that is, orders which combine legal custody and physical custody to one parent (reasonable access is usually awarded to the other parent). Until quite recently sole orders were generally taken as granting the custodial parent control over almost every aspect of a child's life (save changing his/her surname and taking him/her to live abroad). A decision in the Court of Appeal, however, generated some confusion and doubts as to the powers previously believed to be embodied in a sole custody order (*Dipper* v. *Dipper* (1981) Fam. 31). The confusion concerns the degree of independent action a sole custody order actually gives the custodial parent (usually, of course, the mother), the degree of consultation into which she should enter with the non-custodial parent, and the power of veto which the non-custodial parent might have over any strategic or important decisions concerning the child. To make consultation obligatory (as was suggested in the *Dipper* decision), and indeed to give non-custodial fathers powers of veto over decisions made by mothers, in effect makes sole orders a nonsense. Moreover, it may well return many mothers to the very power structures which they as mothers (as well as wives) experienced within marriage. This is a situation which can consist of substantial inequalities in the distribution of power and responsibilities between parents, whereby fathers retain the power to make final important decisions but continue to allocate to mothers major responsibility for children's daily care and needs. Ironically this may have been the very situation which drove such mothers finally to seek a divorce as a solution (Piper, 1985).

The desire for a clarification of parental powers occurs within the context of a broader mounting criticism of trends in court orders.

Trends in court orders – sole orders to mothers

The divorce court in Britain has wide discretion to organize the custody of children in whatever way it thinks fit. Increasingly in the postwar period, legal custody and physical custody have with certain exceptions (see Brophy, 1987a) generally been awarded as one 'package' in a sole order to one parent. Access for the non-custodial parent is sometimes defined (specific arrangements appearing on the order), but frequently it is simply noted as 'reasonable access' and left to parents to organize.

Much of the criticism from almost all those engaged in the joint custody debate focuses on the predominance of sole orders. It is argued that these orders, usually in favour of mothers, indicate substantial discrimination against fathers by courts. Judicial statistics from the Lord Chancellor's Department (1988) indeed confirm that the most usual order of the courts is for sole custody to mothers. For 1987 some 83 per cent of custody orders were in fact sole orders, 74 per cent being sole orders to mothers and 8.3 per cent sole orders to fathers. But the reasons underlying this trend are seldom addressed in any detail by the critics of sole custody. It is assumed that these figures can simply be read as indicating substantial discrimination against fathers and favouritism for mothers on the part of courts. But although the divorce court does have powers to arrange custody of children in whatever way it thinks fit, in practice it seldom interferes with the arrangements arrived at through pre-court negotiations. In theory, couples cannot at present obtain a full divorce until the court is satisfied that the arrangements for children are the best that can be achieved (s. 41 Matrimonial Causes Act 1973).[2] In practice, however, the 'children's appointment' is often a rubber-stamp procedure (Davis et al., 1983; Maidment, 1976; Dodds, 1983). In the main, courts usually ratify the arrangements for children as they are set out in a parent's divorce petition. Moreover, in the vast majority of divorces the future custody of children is not fully contested in court. Indeed some 94 per cent of all cases concerning children are settled out of court; only 6 per cent are fully contested by parents before a court and require a judicial decision (Eekelaar et al., 1977).

In addition, trends in court practices in both contested and uncontested custody hearings alike indicate that (physical) custody usually goes to the parent who has care of the child at the time of the decision. This is referred to as the *status quo* factor, and research in the 1970s demonstrated that the children's residential *status quo* is the strongest single factor determining custody of children on divorce. Issues of the age and sex of the children, and claims of favouritism for mothers and discrimination against fathers, all give way to the weight of the *status quo* factor (Eekelaar et al., 1977; Maidment, 1976).

The complexities and inconsistencies of current statute law

The area where all critics of current custody practices tend to be most in agreement is in their view of statute law itself. They argue that it is far too complex, and there is a consensus that a review of child law generally is long overdue. Both the courts (*Re C. Wardship and Adoption* (1981) 2 F.L.R 177) and the Law Commission (1986) acknowledge that there are many gaps, inconsistencies, and unnecessary complexities in this sphere of family law.

There are currently some twelve provisions under which courts can make orders for the custody, maintenance, and access of children. There is no clear overriding definition of custody, and it is subject to different interpretations depending upon the particular legal jurisdiction invoked by a parent. For example, parents may make applications regarding the custody of children in both the magistrates' court and the divorce county court. Under the Guardianship of Minors Acts 1971-3 and under the Domestic Proceedings and Magistrates' Courts Act 1978, the court cannot grant legal custody to more than one person and cannot in principle split legal custody from actual (i. e. physical) custody. In theory this means that when hearing applications under these acts the court cannot treat legal and physical custody as separate entities, although in practice it can arrive at a similar solution.[3]

Under divorce jurisdiction, however, courts have powers to award legal custody to more than one person, and to split legal custody from actual custody. Thus a range of orders for children is possible, for example: joint legal custody – physical care and control to one parent; a 'split' order – legal custody to one parent, care and control to another; a sole order – legal custody and physical care and control to one parent; finally, the divorce court can simply make an order for daily physical care and control, leaving the legal status of parents as joint legal guardians intact, maintaining the legal position which existed during their marriage. It is not therefore surprising that both academic and practising lawyers and conciliators have become increasingly reticent to give a precise definition of custody (Cretney, 1984: Westcott *et al.*, 1988; Parkinson, 1988). This *ad hoc* development of statute law could be resolved simply by streamlining legislation across all jurisdictions. Issues of complexity and inconsistencies, however, are only a part of the criticisms surrounding custody of children. The impact of legal practices and procedures on future parenting behaviour now forms the central concern.

Legal practices and their impact on parental behaviour

Two concerns dominate legal discourse with regard to the relationship between law and parental behaviour. One concern, emanating from within the liberal legal tradition, is with the impact of legal practices and procedures on the successful adaptation of children to divorce. The other concern, originating primarily from the fathers' rights movement, is for the diminishing rights of fathers. To understand the groundswell of general support for joint legal custody in Britain, it is important to recognize how these initially separate concerns have now become merged so that the interests of children have now become firmly identified with enhancing the legal status of fathers.

First, within liberal law reform in Britain there is a tradition of ever-increasing concern about the impact of divorce on children. Opinion has largely moved away from a view that all divorce should be opposed or prevented, and the primary focus is now concerned with attempting to ameliorate some of the effects of divorce. Thus the focus is on identifying and preventing emotional and psychological traumas which children might suffer following their parents' divorce. Discussions have been greatly influenced by the psychoanalytic study of children of divorced parents in the United States (Wallerstein and Kelly, 1980). It is now widely maintained that, so far as the successful emotional adaptation of children is concerned, a lack of hostility between parents is of major importance. Joint custody eventually became seen as the legal vehicle through which it was thought a reduction in hostilities could be achieved.

This view of the importance of a conciliatory attitude between parents focused enormous attention on the relationship between legal practices and procedures and parental behaviour. Some writers argued that the adversarial system, by its very nature, exacerbated hostilities between divorcing parents and was therefore an inappropriate forum for dispute settlements over children (Parkinson, 1983a, 1983b, 1983c, 1986). This position underscores the development of a strong movement in favour of conciliation schemes in Britain, where the emphasis is upon reaching a settlement by agreement 'for the sake of the children'. It was also argued that sole orders to mothers, because they in effect disenfranchise fathers and make them feel redundant, also increase conflict between parents (Maidment, 1984; Parkinson, 1988b). In addition, a child-centred approach within the liberal legal tradition resulted in an examination of the substantive position of children in the divorce process. Research examined the impact of divorce on children (both emotionally and financially) and high-lighted the general failure of most fathers to maintain their children adequately following divorce (Gibson, 1982; Eekelaar and Maclean, 1982) . It also examined children's sharply declining contact with non-custodial fathers after divorce (Maidment, 1976; Eekelaar *et al.*, 1977; Richards and Dyson, 1982; Mitchell, 1985) and conflict between parents (Walczak and Burns, 1984). It was through these avenues of enquiry that writers in the liberal tradition came to address the problematic father–child relationship and to speculate on the impact that joint custody could have on improving that relationship.

Since its inception in the mid-1970s, the fathers' rights movement (Families Need Fathers, FNF) has attacked sole custody orders, on the basis that such orders demonstrate the courts' discrimination against care by fathers. Sole orders were also seen as empowering mothers (by giving them what was then perceived as sole decision making power), and systematically reducing the power and traditional authority of fathers (Benians *et al.*, 1983). Families Need Fathers argued that mothers utilized their sole powers to obstruct or regulate fathers' access contact with children, and that such orders gave fathers no legal rights to enforce access orders, to intervene, or to be consulted about issues, particularly education. This in turn, it was argued, increased conflict and hostility on the part of fathers. Moreover, FNF increasingly argued that, in the allocation of custody, men are the perpetual 'losers', losing both home and children. Mandatory joint legal custody of all children following divorce became their simple solution to these problems and formed the central demand in the fathers' rights campaign.

Although the initial concerns of the liberal lawyers and FNF were largely different, the former eventually came to focus on the position of non-custodial fathers. Both came to the same ultimate solution, namely joint legal custody of children on divorce, either as the preferred outcome or as a mandatory outcome. It is important to note the very restricted way in which proponents of the liberal legal tradition continue to view these problems (see Freeman, 1983; Eekelaar, 1984; Parkinson, 1986; Maidment, 1984). For example, in addressing the failure of the vast majority of fathers' access arrangements, such writers have been drawn into a general but powerful argument initiated by the fathers' rights movement, namely that fathers are alienated in their parenting role primarily by law and legal practices which render them powerless. Factors such as the social structure of parenting generally and previous level of activity in the pre-divorce parental role, or the impact of money, housing, employment, and re-marriage, on father–child contact have received little attention. Equally little consideration is given to the way in which arrangements frequently provide opportunities for the harassment, intimidation, and undermining of ex-wives, except to say that these represent exceptional rather than normal cases.

In a sometimes desperate attempt at a solution there has been a largely uncritical acceptance of the idea that there is a direct relationship between types of court orders and the attitudes and parenting pattern of fathers. Some also talk in terms of a 'gross failure of parenting' in society, and ultimately concur with FNF and other campaigning groups (themselves of quite different political persuasions) under the slogans 'parents are forever' and 'divorce ends a marriage not parenthood'. It was at this point that joint custody became seen as the panacea to the whole range of problems it was presumed were experienced both by fathers and children.

In this debate, a central powerful role is attributed to law in the reconstruction of parental behaviour. Lawyers and professionals in the field of conciliation began to rehearse traditional arguments about how to utilize law to instil 'parental responsibility'.[4] Indeed some contributors suggested a form of therapy for those parents who continued to disagree or rejected new legal solutions to their problems (Maidment, 1984, p. 27). Within this perspective, law is identified as having both a symbolic and an educative function. It is perceived somewhat simplistically as a mechanism in social engineering which can be utilized to halt a regression in parental responsibility. Susan Maidment's work on legal policy (1984, p.

278) is one example of this position. She states that non-custodial parents (usually, of course, fathers) should simply not be allowed to abandon a parenting role, nor should divorce alter a parent's formal legal status. Since parents are equal legal guardians of their children during marriage (Guardianship Act 1973) she sees no reason why divorce should alter this situation. She argues first that the current court practice of sole orders (to mothers) encourages parental irresponsibility, and second that access should not be a matter of parental choice but should, in the interests of children, be mandatory. Leaving aside the enormous problems of enforcement and its consequences for father–child relationships, this position leads Maidment away from her original support for joint (legal) custody, since it would in practice add nothing to parents' status (it would simply 'return' them in many respects to their pre-divorce position). She concludes that the court should refrain from making any order with regard to legal custody; it should simply allocate the physical residence of children (Maidment, 1984, p. 279).

It is important to recognize that for parents, joint legal custody and 'no court order' for custody may amount to the same thing. Both measures avoid giving the custodial parent ultimate control, and both measures locate the court as the final arbitrator where parents do not agree. Most supporters of joint legal custody or 'no court order' express a form of hope – a wish fulfilment – that this measure will, of itself, affect fathers' behaviour. This position is well expressed by Greif, who argues that 'the more opportunity fathers have to act as fathers, the more they see themselves as fathers and seek to continue that involvement' (1979, p. 313).[5]

The liberals hope that preserving the formal status of parents (as equal) after divorce will have three beneficial effects for fathers. First, that it will lower the stakes at risk in custody cases by partly eradicating the winner/loser dichotomy. Second, that this situation will reduce conflict between parents (because fathers will feel less hostility towards mothers since they have retained legal power and status). Third, that such an arrangement will convey important symbolic messages concerning what Maidment refers to as the 'continuity of parent-relationships and their immunity to the breakdown of marriage' (1984, p. 281). Indeed Maidment concludes that such an approach will 'doubtless also increase the number of cases where co-operation is feasible; the symbolic and educative function of the law should therefore have a powerful influence over parental behaviour in relation to their children after divorce' (1984, p. 281). This is an idealistic approach to the role of law which bears little relationship to the material position of women and children and ignores the development of trends in child care generally. I shall now turn to an examination of these trends in the context of the political economy of Britain under the New Right.

PARENTING AND 'EQUALITY': PERSPECTIVES FROM THE NEW RIGHT

A major consequence of the conflation of the problems discussed above has been the domination of legal discourse by a concern about the impact of law on father–child relationships. This has resulted in a situation in which the interests of children have now become almost exclusively identified with enhancing the legal status of fathers.

This particular perspective on the father–child relationship is not of the same order as the critical analysis of men's role and commitment to children, which was developed by the women's movement in the late 1960s (Nava, 1983). It is important in terms of feminist responses to recognize the differences. For example, neither the fathers' rights movement nor the joint custody supporters within the liberal legal tradition address questions about the quality and availability of public child care provision, workplace nurseries, or maternity provisions in Britain. Indeed there is a resounding silence on child care issues generally. They have specifically failed to address the way in which responsibility for child care forms a central key to understanding not only the economic relationships between men and women, but also between individuals and the state (Mottershead, 1987). The timing of the renewed identification of common interests between men and children is particularly significant for women because of the force of dominant ideologies of parenthood and contemporary politics in Britain. The New Right have demanded policies in both private and public law which demonstrate a positive commitment to traditional authoritarian family values and morals and a rejection of any alternative domestic arrangements. Thus a range of taxation and social security changes have been demanded which would benefit married men and penalize single female-headed households (Ellis-Jones, 1986; Morgan, 1986). Within this demand for a 'return to morality', fathers are identified as the appropriate focus for the distribution of money and state benefits within the family and as the rightful purveyors of dominant social values. The fathers' rights movement utilized a similar model of the function of fathers within families as a justification for the continued control of fathers by means of joint custody orders (Benians et al., 1983; Lettington, 1983). This is not to suggest a conspiracy between these two distinct movements, but rather to demonstrate how dominant ideologies of parenthood can operate in different spheres but to similar ends.

Much to the delight of the fathers' rights movement, the New Right has been critical of the research and writings of feminists and liberal social scientists. Wide-ranging research on the family and child care policies has been attacked partly because it is viewed as an attempt to expel fathers from the family by demonstrating the limited role which many men play within the domestic economy (Morgan, 1986) and also because it is seen as part of a wider attempt to shift financial responsibility for children from individual men to the state.

This backlash against progressive social policies resulted in a resurgence of research which posits the centrality of the role of fathers to children – for 'better' socialization, higher identification with conventional social values, family stability, and appropriate sex role behaviour. Single (mother) headed households are identified with long-term delinquency, under-achievement, and future social, emotional and indeed political unrest (Benians et al., 1983; Ellis-Jones, 1986; Morgan, 1986).[6]

Utilizing the equality argument as a justification for extending the rights of post-divorce fathers is particularly ironic at this stage in British politics. The British government continues to reject equal opportunities and positive action programmes which would benefit working mothers (Mottershead, 1987). Hence, the structural nature of the sexual division of labour with regard to child care continues to ensure that it is women who overwhelmingly provide primary care for children (Henwood et al., 1987) and who continue to bear the social and economic consequences of that responsibility (Roll, 1986; Joshi, 1985, 1987; Newell and Joshi, 1986; Martin and Roberts, 1984). This is not simply a matter of historical development. Child care in Britain continues to be seen as a personal matter for women, and not the responsibility of men, employers, or indeed the state (Moss, 1987; Cohen and Clarke, 1987; David and New, 1987). Traditional views on care by mothers in the home continue to form the basis of domestic economic and social policies of the Thatcher government. In comparison with the European Parliament commitment to positive action for women, Britain's stance is far from encouraging. Indeed where it does not actually contravene the letter of anti-discrimination and equal opportunities directives of the European Economic Community (EEC), it certainly contravenes the spirit of such moves, for example in reducing the limited employment protection for women who work part-time, blocking EEC directives on *pro rata* part-time employment rights, and parental leave, and introducing taxation of workplace nurseries.[7]

Extending equality for fathers therefore arrives on the political agenda at a time when national legislation blatantly and effectively thwarts EEC aims to extend equality to working mothers, and when domestic laws and practices on sex discrimination and equal pay and the industrial tribunal system have largely failed women (Equal Opportunities Commission 1986, 1988). In addition the Social Security Act 1986 introduced yet further complex regulations abolishing universal maternity grants and reducing maternity pay and employment leave entitlement.

There is therefore not only a lack of evidence of a radical shift in substantive child care roles between men and women, but in addition the absence of a political climate which takes child care issues seriously enough to encourage fathers, via state policies, to take an equal share in child care responsibilities.[8] Indeed the structural prerequisites for that shift do not currently exist. In these circumstances it would be a folly for women to accept joint (legal) custody (and a consequential loss of autonomy and power over decision making) in the hope that progressive changes in the division of labour in relation to child care may follow. All the indications are, in fact, to the contrary.

THE LAW COMMISSION AND CHILD CUSTODY

In its review of custody law and legal practices, the Law Commission acknowledges many of the criticisms raised by contributors to the joint custody debate with regard to court orders (Law Commission, 1986, Part IV, C.116). It concludes that there are three possible future options. It could recommend that courts have a completely free choice in making custody orders; it could recommend that current types of custody orders should continue but with clarification as to their practical effects; or it could attempt a completely new approach. Rejecting the first two options, the Commission propose a new approach. This new approach to custody is based on an attempt to change existing parental conceptions of the differences between legal custody, physical care and control, and access. The Commission argues that parents now wrongly perceive these legal terms to imply a bundle of powers and responsibilities for children – in a descending hierarchy of importance (Law Commission, 1986, para. 153).

The Commission decided that a parent who is exercising access for whatever period of time must have all the rights and responsibilities of someone with actual custody. Thus it argues that a father exercising access must have full responsibility for, and power to decide, whether a child goes to church, what she/he does with her/his time, whether to summon medical attention, the control of bed times, television viewing, and so on. Indeed the Commission further suggests that the division of responsibility between parents with custody and care and control or access respectively is merely temporal rather than qualitative. It concludes that these legal concepts, in practice, simply amount to a form of 'time sharing' between parents (Law Commission, 1986, pp. 135-6). Within this reconceptualization of existing arrangements, the Commission proposes that the new task of courts should be to 'decide in general terms the allocation of a child's time between his [sic] parents each of which should have care and control while he [sic] is with them' (p. 136, para 4.52).

This arrangement would not, however, amount to shared care and control, but rather 'residential care and control' and 'visiting care and control'. In effect, the Commission proposes to append decision making power to the physical location of the child. Whichever parent then has responsibility for the child also acquires decision making power, so that power and responsibility go hand in hand and 'run with the child' (p. 136, para. 4.53(d)). Like those campaigning for joint (legal) custody, the Commission sees the elimination of the notion of a contest as a major benefit arising from these new proposals. It argues that the courts would not have to make invidious allocations of power and responsibilities between parents (although of course courts seldom do that anyway). But in addition, the Law Commission argues that implicitly within this reinterpretation, there may be some encouragement towards a more equal distribution of time and day-to-day responsibility for children.

The Commission repeatedly states that the central aim of the proposals is to encourage parental responsibility. The upgrading of access clearly forms a major part of this endeavour. It is hoped such a move will reduce some of the problems said to face non-custodial fathers. Indeed in many respects the Commission's proposals for court orders pay 'lip service' to the demands embodied in the joint legal custody campaigns of the fathers' rights movement, in the expectation that added legal power and status will induce a sense of paternal responsibility. In line with the development of liberal legal tradition, the Commission uncritically accepts that an extension of the concept of formal equality to the post-divorce status of parents forms a major part of the solution to problems in this field. Thus, it is proposed that each parent should retain his [sic] parental status with those powers of independent action which existed during the marriage. In the event of a dispute, recourse could be made to the court (Law Commission, 1986, p. 137). But the concept of legal custody would disappear. Parental rights previously encapsulated under the term would be dealt with by statute or, where necessary, spelled out in the new form of court order. So, for example, an order for 'residential' and 'visiting care and control' could also specify those issues (previously part of legal custody) over which a particular parent would not have control. The Law Commission recognizes that orders dealing with these important issues may be necessary 'where a parent may flout the other parent's wishes in a matter' (p. 139).

A major problem arises from this proposal. Parents will have equal powers and be able to act independently of one another 'unless and until otherwise provided' (p. 140). Thus it will be up to mothers as primary carers to return to court where a father flouts her wishes. Under sole orders the onus is on the non-custodial father to make an application to the court if he disagrees with decisions taken by a custodial mother. To change this situation is to add yet further responsibilities to the role of mothers where they already carry the major daily responsibility for children (and, in effect, places the child between what may be two entirely different approaches to child rearing). Moreover, the proposal that, where there is disagreement, either parent has recourse to the courts does not remove the bones of contention between warring parents where ultimate authority has been removed. It simply shifts the battle 'underground' – in effect back to the very scenario from which it arose, namely back to the parents, where mothers may have to continue the very power struggle they experienced during marriage. 'Sequential custody' will not eradicate these problems, and it is highly problematic to suggest that in such circumstances recourse should be made to the court. This avenue for the resolution of disputes concerning children within marriage has existed since 1973,[9] but not surprisingly it has never been used by parents (Law Commission, 1986). It could of course be argued that both parents might be more willing to invoke the law once they had separated or divorced, but equally there are also reasons why a mother might be extremely reticent to involve the court, not least because of the financial implications. These arise partly as a consequence of the general drift towards conciliation and the way in which conflict is negatively viewed, and partly as a consequence of how insecure a woman may feel in the face of a father threatening to contest her primary care of the children. Briefly, in a system increasingly dominated by the ideology of conciliation, which advocates consensus between parents 'for the sake of the children', dealing directly with conflicts of interest between parents is becoming increasingly difficult. It is likely that within this approach to conflict, a mother who perhaps continually returns to court because of a 'vexatious and difficult' father will herself be regarded in precisely those terms by courts and welfare agencies because it is she who brings the matter before the court. This situation may ultimately prevent her from bringing problems before the court, especially if she fears that it may lead to a reconsideration of her role as the children's primary carer. In effect, therefore, this proposal would reduce the autonomy of divorced mothers from both men and the state, while at the same time increasing her responsibilities.

CUSTODY LAW AND 'CO-PARENTING': LEGAL REGULATION OR SOCIAL ENGINEERING?

It is important to identify certain inconsistencies and ambiguities in the Law Commission's approach to the use of custody law and equality of responsibility for child care. These are particularly salient to the development of a feminist perspective in this area.

First the Law Commission is not consistent in its approach to the use of law in attempting to achieve co-parenting. For example, the Commission states that it is an important function of law to provide a model of behaviour which is generally believed to be desirable (Law Commission, 1986, p. 106). It demonstrates clear support for shared parental responsibilities as the preferred model at several stages in the working paper (e.g. p. 136, para. 4.53(b); p. 140, para. 4.58). However, the Commission then retreats from the assertion that shared parenting should be the norm (perhaps in a last-minute realization that family law cannot in practice enforce this model). But this retreat undermines much of the Commission's original argument regarding the function of law in this area. Law either does or does not set standards. Here the Commission adopts an untenable position – the law sets standards unless a parent disagrees with these standards. The initial premise is itself highly questionable, namely that one can in fact utilize custody law at the point of marriage breakdown to achieve co-parenting. Nevertheless, if that perspective is adopted, it does require consistency in the face of possible opposition. This is primarily because, given the economic consequences of child care, most fathers may prefer existing arrangements whereby mothers carry the major responsibility. Given this situation, it appears from the Law Commission's proposals that the interests of fathers would continue to prevail.

The second point concerns the theoretical position taken with regard to the role of law generally in relation to co-parenting. There is ambiguous support in the working paper for the notion of co-parenting. But it is doubtless the case that, in the vast majority of divorces, this model bears little relationship to the pattern of child care carried out within most marriages. This raises important questions about the function of custody law at the point of marriage breakdown. To expect custody law to instigate new patterns of parenting (even assuming that to be possible) is clearly a very different function to that of providing a framework for existing patterns to continue. Co-parenting, like joint (legal) custody, assumes and thereby attempts to impose a particular model of parenting on divorcing parents whose marriages, for the most part, lack both the formal structures and mutuality necessary to achieve this ideal. Thus a legal presumption based on the notion of existing co-parenting may simply be a presumption to continue substantial inequalities of power and responsibilities.

Third, it is necessary to challenge the Commission's ultimate objective in the reinterpretation of existing legal concepts of custody, care and control, and access. The Commission argues that these concepts are now wrongly conceived by parents as denoting a hierarchy of power. Rather it argues, what now exists between parents is simply a form of 'time sharing' with regard to child care on divorce. This reconception is a fundamental misrepresentation of the organization of child care. Examination of current responsibilities for, and consequences of, child care between fathers and mothers following divorce (or indeed within marriage) demonstrates this. There is necessarily both an implicit and an explicit hierarchical relationship in post-divorce parental positions. This situation is established by the structure of both private and public law. For example, it is the (private) responsibility of mothers as custodial parents to ensure that children are cared for before and after school hours – public law makes no national child care provision. It is generally expected that a parent exercising access will act as a responsible parent. Nevertheless, outside periods of access (most usually weekends and school holidays) non-custodial parents (usually fathers) do not carry responsibility for, or indeed anticipate, children's daily needs. Nor are non-custodial parents expected to accept immediate responsibility where those needs change. So, for example, they are not expected (by employers or the state) to take time off from work in periods of children's ill health, statutory school holidays, visits to doctors, dentists, and so on. Fathers on the whole do not negotiate full-time work with daily responsibility for child care, especially very young children, either during or after marriage.

Thus primary responsibility for children means that the majority of mothers have to arrange employment around child care. And women's employment patterns in Britain demonstrate that mothers frequently take part-time, low paid, insecure jobs, with little chance of training, promotion, and long-term job security (Martin and Roberts, 1984). In addition, labour market requirements such as overtime, evening and weekend training, shift work, evening meetings, extensive travel, and conferences are impossible for most working mothers. The same is not true for fathers. Fathers' responsibilities for child care are clearly limited, often in terms of their own expectations, and almost always in terms of the expectations of employers and the state. These expectations are built upon the idea and the reality that women are the primary carers and will meet children's everyday changing needs (Moss, 1987). This hierarchy of responsibility between parents applies within marriage, but it is even more pertinent on divorce where there is inadequate child care provision, and where geographical location, re-marriage, and employment demands are additional complicating factors (see Pearson and Thoennes, 1985; Steinman, 1981, 1983). Even where mutuality might exist between parents, employers and the state operators on the basis that mothers are, and will continue to be, the primary carers of children.

To develop legal policies which ignore these concrete realities with regard to child care is not in children's nor in women's interests. Moreover, to do so in effect sustains and perpetuates those inequalities which the Law Commission hopes are changing. Child care on divorce is not therefore simply a form of 'time sharing'. This perception suggests there is a freedom of choice as to the precise timing and nature of the 'contract' and also an equality of bargaining power between parties. This is clearly not an accurate representation of how child care is organized between parents, either during or after marriage.

My main argument is that it is beyond the scope of family law radically to transform structural differences in child care.[10] The Law Commission engaged in some skilful legal and conceptual manoeuvres in response to the criticisms outlined in my introduction. But it failed to give clear recognition to the fundamental point of the likely impact of new proposals on the child care role of fathers. Without comprehensive changes in provision for all children (so that responsibility for them is not seen solely as the private responsibility of mothers), then divisions of responsibility with regard to child care will remain broadly the same for the vast majority of parents in Britain. In developing future policies, therefore, it is clearly inadequate to proceed as if parents are completely interchangeable free-floating agents while the actual practices and expectations of all those concerned clearly demonstrate that parenting roles remain specific.

LEGAL POLICIES AND FEMINIST POLITICS

A major problem for feminists working in this field of family law is that we continually address a situation in which we have to respond to fairly narrow and specific proposals. This is increasingly the case in the shift to the right in British politics. Few feminists retain the optimism experienced during the women's movement of the late 1960s and early 1970s with regard to the impact of progressive feminist proposals on the structuring of social policies. I am not, however, arguing that the demands of the 1960s–1970s women's movement for equality of responsibility for child care are now redundant or misguided (see letters, *Everywoman*, November 1986). Rather, I am arguing that it is theoretically inaccurate and politically ill-advised for both the Law Commission and indeed feminists (e.g. Bruch, 1978) to attempt to utilize custody law at the point of marriage breakdown as a mechanism to achieve joint or equal child care responsibilities. There is an understandable demand for a redistribution of daily responsibility for children. This has led to an approach which moves between forms of pragmatism in some instances and a reification of the influence of law in others. But court orders cannot force parents to agree where they do not, and, where they do, court orders are largely unnecessary. Moreover, whatever the social ideas set by more traditionally minded reformers in this field (e.g. restricting the grounds for divorce, suggesting increased state intervention in families to prevent divorce and educate parents) people seldom react to such reforms in the manner expected.[11] This is especially the case when the ideals embodied in new reforms are far removed from the everyday experiences and realities of people's lives.

Although it is important to look at women's needs as primary carers in the divorce process, there is little research which avoids idealized notions of parenting on divorce and focuses on women's experiences of law and legal practices. Three major points arose from my own research which included a small sample of interviews with divorced mothers (Brophy, 1987a). First, there is a tendency for courts faced with a fully disputed case to undervalue previous responsibility for child care as an indicator for future care. As one mother commented:

> there was no discussion of things when I went to court ... of things like who meets a child from school, takes it to the doctors and things like that, I mean those are the things which I would have thought important but the courts don't see it that way. (Brophy, 1987a, p. 226)

Second, fathers continue to rely on proving the mother unfit as a method of establishing their own claims to custody of children. Historically of course fathers relied on wives' adultery to establish they were unfit as mothers. That avenue no longer exists, but the defects approach is still utilized to usurp mothers' claims, and issues such as mental instability, responsibility for marriage breakdown, choice of cohabitee (Maidment, 1981) and sexual orientation and lifestyle form avenues through which fathers seek to establish a mother's unfitness (Brophy, 1987a). In general fathers do not argue their case for the custody of children on the basis of a history of shared child care: rather they attempt to discredit the mothers.

Third, the current tendency of courts to ignore or undervalue women's previous child care responsibilities has implications not simply for those mothers facing a real challenge to custody, but for all mothers on divorce or separation. This is because legal practice in contested cases influences the climate of bargaining in pre-court negotiations (Mnookin, 1979). Thus where a mother fears a contested case, she may well feel compelled to accept an inadequate settlement in other areas of ancillary relief (e.g. maintenance and lump sum settlements, share of the matrimonial home) rather than risk a contest over custody. The Law Commission proposals on court orders discussed above may eradicate the worst excesses of a contest so far as fathers are concerned; however, they do not address the essential elements of a contest so far as mothers are concerned. Nor indeed does the Commission consider the benefits which accrue to men as a consequence of a legal code which in effect ignores previous responsibility for children, or the way in which it could operate as a disincentive to more equal child care between men and women.

A further area of concern for mothers following divorce is that of access. Although the major trend in debates over access point to more and not less access for non-custodial fathers (and the Law Commission in principle supports this approach), little attention has been given to the problems for both mothers and children which arise where men utilize access to continue to harass and intimidate mothers.

Access problems can affect all custodial mothers regardless of race or class. The experiences of some black and Asian mothers, however, demonstrate additional problems which in turn highlight the limited way in which the 'access problem' is currently perceived. All mothers face enormous difficulties in leaving the matrimonial home with children, and this is likely to increase as the housing crisis in Britain worsens. But black and Asian mothers can face additional problems, particularly when leaving violent and abusive men, because of pressures exerted by some sections of the ethnic communities who are opposed to divorce[12] (see also Chapter 8 in this volume). Many women are indeed successful in leaving their homes but the struggle is frequently protracted and complex. Often the only safe solution to continued control and abuse by husbands is for women to move away completely from their own communities and friendship networks. While this move brings isolation (and perhaps for Asian and black mothers and children less protection from expressions of racism), it can bring safety from violent men.

Two points arise out of this situation which affect access arrangements. First, it is not generally accepted (by courts or indeed welfare agencies) that for children to witness the physical and/or emotional abuse of their mother is itself a form of child abuse. Second, in awarding access to vindictive and violent men, courts are not sufficiently sensitive to the way in which fathers utilize these periods in a continued war of attrition. Courts frequently put the onus back on mothers to facilitate access, either by revealing her address or ordering her to take the children to the father's home. In both situations mothers are again at risk of further intimidation and abuse. If courts continue to award access in these circumstances, and it seems likely that they will (Law Commission, 1986, p. 123), then proposals are necessary to protect mothers. One possible solution is 'supervised access', and neutral access facilities. Currently, this role falls to a few voluntary groups, but this is clearly an inadequate arrangement in a situation where access is receiving such attention and upgrading. It is indeed ironic that the very women's groups who provide the support and refuges for women to leave violent and abusive men now find that, in a further effort to protect such mothers, they have to provide a supervised access facility to the very men who have forced these women and children to leave their home. It is inadequate to 'leave it to the courts' when these situations arise since courts cannot compel men with a history of violence to behave in a responsible manner, and in any case can act only after the injunction or non-molestation order has been broken. However unpalatable it may be to those advocating conciliation at all costs, supervised and neutral access facilities can offer benefits to all mothers where there is continued conflict and hostilities.

Finally, it may appear that in certain respects feminist responses seem more concerned with the 'damage limitation' than with creating new policy developments. This limited response causes frustration, particularly for those feminists who see custody law as a central force in the struggle towards real equality of child care. Equally, contributors to the liberal legal tradition may argue that my perspective relocates children within a 'bargaining climate' and therefore flies in the face of the whole development of postwar welfarism in this branch of law. However, it is not possible either in theory or practice to isolate children from the social structures and institutions within which they are reared. Policy development must take as its starting point the material reality of child care. Moreover, it requires an understanding of the limitations of family law within the social structure, and in addition must be based on consultation and dialogue with those most centrally concerned – namely mothers. In other words, policy must reflect the concrete needs of women as primary carers, and not hypothetical wish-fulfilment or 'social engineering'. This does not necessarily mean forgoing ideals with regard to child care, but it does mean continually reassessing those ideals while remaining firmly rooted in the political economy and the everyday lives of women and the consequences which follow from being primary carers.

ADDENDUM

Following the writing of this chapter the Law Commission

produced a final report and recommendations for legislation (Law Commission 1988). It remained essentially committed to the role and function of law as outlined in the Working Paper. Although the Commission acknowledged the limits of law in altering human relationships, it added the rejoinder that '[law] should not stand in the way' (p. 23). The Commission remained convinced by the major arguments that current custody law and legal practices limit the role of fathers after divorce and exacerbate the problems between parents. The recommendations were, therefore, broadly in line with the proposals outlined in the Working Paper. The position of the non-custodial parent was substantially upgraded. However, there were some changes in terminology, and some protection against intervention.

The Commission recommended the terms custody and care, and control and access, be abandoned. Parenthood should become the primary concept, and the legal status of parents in relation to the care and upbringing of their children should be termed 'parental responsibility'. Parents with parental responsibility should have equal status, each should be able to act independently in carrying out that responsibility. Where there is disagreement, it was recommended the court should act as the final arbiter.

On relationship breakdown it was recommended that the court should have a duty to consider the arrangements made for any children but it should not have to make an order in every case (p. 14). Where orders are thought appropriate, the new range of orders recommended were, in effect, broadly the same as those proposed in the Working Paper and amount to sequential custody. The terminology recommended was, however, different. The orders recommended were:

a 'resident order' which would prescribe with whom the child is going to live;

b a 'contact order' requiring the person with whom the child lives or is to live, to allow the child to visit or otherwise have contact with another person.

Where there are problems or interference by a parent, the Commission recommended the courts should issue:

c a 'specific issues' order, resolving a particular aspect of parental responsibility;

d a 'prohibited steps' order specifying that a particular step should not be taken without the consent of the court.

Under these recommendations a (custodial) mother would be free to exercise her full parental rights and authority without consulting the father. A father would, however, retain parental rights and authority (other than the right to actual possession of the child). He would be entitled to his own point of view on the way in which the child was being brought up. And, where he disagreed with a mother's decision, he would not have a power of veto, but he would have the right to apply to the court for a 'specific issues' order. This recommendation represented a new right for non-custodial fathers. Under a 'contact order' (which would replace access orders), a father would be entitled to exercise all his parental rights and responsibilities. The Commission stated that in doing so, he 'must not do something which is incompatible with the order about where the child should live' (p. 27). Some fairly straightforward examples of this appeared in the Report, but more complex issues about the incompatibility of different life-styles and methods of child rearing were not addressed. And it may well open up, rather than reduce, areas of potential conflict. For those cases where there are particular anxieties or bones of contention between parents, the Commission recommended courts should attach certain conditions to residence or contact orders. However, it stated these should rarely be required. But the court could, for example, attach a condition to a 'residence order', such that a mother may not take certain decisions without informing the father or giving him the opportunity to object. In effect, therefore, this type of condition could amount to a form of mandatory joint custody over certain issues. It differed slightly in that it did not give one parent in *advance* the right to be consulted on *all* important decisions which the other parent will have to put into effect.

Clearly the Commission remained committed to upgrading access and in the Final Report it emphasized the hope that these recommendations would reduce the issues at stake between parents. Certainly in the case of fathers this is so. Equally the Commission remained hopeful that this in turn would encourage more 'responsible parenthood' on the part of fathers, but this does not necessarily imply more daily care. Indeed, the Commission now gives uncritical recognition to the fact that 'clearly in most cases one parent carries a much heavier burden of responsibility than does the other' (p. 24); however, references to co-parenting were absent. The Commission simply argued that 'the practical question for courts is to decide where the child is to live and how much he or she is to see of the other parent' (p. 25). In December 1988, the government produced a Bill: Children Bill [H.L.] 1988 containing the above recommendations.

NOTES

1 The Law Commission was created by Act of Parliament in 1965 for the purpose of promoting law reform and to consider ways of updating and simplifying law.

2 This condition resulted from the Royal Commission on Marriage and Divorce in the postwar reconstruction. It was an attempt to prevent parents divorcing but, where they did, to prioritize children in the legal procedure and give the court complete control over the arrangements for all children, including those whose custody was not contested. However, it has always remained a problematic provision, lately subject to much criticism. The Booth Committee made several recommendations for improvement in 1985, and the Law Commission (1986, pp. 108-9) proposed a less stringent arrangement. Formal court scrutiny of all arrangements would remain, but the court's new duty would simply be to decide whether there are circumstances requiring an order to be made; it would not have to express a view as to how satisfactory a solution could be achieved.

3 For example, what the court can do under these jurisdictions where it grants legal custody to one parent is to order that the other parent retains specified rights, sharing them with the custodial parent (Domestic Proceedings and Magistrates' Courts Act 1978 s.8(4); Guardianship of Minors Act 1971, s.11 (A)).

4 Such objectives and arguments can be identified in attempts at law and legal procedure reforms in the postwar economy (*Report of the Committee on Procedure in Matrimonial Causes* (Denning, 1947); *Royal Commission on Marriage and Divorce* 1951-5 (Morton, 1956); Brophy, 1987a, pp. 77-87).

5 It could of course be pointed out that fathers within marriage have always had that opportunity – and in (arguably) more ideal circumstances. Yet as research continues to demonstrate (Henwood *et al.*, 1987), this has not led to a substantial shift towards a more equal division of responsibilities for child care.

6 This is despite the fact that the Home Office in its 1985 review of the relationship between parental supervision and juvenile delinquency rejected such a position (Riley and Shaw, 1985).

7 For example the government rejected the EEC directive on parental and family leave which proposed paid leave entitlement to parents in the first two years of children's lives plus a minimum number of days'

leave per year for family reasons. The aim of the directive was to promote equal opportunities by making it easier for women to combine work and child care and to encourage men to play a greater role in looking after children. The British government rejected the proposal on the basis that these measures 'are best pursued by voluntary negotiation between employers and employees. [It] welcomes U.K. endeavours to encourage instead community initiatives which enhance job prospects for men and women.' Indeed the very notion that men should become involved in child care received substantial ridicule from members of the government (see comments of Beaumont-Dark, Parliamentary Debates (1985) H.C. *Hansard*, 26 November).

8 This is not to say that there are not a minority of men who nevertheless attempt – within those constraints – to take a share of child care responsibilities. However joint custody orders cannot force those who do not to begin/attempt to do so, and where they already co-operate a joint custody order is unnecessary.

9 Guardianship Act 1973.

10 Ironically the Law Commission (1986) acknowledges work which makes this point early in the working paper (pp. 130-1, para. 4.45) but then fails to bring that point to bear on future policy proposals.

11 One example of this is the general failure of the stringent procedures discussed in note 2 above actually to prevent the rising rate of divorce in Britain.

12 Points raised in discussions with author by the Asian Women's Network and Southall Black Sisters (Brophy, 1987b, p. 17).

CASES

Dipper v. *Dipper* [1981] Fam 31.
Re C. Wardship and Adoption (1981) 2 F.L.R., 177.

STATUTES CITED

Matrimonial Causes Act 1973.
Guardianship of Minors Act 1971.
Guardianship Act 1973.
Domestic Proceedings and Magistrates' Courts Act 1978.

Chapter Ten

WHAT ELSE IS NEW? REPRODUCTIVE TECHNOLOGIES AND CUSTODY POLITICS

JULIETTE ZIPPER

Child custody is not only a problem when it comes to divorce. Custody also has to do with other issues around care, control and 'access' to children. With the emergence of reproductive technologies, a new field of legislative and regulatory activities is created. In turn this raises the question as to what the implications will be for the power relations between women and men. Although legislative and other measures directed at the regulation of reproductive technologies affect a relatively small number of people, they do have wider ramifications. Discourses on motherhood and fatherhood in relation to reproductive technology fit into a general debate on parental rights and duties.

This chapter is written from a particular perspective – the debate in the Netherlands on legal consequences of reproductive technologies is taken as the starting point for a more general consideration of the issues. The debate has been started by the availability of new reproductive technologies in the Netherlands and abroad, and the reactions of governments, and of those who advise governments, have swiftly taken the form of proposals for legislation. I will therefore refer to proposals for legislation in the Netherlands, in other western countries, and to proposals for supranational legislation such as those which have been made by a special committee of the Council of Europe.

What are the general connections between reproductive technologies and issues concerning the field of custody? There is a long-standing connection between fatherhood and filiation in relation to married and unmarried men. A comparison between historical debates on artificial insemination in the Netherlands and in the United Kingdom sheds a new light on the more recent debates about reproductive technologies. Nowadays legal and social father-hood is not the only problem: motherhood is the subject of concern too, in particular when it comes to surrogate motherhood, which can entail many legal as well as other problems. In many countries proposals have been made for legislation to regulate reproductive methods. What can be the effects – if any – of these proposals? What trends towards a supranational jurisprudence on reproductive technologies can be perceived? And what does it all mean for the legal relations between women and their children?

REPRODUCTIVE TECHNOLOGIES AND FAMILY RELATIONS

Contraceptives created the potential for sexuality – that is, hetero-sexuality – without procreation. Reproductive technologies have loosened the ties between procreation and sexuality even further. The ties between biological and social parenthood seem to have been severed, if not in practice, at least potentially. Ongoing developments in the field of reproductive technologies have generated debates on several levels. Doctors commit themselves to the practice of the technology; the media are on the alert for every new invention; lawyers are studying the legal consequences of the new forms of parenthood. There are public debates about particular cases and legal debates on proposals for legislative reforms. Repeatedly the question emerges of whether everything that is technically possible should be permitted. Experts in the field of medicine, law, and ethics, among others, debate about norms and values that ought to be the underlying principles for research and employment of reproductive technologies. Further-more, there are debates among legal experts about the international aspects of future legislation.

What can be the consequences of the developments in the field of reproductive technologies with regard to custody politics? This may seem a rather far-fetched question. In the public debate on reproductive technologies the question of custody does not take central stage, but the issue slips in by the back door, for example by proposals to change rules of filiation. In cases of sperm and/or egg donation, filiation and thus parenthood can become obscure, which can sometimes result in tugs-of-war over the child. In a more implicit way custody politics is a relevant issue because of the conditions and qualifications that are demanded of those who want admission to a clinic for artificial insemination or to participate in an *in vitro* fertilization programme.

Both sexuality and reproduction are by and large supposed to take place within marriage, or at least within stable heterosexual relationships (see Warnock, 1985). Reproductive technologies that are applied in combination with non-traditional forms of motherhood and fatherhood may obscure who is related to whom, in other words who has certain rights and duties in regard to whom. In the actual political circumstances this may have consequences for duties of child care, maintenance, of custody, and parental power (Chapter 3 in this volume). Dutch family law is rather complicated when it comes to the relations between legal, biological, and social parenthood. Although at first sight blood-ties form the basis of filiation rules, to a certain extent fictions of biology are always involved. A paternal presumption is the rule, in that the husband of the woman who gives birth to a child is supposed to be the father, whereas the law also presumes that the woman of whom the child is born is going to mother it. The introduction of new reproductive technologies, as well as the regulation of some older unorthodox methods of procreation, may become vehicles to bring biology into filiation law in a way that it never was before. Furthermore, ova and semen need not necessarily be the genetic material of the parents concerned.

Reproductive technologies do not develop in a social vacuum, but against a background of changing notions of motherhood and of anxiety about the decline of the traditional family and the meaning of fatherhood (Vilaine *et al.*, 1986). It is this background and these anxieties that we have to keep in mind when we examine the debates around reproductive technologies. Can the efforts to regulate reproduction and reproductive technologies perhaps be interpreted as the last effort to uphold traditional values?[1]

More often than not medical institutions in the Netherlands and elsewhere demand a marriage certificate from a woman who wants artificial insemination or *in vitro* fertilization. Heterosexual couples are admitted to *in vitro* fertilization programmes after consultation with a psychologist or psychiatrist who has declared them a 'proper couple' and 'fit for parenthood'. The notions of a 'proper couple' and 'fit for parenthood' imply discourses on 'normal' femininity, 'normal' family life, and 'normal' hetero-sexuality. In particular the discourses on femininity figure strongly in the 'medical' evaluation, together with norms about the sort of family children 'need and have a right to'. Supposedly children have a right to a family that it is constituted by '1) a loving and monogamous relationship, 2) between a man and a woman who 3) want to embody their sexual-biological experience in a child' (Christiaens, 1986). Dutch theologian M. Christiaens calls this the 'safe cushion of the family triangle' and says that this model has a normative character, which is as it should be (Christiaens, 1986).

Normative opinions are also expressed in the discourses on femininity. In these discourses, fertility and infertility have to do with the acceptance of 'normal femininity' and the 'normal feminine role'. For example, some research has indicated that there is a significant correlation between infertility and menstrual disorders on the one hand and a negative self-image that women have (the result of their relation with their mothers) on the other hand. After some testing, Austrian endocrinologist Kemeter (Kemeter et al., 1985) came to the rather startling conclusion that infertility in women is connected with the rejection of femininity and female sexuality and, as if this is not enough, with prudishness and a neurotic character structure. In short, it is argued that women with fertility problems have personality problems.[2] Psychotherapy is the solution, and when a deeper understanding is acquired the problem of infertility will vanish (Kemeter et al., 1985). But there is more to it; to become a mother, a woman must be prepared to give up some things to deserve motherhood: 'all who treat infertility are familiar with the woman who doesn't achieve a long-cherished pregnancy until she gives up her career' says Christie (1980). This Australian psychiatrist also offers his opinion on the suitability for parenthood of a couple who want infertility treatment. This suitability depends on the sexual relations of the couple, or, to be more precise, on the sexual responses of the woman: 'It is only when a good sexual relationship is re-established ... that the true generative urge can reappear. A child has a right to parents, and a good parent is, primarily, a good partner' (Christie, 1980). In regard to what is known about the strains that infertility treatment put upon women and the effects this has on their sexual life (Pfeffer and Wollett, 1983), the demands that this 'expert' makes can hardly ever be fulfilled.

And even if some treatment is allowed and it succeeds, the

'expert's' standards for motherhood are not always met. English gynaecologist M. E. Pawson expressed doubts whether 'infertile patients ... do ... really want a baby at all' and concluded that 'women who force themselves, or allow doctors to force them, to be mothers do not do well as mothers' (Pawson, 1981).

Not all 'experts' in the field of fertility and infertility are as outspoken as those quoted, but their judgements are typical of a certain mood, and they represent the dominant perspective. There is a school of thought in which the 'normal family' figures as the leading theme. And the creation of such a 'normal family' is the one thing that legitimates the use of reproductive techniques.

FILIATION AND FATHER RIGHTS

Through the use of diverse techniques a child can still be the 'genetic' (or biological) child of the people who are going to raise it. In that case genetic and social parenthood coincide. Although medical intervention may take place, there need not be any legal problems. But the use of donor gametes is possible and then legal complications may result. However, the possibilities to combine ovum and sperm do not say anything about who is going to bear and/or rear the resulting child. Nor do they say anything about the filiation rules that will be applied, whose name the child will bear, or who is going to have parental power or custody.

In contrast to the new question 'Who is the mother?' in cases of ovum-donation and/or surrogacy, the question 'Who is the father?' is an old one. Fatherhood has always been an uncertain factor; hence the laws on marriage, filiation, and the measures against adultery by women. Adultery by women could bring 'foreign blood' into the family and thus endanger the male line.

In the Netherlands the answer to the question 'Who is the father?' is grounded on a presumption of paternity in marriage. This means that as a rule *pater est quim nuptiam demonstrat*, the father is he who is married to the mother [art. 197 BW]. (Unless he denies fatherhood, but that is another story.) In Dutch law fatherhood outside marriage can be established by legal recognition of a child by anyone for whom there are no legal bars to marrying the mother of that child. Fatherhood can also be established by a paternity suit (Sevenhuijsen, 1987). Legal recognition does not necessarily have to be based on a biological fact; a man can also recognize a child of whom he is not the begetter. In that case fatherhood is based on a legal construction. One thing still stands out in Dutch law; a man needs the written permission of the mother of a child before he can recognize it. The permission can be given either before or after the birth of the child.

Until recently the institution of marriage functioned as a mechanism to secure fatherhood in the biological and social sense, even though marriage has had a different meaning in different times and societies. Marriage is a historical social construction (Sevenhuijsen, 1987; Smart, 1984). The traditional nuclear family with the traditional division of labour is on the decline (CBS, 1987). Writing about the situation in the United States, sociologist Barrie Thorne stated that 'While the ideology of The Family is still strongly embedded in cultural ideals, government politics, the organization of the economy and "pro-family" political movements, in fact only a minority of U.S. households fully resembles that form' (Thorne, 1982). This is not only happening in the United States, but in most western societies as well: 'there is today a moral panic over the increase in the number of divorces' (Brophy, 1985). Arguably, legal marriage does not function any more as the mechanism that gives certainty about paternity.

There have always been conflicts between individual women and men about parental rights and duties, most clearly in cases of divorce, custody, alimony, and visitation rights. However, since the changes in divorce law in the second half of the twentieth century, the character of these conflicts has changed; custody has become a political issue. The wishes of various interest groups in the field of custody and parental rights are often mutually exclusive (Zipper and Sevenhuijsen, 1987). It would appear that it is mostly those 'wishes' that are expressed by fathers that become transformed into legal rights (see Chapter 3). In addition to the extension of rights of men as fathers outside marriage, there are indications of an extension of the rights that men have, based on the simple act of begetting (De Hondt and Holtrust, 1986a). The extension of rights is sometimes accompanied by an extension of financial duties; for example, the Dutch government recently proposed that 'natural parents' (by which they meant begetters) should be made to contribute to the cost of the education of their children.

Some men feel threatened by anything that they perceive as an infringement of their rights as men and fathers, particularly by women who demand rights as women and as mothers in custody disputes (Goode, 1982). In the United Kingdom these men have organized campaigns such as Families Need Fathers, which as Brophy (1985) argues is an example of 'an interest group representing male interests'. The fathers' rights movement in the Netherlands consists of a loosely organized power elite that dominates the field of family law and has a strong lobby in the Dutch Ministry of Justice. Prominent fathers' rights advocates appoint themselves 'experts', for example as psychologists who talk about vengeful, wicked mothers who keep children away from their divorced but nevertheless doting fathers. The fathers' rights movement is organized on various issues, reproductive technologies being one among many. According to the fathers' rights movement men should have a dominant voice in matters of fatherhood around reproductive technologies. This includes interference with a woman's right to have an abortion if she so wishes. It is therefore not surprising to find the right-to-life movement on the side of the fathers' rights movement, as became clear in a much-publicized case in Oxford where a man tried legally to prevent his former girlfriend from having an abortion (The *Guardian*, 25 February 1987).

In the Netherlands a self-appointed study group of members of the Society for Family and Juvenile Law (Vereniging voor Familie-en Jeugdrecht, SFJL) wrote a report on reproductive technologies and some of the legal problems involved (Hammerstein-Schoonderwoerd *et al.*, 1986). This report, immediately dubbed 'the experts' report' in the media, stressed the importance of (at least legal) fathers for children. On the whole it was rather hostile to autonomous motherhood, implying that women should not be allowed to have children without male supervision (De Hondt and Holtrust, 1985). Unmarried women must have the permission of a man for artificial insemination, stated the SFJL. Subsequently the man who has given permission then has the right to recognize the child legally. If it were not for the possibility of insemination *in vivo* and self-insemination, regulations like this could make it hard to become a mother without a supervising man. Or, for that matter, to have a child that takes its mother's name.

It is difficult for feminists to intervene and participate in the legal debate and therefore it is hard to influence policy making. Feminists are often explicitly excluded from this form of opinion making. A member of the special study group of the SFJL, professor of juvenile law J. E. Doek, was asked why there were no feminist voices, which would not stress fatherhood so much, to be heard in the consultation procedure. The professor answered that the members of the group were not waiting for 'another minority point of view' (*Trouw*, 1985). Not only does this remark reveal his attitude to feminists; it also tells something about the construction of feminism as a phenomenon that ought to be opposed.

'Experts' stress the importance of a family consisting of a man, a woman, and their offspring; thus the importance of the heterosexual nuclear family is reinforced. In the Netherlands article 8 of the European Declaration of Human Rights is used by the SFJL to 'repair' the rights of men as fathers. Husbands and male stable partners have to give their permission for medical treatment of the woman for infertility, and men as donors must be guaranteed the right to remain anonymous.[3] On the one hand the study group of the SFJL proposed that legal recognition by the donor as well as visitation rights must remain possible, based on 'the right to a family life'. On the other hand they also proposed that a surrogate mother had no such rights and responsibilities, because at the moment of conception she had no intention of creating a family life. As Dutch lawyers Ineke De Hondt and Nora Holtrust have argued: 'A man has the right to a family-life that must be protected, based on one ejaculation, whereas a woman who has been pregnant for nine months does not have any right' (De Hondt and Holtrust, 1986a). It is rather amazing indeed that there is such a disparity in (proposed) rights while the investment in time and energy is inversely proportional. Although the trap of biological and moral arguments about motherhood must be avoided, one has to recognize the difference between the donation of a little bottle of sperm and the delivery of a baby carried for nine months. And it is strange that this difference results in such very unequal proposals. The disparity in proposals reflects the different legal status accorded to female and male parents. The SJFL has purposely omitted to claim equal rights for egg-donating women, probably because in their opinion women have nothing to do with filiation.

In the not so distant past unmarried motherhood was cause for social condemnation. An unmarried mother was perceived as a 'fallen woman' and 'sinner', who most certainly ought not to have a chance to claim a wealthy man as the begetter of her child and consequently blackmail him and even ruin his marriage. Unmarried mothers and their children were often in dire straits (Sevenhuijsen, 1987). Feminists, politicians, and reformers in general agitated to take care of unmarried mothers and re-educate them, and for legal reforms in regard to their children (Sevenhuijsen, 1987). In former days, unmarried women who wanted their children to have a legal father were prohibited from filing a paternity suit. Now it is exactly the other way around and unmarried women are forced by law to name the father of their children. In the Federal Republic of Germany, for example, women who refuse to name the father at the registration of births are denied custody as well as financial benefits for child care (Holtrust, 1986).

It seems as if there has been a complete turn about in the ways women want to organize their motherhood. Therefore the fathers' rights movement tries to secure, if not the foundations of marriage, then at least the rights of fathers. The foundations of marriage and uncertainties for men as a result of the use of a reproductive technology, however, have been themes of former debates on artificial insemination.

THE CASE OF ARTIFICIAL INSEMINATION

The recent commotion around reproductive technologies may sustain the idea that all these technologies are very new and very revolutionary indeed. Aspects of the technologies are, however, not that new. Artificial insemination, for example, has been the subject of legal and political debates for several decades in several western countries. The debates on artificial insemination during the 1950s involved questions of whether artificial insemination should be regarded as marital misconduct or adultery and hence a ground for divorce; the consequences it held for filiation, blood relationship, legitimacy, and duty to child support were also salient (see Smart, 1987). At the same time the debates provided ample opportunity for airing opinions on the psychology of marital relations, motherhood, fatherhood, femininity, and sexuality. Since the 1960s artificial insemination has been regulated by law in a number of western countries. But most governments seem to think that, in the wake of debates on *in vitro* fertilization, a reconsideration of artificial insemination is due.

In the Netherlands the postwar debates on artificial insemination were at first held mainly among the clergy, in so-called 'ethical committees'. Later government committees were appointed, whose task it was to advise on policy and to propose legal measures.[4] Between 1955 and 1965 various committees in the Netherlands studied the question of artificial insemination.[5] Like almost any ideological question in the Netherlands, it was determined by the typical Dutch phenomenon of so-called pillarization, which is not just a division of religious denominations but a politically institutionalized way to deal with potential conflicts (Lijphart, 1968). The terms of the debate were predominantly set by various religious convictions. Not only were there several religious convictions, but the religious groups were divided into various denominations with different opinions on any given problem. The Roman Catholic doctrine on artificial insemination was – and still is – based on natural law doctrines, and forbids any form of procreation that is not performed by the *actus conjugalis* – sexual intercourse by a married couple (Petit, 1961; Ratzinger and Bovone, 1987). The Protestant churches were more amenable to the emerging psychological arguments; some of them even thought that artificial insemination with sperm of the husband was permissible in very special cases, although other Protestant groups were – and still remain – strongly opposed to reproductive technologies (Zipper, 1986).

The arguments that lawyers gave for making artificial insemination a criminal offence were based mainly on clerical dogmas on marriage. Proposals to criminalize artificial insemination were made by a prominent Roman Catholic professor of law, Ch. J. J. M. Petit, even though it was very clear to him and his committee that control was practically impossible. The husband was outside the scope of all the proposals, whereas the doctor, the donor, and the woman were to be convicted, even to risk imprisonment (Petit, 1961). The husband was seen as the victim of his wife's wish for a child. One Protestant committee in particular was rather worried about the psychological effects that committing a crime – making a 'false' registration on the birth certificate – could have for the husband (Hijmans, 1958). Those who were opposed to artificial insemination by donor often interpreted it as adultery, which in its turn gave rise to another dilemma for those who opposed divorce, for example on religious grounds. (More often than not the two groups overlapped.) But in spite of the harsh terms, legal grounds for penalizing artificial insemination were hard to find, especially where artificial insemination with the sperm of the husband was involved.

The one thing on which all experts agreed was the subject of artificial insemination of single women, namely that it ought to be prohibited. Although the 'experts' made some reference to the wish of a single woman for a child, these references were followed immediately by the advice not to take that wish seriously. A woman who wanted a child without a man could be nothing else but a frustrated man-hater; therefore she was no doubt neurotic, and thus not fit for motherhood at all. Artificial insemination for single women should be impossible because otherwise an 'artificial matriarchy' would threaten society as a whole (Zipper, 1986).

The donor was generally seen as a 'dubious figure', an attitude that results in a continuous confusion about the right terminology to indicate the donor. He is alternately called 'the sperm provider' or 'begetter', sometimes 'the biological father' or 'the real father', or even 'the lover that is shrouded in the fog' (Zipper, 1986). The notions about fatherhood were rather foggy.

Questions in parliament in 1957 prompted the Ministers of Justice and of Social Affairs and Health to set up two committees: one of the Health Council (Gezondheidsraad), where physicians had to advise on the health aspects; and a second one, a general governmental committee, that had to advise on policy measures with regard to the conclusions of the medical committee. The general committee finished its report in 1965 (Verveen, 1965). The majority of the committee reached the conclusion that artificial insemination by donor was not to be made a criminal offence, in spite of the fact that this majority had many objections to it. Penal law was not to be extended to artificial insemination and in such cases registration on the birth certificate was not to be considered false (art. 227 Sr WvS), nor punishable as 'obscuration of lineage' (art. 236 WvS). In the opinion of the majority of the committee a prohibition could not prevent the practice of artificial insemination by donor. Quite the contrary; the authority of legislation in general would be undermined by a penal provision that could not be maintained. As the committee clearly recognized, the application of artificial insemination is very simple indeed and they predicted a 'dangerous' situation in which people would turn to quacks (not to mention the possibility of self-insemination). Furthermore, artificial insemination was practised abroad. And, last but not least, women might turn to 'natural insemination' by a man other than the husband. The committee therefore thought it best to let sleeping dogs lie; legislation just might put ideas into the heads of some people.

There are obvious similarities in argument and lines of reasoning between the English Feversham Report on artificial insemination (1960) and the Dutch Verveen Report on the same subject (1965). For example, both reports question whether or not artificial insemination by donor is a form of adultery and thus a ground for divorce, and whether a child begotten by donor insemination thus would be illegitimate. The psychological chapters of both reports are highly speculative about the sexual aberrations which undoubtedly motivate sperm donors, as well as condemning the women who, by demanding children by artificial insemination, force their husbands to agree to a humiliation of his manhood. Both reports state the importance of marriage as a pillar of society and perceive artificial insemination as a threat to marriage and consequently as a threat to society. These similarities notwithstanding, the conclusions of the respective reports have not resulted in identical legislation of artificial insemination in the two countries. In the United Kingdom where the husband of the mother is named as the father on the birth certificate of a child who has been conceived by artificial insemination by donor, an offence has been committed because he who is named as the father is not the begetter (Warnock, 1985, 4.25). Furthermore, since 1949 English men have had the possibility of denying fatherhood within marriage in cases of artificial insemination (Smart, 1987).[6] In the Netherlands a married man also has (since 1837) the possibility of denying the fatherhood of a child born to his wife. In 1970 this possibility was restricted; the law was extended by an amendment that was especially directed at artificial insemination. A man can deny fatherhood within marriage, but not in cases where he has consented to 'an act that may result in the conception of a child' (art. 1:201 BW).[7] The legislator consciously used this formulation to pass over in silence which acts were particularly referred to – both artificial insemination as well as adultery with permission of the husband (Asser, 1978). Once permission for the act is given, the husband has no legal possibility whatsoever to deny paternity afterwards. This means that if a couple with a child born as a result of artificial insemination by donor divorce, the man cannot try to evade paying alimony by claiming he is not the biological father of the child. He has become a father, not by biology but by consent.[8] This again shows the peculiar mixture of biological, social, and legal parenthood in Dutch family law.

The family stood at a point of intersection of psychological and pedagogical theories that emerged in the 1950s. The emotional relationship between wife and husband became important for the functioning of the family. Female sexuality achieved a new role in marriage; the only way to be a good mother was to be an enthusiastic sexual partner (Akkerman, 1982; Wilson, 1980). The emergence of psychological and pedagogical theories also gave a new meaning to fatherhood; fatherhood became important in the education of children, especially with regard to the learning of the 'right' gender identification (Knijn and Mulder, 1987). Fatherhood thus acquired the status of 'pedagogic principle'. These prevailing psychological theories in regard to marital relations, motherhood, femininity, fatherhood, and masculinity were brought up in the debates on artificial insemination.

Contrary to the debates on artificial insemination in the 1950s, the recent debates on reproductive technologies are public debates. In the 1950s the debate took place amongst a small group of lawyers, physicians, and theologians. The mass media, at least in the Netherlands, never wrote about such 'sordid' issues. But although it was not a wide public debate, and we cannot speak of a moral panic, moral fears about the decline of marriage and the family became very clear. Those fears notwithstanding, artificial insemination was ultimately permitted within marriage. It is highly probable that this reform was the result of a particular construction of the wish for a child as well as the dominant family ideology which meant that a family without children is not complete.

After 1965 the question of artificial insemination faded out of politics in the Netherlands, only to emerge halfway through the 1970s. However, the issue then at stake was not so much the reproductive method as such, but the fact that single and/or lesbian women who wanted to become mothers practised artificial insemination. In 1982 artificial insemination again became a subject of Dutch governmental anxiety. The Under Secretary of Health appointed a committee to evaluate reproductive technologies and recommended that artificial insemination was one of the subjects that the committee should look into. As in the 1950s, the legitimacy of the methods and the possibility of regulating them were at stake. In the recent debate some of the old arguments were brought up again; for example, the question of the right to anonymity of the donor *versus* the right of a child to know about its male lineage (D'Adler and Teulade, 1986).[9] The SFJL want to have their cake and eat it; they propose to keep the genetic data of the donor in a central register as well as guaranteeing anonymity. The Health Council rejects mixing of sperm, because this makes it impossible to trace the male lineage. The child and its parents do have a right to knowledge about the genetic identity of the donor, says the report, but not the right to know his personal identity (Gezondheidsraad, 1986).

In the Dutch debate in the 1950s the unlawfulness of 'obscuration of lineage' was stressed, whereas nowadays the supposed right of a child to knowledge about her or his genetic lineage (in the male line) is raised to reject artificial insemination by an anonymous donor. This supposed 'right to knowledge', 'right to know who is the father' in order to 'know who one is', is then linked to a 'right to have' a father (Zipper and Sevenhuijsen, 1987). There is a difference between 'absolute rights' and 'legal rights'. The first functions as a 'statement of principle' and cannot always be translated into the latter, or 'into a set of concrete proposals' (Kingdom, 1985; Leenen, 1980).

The presence of a father, or at least a 'father figure', is seen by some psychologists as essential for the normal, healthy (i.e. heterosexual and heterosocial) development of a child. The other side of the coin is the wish of the donors, and it seems as if they do not care very much for registration. The example of Sweden can be enlightening. The number of available donors rapidly diminished when in March 1985 a law was passed that gave children the right to know the identity of the donor upon reaching the age of 18. Nine out of ten Swedish sperm banks have been closed since (Heida, 1986).

Another debate that is revived is whether or not there is such a thing as a 'right to have children'. In the 1950s involuntarily childless people were directed to the possibilities of adoption or of step-parenthood and they were urged to accept their fate. This was done with an appeal to God. Nowadays acceptance is brought up with an appeal to nature or the necessity to set priorities in the system of health care (Zipper, 1987). In times of economic recession and a restricted health budget, infertility problems are perceived by some as luxury problems. The argument of 'nature' is used by those who advise involuntarily childless people to accept their biological fate as 'given', to resign themselves to this fate, and eventually to adopt (Meer, 1986). But not everyone takes their biological givens of nature for granted. And although some people do resign themselves and/or adopt, others try a less orthodox method for having a child, by what is currently known under the suggestive name 'surrogacy'.

SURROGACY PROBLEMS, OR WHAT IS A MOTHER ANYWAY?

Surrogate motherhood is often mentioned as one of the reproductive technologies, although it does not have to be a technological method at all. As with the creation of other pregnancies, in principle any of the usual methods can be applied. More important than the technologies concerned in particular cases are the relations and arrangements around surrogacy in general (Zipper and Sevenhuijsen, 1987). Cases of surrogacy have given rise to heated debates about the meaning of motherhood. Surrogate motherhood seems to evoke a moral panic and is increasingly becoming a subject of popular fiction, both 'romantic' (Moggach, 1986) and 'horror' (Atwood, 1985; Clark, 1980; Klein, 1980).

In former days it was the filiation on the father's side that was problematic, whereas nowadays the question of who counts as the mother of a child is raised. With the introduction of the possibility of combining *in vitro* fertilization and surrogate motherhood, the definition of the 'real' mother can pose a problem (Heida, 1984; Zipper and Sevenhuijsen, 1987). Fatherhood has been split into biological, legal, and social aspects for a long time. Motherhood, on the other hand, was a monolithic, undivided affair, at least in countries where the *mater semper certa est* rule was applied. The emergence of reproductive technologies enables us to raise legal questions about motherhood that thus far could only be raised about fatherhood. However, because of the ideological differences in the meaning of motherhood and fatherhood, the meaning of this questioning differs. The old rule *mater semper certa est* (the woman of whom the child is born is the mother) suddenly seems outdated.[10] What can be the future consequences for the *mater semper* rule in countries where such a rule currently exists? For example the Dutch professor of family law M. Rood-de Boer proposed to abolish, or at least amend, the *mater semper* rule and introduce a 'presumption' of motherhood as well as a possibility of denying motherhood. She thinks the donation of an ovum is essentially very different from the donation of sperm, and this difference should be reflected in law. That is why she wants the judge to decide who is the mother in cases of so-called full surrogacy (Rood-de Boer, 1984b).

As mentioned above, the question of custody is not a central issue in the debate on reproductive technologies, except when it comes to surrogate motherhood, or rather when surrogacy arrangements go sour. The surrogacy arrangements that have a happy ending seldom get the media coverage received by cases that go wrong.

There was much publicity about Kim Cotton, the first English woman who was known to have a commercial surrogate contract. The child she was bearing was made a ward of court immediately after the delivery. Soon afterwards the commissioning couple were awarded custody of the child (Cotton and Winn, 1985). Alarmed by the publicity and the resulting moral panic, the government reacted immediately. Hasty proposals to prohibit surrogacy were made. In July 1985 the Surrogacy Arrangements Act 1985 became effective. All commercial surrogacy actions in the United Kingdom are forbidden and third parties are not allowed to give information about negotiations for or the entering of surrogacy contracts. However, the law does not protect either the surrogate mother or the commissioning person(s) from taking advantage of one another (Heida, 1987). Furthermore the Act is rather vague on motherhood, while surrogacy in combination with artificial insemination or with ovum donation are not differentiated (Payne, 1987). Although this Act to prohibit commercial surrogacy arrangements may function to deter some people, it cannot stop individual arrangements effectively:[11] quite the contrary, this legislation may just drive the practice of surrogacy underground.

Another English surrogate mother had foreseen the commotion that followed the birth of Kim Cotton's baby and, in order to avoid it and legal and medical interference, Kirsty Stevens (a pseudonym) decided against artificial insemination. Thus the classical method of procreation ('insemination *in vivo*' by sexual intercourse) was used. Both the surrogate mother and the commissioning couple feared that otherwise their identities might be revealed by doctors and that a child would be taken away by the social services (Stevens, 1985; Dally, 1985).[12] Their fear seemed justified, for this was exactly what was threatened with 'Baby Cotton'. More than two years later, however, and in spite of the Surrogacy Arrangements Act 1985, their precautions and the careful way they went about it were rewarded – and complimented – by the judge, who decided that they had not acted against the law. Besides, no profit or financial reward was involved. The surrogate mother had even refused part of the money which she would receive to cover her loss of earnings, because she made money from a book about her experiences. The judge granted the commissioning parents the adoption of the child (*Re an adoption application (surrogacy)* [1987] 2 All ER 826).

There have been several cases where the surrogate mother did not want to give up the child. A French woman became a surrogate mother because it gave her 'warm feelings that women still did things for each other, voluntarily and for love'. The commissioning couple, however, did not give her 'warm feelings' at all; she thought the woman sober, sharp, and cold. As a mother of a child with a handicap, she was particularly offended when the commissioning couple assured her that if the child had a handicap, they would send it to a good institution. After some media appearances in which she was portrayed negatively, she became rather angry. She then realized she had wanted a second child anyway, but as an unmarried woman she would probably have no access to a clinic for artificial insemination. She decided to keep the child: 'I always knew you do not sell your own baby.' She saw it as a kind of revenge on the doctor and on men in general (who never wanted a relationship with her because of her child with the handicap) to keep both the baby and the money (*Viva*, 1986).

An Australian surrogate mother who kept the child had a strong legal case. She was married and, because of the paternal presumption, her husband became the legal father of the child.

Had the child been begotten by insemination *in vivo*, then the aspiring father might have won the case. But according to law in New South Wales, artificial insemination with permission of the husband gives the husband, and not the donor, rights to the child. The question became a conflict of interests between two men, in which the law gave prevalence to the rights of the married man. Had the surrogate mother not been married, it might have ended otherwise.

A very unhappy arrangement for all parties was the case in the United States where the surrogate mother gave birth to a baby with a handicap and the commissioning couple refused to accept it. The commissioning man then appeared on a live television programme and gave the result of blood tests to prove that he was not the begetter. All kind of sordid details were made public. After that an almost endless series of court cases started, in which each party sued the other (Singer and Wells, 1984).

Finally there was the case of Baby M in the United States, a case that made headlines all over the world. Surrogate mother Mary Beth Whitehead, after the birth, decided that she would rather have the child than the money and she 'kidnapped' the child. The commissioning couple, Mrs and Mr Stern, then hired detectives, who found her and the baby. The case became a typical example of classist and sexist law. The question was, who deserves motherhood, which woman is a good, deserving mother, and which woman is a bad mother? Elizabeth Stern was asked why she had postponed having a child. Was this because she put her career first and motherhood second? Mary Beth Whitehead was said by psychologists to be an exploitative mother, married to an alcoholic whom she dominated (Broekhuijsen-Moolenaar, 1987). She was also accused of being narcissistic because she dyed her hair (Chancellor, 1987). (Presumably she would have been accused of an unkempt appearance and of being unfeminine had she not dyed her hair.) The judge decided that the child should go to the Sterns; a contract, he stated, was a contract. Mary Beth Whitehead was not even granted visitation rights – all supposedly in the 'interest of the child'. Immediately after the verdict the judge took Elizabeth Stern to his office and 'performed a record-speed adoption' by which she became the legal mother of Baby M (Levine, 1987). Mary Beth Whitehead appealed to a higher court to try to get the baby back.

In January 1988 the New Jersey Supreme Court declared all surrogacy contracts null and void, because the law prohibits payment for adoption. The adoption of Baby M by Elizabeth Stern was declared to be not legally valid. Mary Beth Whitehead and William Stern then had to negotiate as any divorced couple over visitation rights. Mary Beth Whitehead was granted two hours a week visitation rights. The child stayed with the Sterns, once more the argument of the 'best interests' was brought forward; the court thought the Sterns would offer the child a better future.

Contract law has more weight in the United States than it has in most other western countries, yet in this case contract law was not conclusive. This dismissal of the freedom of contract may be caused by ideological influences of the Moral Majority, a group that is strongly opposed to surrogacy and who 'orchestrated by the New Right', appeals 'to some natural order, predicated on the "naturalness" of traditional family relationships' (David, 1986).

In the Netherlands there have thus far been no law suits over surrogacy. Although it is estimated that there are about fifty cases of surrogacy a year, no cases of commercial surrogacy are known. The dominant opinion is that contracts to bear a child are not valid and therefore not enforceable; if a surrogate mother changes her mind and wants to keep the child, she can. If it comes to a legal case, she will win (although undoubtedly her 'mothering qualities' will be questioned). Furthermore, according to Leenen, a Dutch professor in social medicine and medical law, contracts in which the behaviour of a surrogate mother with regard to, for example, dangerous sport or alcohol, or where medical advice is against pregnancy, would be contrary to art. 11 of the Dutch constitution (*de Volkskrant*, 1987). This article guarantees the integrity of the human body. Roman Catholic theologian M. Christiaens on the other hand argues that there cannot be enough regulations; he wants heavy restrictions to deter people from making any surrogacy arrangement at all (*Trouw*, 1986). In the general cry for regulation, the voice of family law professor Hammerstein-Schoonderwoerd is an exception. She proposes to wait and see what the developments will bring; furthermore, she thinks that social opinions on these issues are changing rapidly (*Trouw*, 1986).

Changes in opinions may, however, depend on an evaluation of experiences. But how should experiences be evaluated, allowing for the difference of particular circumstances? Is it even possible to generalize? Some clinics have follow-up programmes to find out if and how *in vitro* fertilization does affect a child and its parents. Here once again 'experts' will evaluate and appraise, according to unstated norms and values. But there are already some first-hand evaluations. Elizabeth Kane, for example, who in 1980 was one of the first women to make the headlines as a commercial surrogate mother in the United States, now strongly regrets her experience. In 1985 during the wave of publicity about Kim Cotton, Elizabeth Kane was interviewed and said that she had changed her mind on surrogacy, would never again do it herself, and discouraged any other woman from being a surrogate mother. On the other hand there is the story of the two Dutch women, where one woman was a surrogate mother for her involuntarily childless twin sister (Zipper and Sevenhuijsen, 1987). Four years later the women were interviewed once more by a woman's weekly magazine. They did not have a moment's regret; in fact they had a unique rapport with each other and with their brothers-in-law. They see each other and their children daily and have fantasies about a big house where they all can live together. These examples may represent extremes, but they also clarify that there is no one conclusive experience on which legislation could be founded. There may be many more 'cosy' cases of surrogacy which never made the headlines, and there may be surrogate mothers who are sorry and have reached private agreements to keep or see the child. It remains to be seen whether legislation should be founded on individual experiences at all, as no issue offers experiences that are unambiguous enough to serve as a guideline.

TRENDS TOWARDS SUPRANATIONAL REGULATION

Proposals for legislation of reproductive technologies have been made in several western countries (Warnock, 1985; Gezondheids-raad, 1986; Benda-berichte, 1985). Many of these proposals for regulation resemble each other. On a national and international level legislators and their advisors realize that the application of reproductive technologies is not confined to one country. People who want to use one of the technologies are prepared to go abroad if they do not succeed or have access to facilities in their own country. It remains to be seen whether or not national proposals for legislation are mutually exclusive or can reach the intended effect, as for example the English Surrogacy Arrangements Act 1985. Legislation that can be evaded on all sides is not very effective.

It is remarkable that something that is neither new nor necessarily a technique – surrogate motherhood – is the issue which causes the most heated debates. This becomes very clear when we take a look at the proposals for regulation of reproductive technologies by legal reform. In western Europe several official governmental committees have broadly come to the same conclusions, which may have something to do with the influence of the British Warnock Report that served more or less as an example for other committees.

Reproductive technologies were in the first place only to be allowed in cases of infertility due to medical causes. Here involuntary childlessness is defined as a medical problem; it is, however, narrowly defined as a very special medical problem because it appears only people with a marriage certificate can suffer from it – unmarried women 'cannot' have this health problem. The definition of childlessness as a medical problem logically leads to the designation of medical practitioners as the experts *par excellence* in the field (Testart, 1986). In the second place most ethical and governmental committees advise that only married couples be admitted to medical programmes. Some state that heterosexual cohabiting couples can be admitted, too, if stability is scrutinized. (Presumably married couples are stable in and of themselves.) Generally there is consensus on the need of a child for a father and a mother. Artificial insemination or *in vitro* fertilization for single women is therefore disapproved of and dismissed.

Proposals for legislation also include rules on surrogate motherhood. Most committees want it to be completely abolished, but they cannot fail to see that that is impossible. To prevent commercialization flourishing as it does in the United States, most European national committees propose regulating bodies comparable to adoption boards to be set up (Rassaby, 1982). In the United States it has been proposed to set up a Surrogate Court of the Family Court to supervise surrogacy arrangements (Broekhuijsen-Molenaar, 1987). Then there are also supranational bodies that occupy themselves with reproductive technologies. In the light of harmonization of legislation between the states and regulation concerning filiation and custody, the developments in this field are interesting because in 1992 European family law has to be harmonized. The Council of Europe has made some efforts to come to a general proposal for the regulation of reproductive technologies (CAHBI, 1986), but it remains to be seen what the results will be.

In April 1987, immediately after the verdict in the Baby M case in the United States, the Christian Democratic Minister of Health of the Federal Republic of Germany announced that she was preparing a law to prohibit surrogacy contracts, in order to 'protect the dignity of women and children'. The Social Democratic Party (SPD) wholeheartedly agreed with the proposal to outlaw all forms of surrogacy as well as all advertisements for surrogacy. But it seems as if this proposal took some time, because in the autumn of 1987 Noel Keane (the lawyer who set up the first surrogate agency in the United States) assisted some German entrepreneurs to set up a surrogate agency called United Families International in Frankfurt. Here European couples could have an informative discussion about surrogacy before flying to the United States. There they could go to Noel Keane's offices, arrange the surrogacy, adopt the child, and fly back to Europe as the parents of a child. The public presentation of United Families International led to legal debates. A German member of the Green faction of the European Parliament consequently proposed to outlaw surrogate motherhood in Europe, a proposal that was supported by his own as well as the Socialist faction (Noorman, 1987). Following the orders of a German court, in January 1988 Keane's office was closed. The argument for closing the surrogate agency was that its activities were contrary to the German adoptive law, where it is not legally possible to adopt children without the assistance of the state Board of Adoption (*De Waarheid*, 1988). Although the proprietors of the agency had foreseen this and called it an 'information centre' instead, they nevertheless lost their case. Free enterprise goes a long way, but clearly this route is shorter in Europe than it is in the United States.

The application of various reproductive technologies is not limited by national boundaries. For a number of years instances of 'reproductive tourism' have become visible, for example between Spain and the Netherlands. Because it is almost impossible to have an abortion in Spain, Spanish women come to Dutch abortion clinics. On the other hand Dutch women travel to Spain for *in vitro* fertilization services in a private clinic, because Dutch health policy has restricted the number of *in vitro* fertilizations. In some other European countries the policy is less severe and the success rates are significantly higher; therefore many Dutch women go abroad to clinics in Austria and the United Kingdom.

It also needs to be considered whether international legislation on reproductive technologies might be incompatible with other laws. For instance international or even national regulation which excludes single women from medical treatment can be contrary to legislation on discrimination. In the Netherlands, for example, it could be interpreted as an infringement of the constitution; article 1 of the Dutch constitution explicitly prohibits discrimination on grounds of (among other things) marital status. It therefore remains to be seen whether total regulation will ever be possible.

Once again the comparison with abortion comes to mind as an instructive example in the field of reproductive rights. Time and again abortion laws in countries all over the world have been evaded by women in a whole range of ways. In countries where abortion was not permitted, some women could have the same medical treatment (D & C, dilatation and curettage) anyway; it may not have been called abortion, but it had the same effect. Women who could afford to do so went abroad for an abortion. 'Reproductive tourism' is already a reality. In the case of an eventual future European ban on surrogacy or on *in vitro* fertilization (for all women or for single women) the realm of control will still be limited. And the wish for a child will not vanish because of prohibitions or inaccessible treatment (Hampshire, 1984; Holtrop and Scherphuis, 1985). There may come into existence some rather exclusive private clinics – say for example in Casablanca – where rich women undergo a rather mysterious treatment and return pregnant or with a newborn child.

CONCLUDING REMARKS

The connection between custody politics and reproductive technologies becomes clear in the proposals to regulate admission for medical treatment and the arguments that are given for those proposals. It is therefore important to analyse the ways in which marriage and the traditional family are stressed in those proposals. The tendency to stress the importance of the traditional two-parent family is also reflected on another level, in the different proposals for legal reforms by national government committees. Legislation proposals to regulate the employment and practice of reproductive technologies are related to general legislation on motherhood and fatherhood. Given the complexity of the matter and the growing complexity of legal systems in general, legislation and regulation seem an almost impossible task. It is still a long way to effective (supra)national regulation. For the time being, it is interesting and important to consider what is behind the eagerness to regulate. So far an atmosphere of strengthening the ideology of the traditional family can be detected, together with a tendency for the imposition of 'family' regulations where there is no nuclear family. There also is an emphasis on blood ties, as well as the construction of the wish for children as a legitimate wish only in the context of the traditional family. As a result of legislation on reproductive technologies the legal concept of paternity may be extended. The regulation of reproductive technologies could thus become a vehicle for a wider policy on paternity – which could well result in a restriction on the possibilities women have for opting for autonomous motherhood.

There are – so far – no rules explicitly meant for diverse situations and all the possible options. Much will depend on the policy makers in the field of reproductive technologies. This then raises the question of whether feminists will be able and willing to influence legislation on the regulation of reproductive technologies with regard to family law and medicine.

Policy makers and other people who enforce regulations have to deal with complexities that turn all the old certainties upside down. These old certainties dealt with questions about which person has what kind of obligations and rights in relation to a certain child; that is, they dealt with motherhood and fatherhood. As the rights and obligations of women and men as parents differ, the old certainties ultimately deal with sex differences, implying a static dichotomy of femaleness and maleness. An important question is whether future rules are meant to preserve the differences between the sexes that are implicit in the old certainties (Vliet, 1987).

As far as the law is concerned, however, the distinction between the sexes and the definition of women and men can only be founded on reproductive capacities and marital state (O'Donovan, 1985). In law women and men can only be defined as women and men in regard to their reproductive capabilities, in terms of parenthood.[13] In law women are defined as wives and mothers; men are defined as husbands and fathers. The law makes a difference between two classes of persons, between two modes of reproduction. Why is it that someone who delivers a child has different rights and duties from someone who begets a child?

In the political struggle over legal rights concerning parenthood, time and again there is a construction of stereotypes in which images of women are incorporated. In the process of regulation of reproductive methods the construction of yet other female stereotypes becomes visible. Following the worn images of fallen women, sinners, and prostitutes, of castrating divorcees and demanding feminists, we now witness the emergence of two new stereotypes. One is the surrogate mother as both a warm and altruistic person, and a cold and calculating person who sells her child. The other is the image of the good mother as a woman who sees to it that her child has a father.

NOTES

I thank Annick Verbraken for giving me legal information, and the Documentation Department of the Emancipation Council of the Dutch Government was kind enough to let me use their library and archives, for which I am grateful.

1 The label 'reproductive technologies' covers a range of interventions in the reproductive capacities. Both contraceptives and abortion can be counted among them, as well as several ways to get pregnant. There is artificial insemination, with the sperm of a male partner or a donor who may or may not be anonymous (Robinson and Pizer, 1985; Saffron, 1986). Then there are the more sensational treatments for involuntary childlessness such as *in vitro* fertilization and embryo transfer. Technically more complicated are techniques like cloning, cleaving, and genetic engineering. These techniques are not a reality for human reproduction yet and it remains to be seen whether they will ever become everyday practice. None the less it is not surprising that a fictional book on cloning could be presented to the public as an authentic documentary story (Rorvik, 1978). Future possibilities of tampering with the creation of human beings have been the subject of novels and horror stories ever since Mary Shelley wrote *Frankenstein*.

Although the imagination may be fired by sometimes rather frightening fiction, in this chapter only those methods that are already common practice in a number of western countries are discussed.

2 Infertility may indeed affect a woman's self-image. But then a change in self-image and maybe even in character is the result of infertility. Some medical and psy-experts argue from another angle and claim that infertility is 'caused' by character. In their view the woman's self-image is the cause, not a result.

3 The same article 8 of the European Declaration of Human Rights however is used in the Federal Republic of Germany to state the right of a child that is conceived by artificial insemination by donor to know the name of the donor.

4 See for example *Artificial Human Insemination* (Archbishop of Canterbury 1948) and the report of the Roman Catholic committee *Kunstmatige inseminatie bij de mens. Wenselijkheid en wettelijke maatregelen* (Petit, 1961). However, the debates in the Netherlands lagged some years behind those in the United Kingdom. For that matter it looks as if history repeats itself; the Warnock Report was presented in 1984, whereas the Report of the Health Council (Gezondheidsraad) was presented in the autumn of 1986.

5 The number of committees can be explained by a typical Dutch political feature – pillarization (see Lijphart, 1968).

6 West German married men also have the legal possibility to deny fatherhood even after they have consented to artificial insemination by donor (Coester-Waltjen, 1983).

7 Furthermore, Dutch legislation concerning the practice of medicine was extended with a provision that made the practice of artificial insemination a medical act. This was done to prevent quacks, as well as self-insemination, both in order to keep artificial insemination under control. Self-insemination is therefore a form of breaking the law in the Netherlands. But as long as insemination *in vivo* by sexual intercourse cannot be controlled, this consequence of the law is of no importance whatsoever.

8 Adoption is another way to become a father by consent, but then this is clear from the birth certificate.

9 The supposed right of a child to knowledge about lineage is increasingly given more weight by the doctors involved, because of a new interest in medical records and hereditary diseases. Medical arguments are a point of impact in the debate; they pretend to give reasons for renewed surveillance. Moral panics about diseases are used as a focal point of old concerns.

10 The only exception to the rule were women who became mothers by adoption, but again this is to be found on the birth certificate of the child. The *mater semper certa est* rule was introduced in Dutch civil law in 1947.

11 A way around the law was found immediately. There is no contract

for surrogacy and the 'production' of a baby, but for the production of a manuscript for a book. The surrogate mother has to keep a diary about her experiences during pregnancy. As it is perfectly legal to pay an author for her literary work, this seems an effective trick. (Information from Women's Reproductive Rights Information Centre, London.)

12 To circumvent problems about adoption, 'Kirsty Stevens' told the doctors that she became pregnant after an affair with a married man who was opposed to abortion but who wished to adopt the child with his wife. On the birth certificate are her name and the name of the begetter of the child (Dally, 1985; Stevens, 1985).

13 This becomes very clear when we take a look at legislation on changes of gender. A trans-sexual person can only legally change her/his sex and name on the birth certificate in Dutch civil law after sex change treatment, when s/he no longer can reproduce her/himself in any way. Otherwise it would be possible for a former woman who is changed into a man to become a mother, a male mother, or for a former man who is changed to a woman to become a female father. Obviously the legislator cannot handle that kind of confusion. Feminists – who have been known to want changes in mothering, fathering, and rigid gender roles – on the other hand might see possibilities.

BIBLIOGRAPHY

Abella, R. S. (1981) 'Family law in Ontario: changing assumptions', *Ottawa Law Review*, vol. 13, no. 1, pp. 1–22.

Akkerman, T. (1982) 'Moeder en minnares. Vrouwbeelden in de ideologie van de NVSH in de jaren vijftig', *Tijdschrift voor Vrouwenstudies*, vol. 12, no. 34, pp. 450–71.

Allen, J. (1985) 'Desperately seeking solutions: changing battered women's options since 1880', in Hatty, S. (ed.) *National Conference on Domestic Violence*, vol. 1, Australian Institute of Criminology, Canberra.

Anders Geregeld (1978) *Tweede Kamer*, no. 15, 401, Den Haag, Staatsuitgeverij.

Anon (1980) 'Lesbian custody: a personal account', *Refractory Girl*, no. 21, pp. 1–6.

Archbishop of Canterbury (1948) *Artificial Human Insemination: The Report of a Commission Appointed by His Grace the Archbishop of Canterbury*, London, SPCK.

Areen, J. (1985) *Teachers' Manual* to accompany *Cases and Materials on Family Law*, 2nd edition, Mineola, New York, Foundation Press.

Ariès, P. H. (1975) *L'enfant et la vie familiale sous l'ançien régime*, 3eme ed., Paris, Seuil.

Armstrong, P. and Armstrong, H. (1984) *The Double Ghetto: Canadian Women and Their Segregated Work*, Toronto, McClelland & Stewart.

Arnup, K. (1984) 'Lesbian mothers and child custody', *Atkinson Review of Canadian Studies*, vol. 1, no. 2, pp. 35–40.

Asser, C. (1957) *Handleiding tot de beoefening van het Nederlands Burgerlijk Recht*, Part 1, 9th printing, revised by J Wiarda, Zwolle, Tjeenk Willink.

Asser, C. (1978) *Handleiding tot de beoefening van het Nederlands Burgerlijk Recht*, Part 1, Personenrecht, eleventh printing, edited by J. de Ruiter, Zwolle, Tjeenk Willink.

Atwood, M. (1985) *The Handmaid's Tale*, Toronto, McClelland & Stewart.

Australian Institute of Family Studies (AIFS) (1986) *Setting Up: Property and Income Distribution on Divorce in Australia*, Melbourne, Prentice-Hall.

Australian Law Reform Commission (1986) *Transcripts of Proceedings, Public Hearings on the Law of Contempt.*

Australian Law Reform Commission (1987a) *Contempt,* Report no. 35, Canberra: Australian Government Publishing Service.

Australian Law Reform Commission (1987b) *Matrimonial Property Law*, Report no. 39, Canberra: Australian Government Publishing Service.

Australian Senate (1987) *Parliamentary Debates*, 20 October, p. 959.

Backhouse, C. B. (1981) 'Shifting patterns in nineteenth-century Canadian custody law', in Flaherty, D. H. (ed.) *Essays in the History of Canadian Law,* vol. 1, Toronto, The Osgoode Society, pp. 212–48.

Badinter, E. (1981) *The Myth of Motherhood*, London, Souvenir Press.

Bahr-Jendges, J. and Bubenik-Bauer (1984) 'Die neue Zeit im Gewand der Mutterlickkeit, Familie und Familienpolitiek in der Bundesrepublik Deutschland', in Haarbusch, Elke (ed.) *Diskurs, Bremer Beitrage zu Wissenschaft und Gessellschaft,* Bremen: Universität Bremen.

Baker, M. (1985) *What Will Tomorrow Bring? ... A Study of the Aspirations of Adolescent Women*, Ottawa, Canadian Advisory Council for the Status of Women.

Baldock, C. and Cass, B. (eds) (1983) *Women, Social Welfare and the State*, Sydney, Allen & Unwin.

Bankier, J. K. (1985) 'Equality, affirmative action, and the Charter: reconciling "inconsistent" sections', *Canadian Journal of Women and the Law,* vol. 1, pp. 134–52.

Barrett, M. and McIntosh, M. (1982) *The Anti-Social Family*, London, Verso.

Bartlett, K. T. and Stack, C. B. (1986) 'Joint custody, feminism and the dependency dilemma', *Berkeley Women's Law Journal*, vol. 2, pp. 9–41.

Bates, F. (1986) 'Australia: the beginnings of a new phase', *Journal of Family Law*, vol. 25, pp. 3–18.

Benda-berichte (1985) *In-Vitro-Fertilisation, Genomanalyse und Genthe-rapie,* Bonn, Bundesministerium für Forschung und Technologie.

Benians, R., Berry, T., Coolins, D., and Johnson, P. (1983) *Children and Family Breakdown, Custody and Access Guidelines: The Need for New Approach*, London, Families Need Fathers.

Berkovits, B. (1980) 'Towards a reappraisal of family law', *Family Law,* vol. 10, no. 6, pp. 164–72.

Boigeol, A. and Commaille, J. (1978) 'Divorce, milieu social et situation de la femme', *Economie et Statistique,* vol. 53, pp. 3–21.

Booth, Mrs Justice (1983) *Committee on Matrimonial Causes Procedure*, Consultative Paper, London, Lord Chancellor's Department.

Booth, Mrs Justice (1985) *Report on the Committee on Matrimonial Procedures,* London, HMSO.

Bottomley, A. (1984) 'Resolving family disputes: a critical view', in Freeman, M. D. A. (ed.) *State, Law and the Family: Critical Perspectives*, London, Tavistock.

Boyd, S. B. (1987) 'Child custody and working mothers', in Martin and Mahoney (1987).

Boyd, S. B. (forthcoming) 'Child custody, ideologies and female employment', *Canadian Journal of Women and the Law*, vol. 3 (1).

Boyle, C. (1985) 'Sexual assault and the feminist judge', *Canadian Journal of Women and the Law*, vol. 1, pp. 93–107.

Broekhuijsen-Moolenaar, A. M. L. (1987) 'Draagmoederschap in Amerika: De zaak "Baby M" in de staat New Jersey en aanbevelingen voor een wetsvoorstel in de staat New York', *Nederlands Juristenblad*, vol. 28, pp. 887–91.

Broom, D. H. (ed.) (1984) *Unfinished Business*, Sydney, Allen & Unwin.

Brophy, J. (1982) 'Parental rights and children's welfare: some problems of feminists' strategy in the 1920s', *International Journal of the Sociology of Law*, vol. 10, no. 2, pp. 149–68.

Brophy, J. (1985) 'Child care and the growth of power: the status of mothers in custody disputes', in Brophy and Smart (1985).

Brophy, J. (1987a) 'State and the Family: The Politics of Child Custody', PhD Thesis, Department of Law, University of Sheffield.

Brophy, J. (1987b) *Co-parenting and the Limits of 'Law': Divorce and Parenthood in the 1990s*, Response to the Law Commission Working Paper no. 96, London, Rights of Women.

Brophy, J. and Smart, C. (1981) 'From disregard to disrepute: the position of women in family law', *Feminist Review*, vol. 9, pp. 3–16.

Brophy, J. and Smart, C. (eds) (1985) *Women in Law: Explorations in Law, Family and Sexuality*, Routledge & Kegan Paul, London.

Brown, C. (1981) 'Mothers, fathers and children: From private to public patriarchy', in Sargent, L. (ed.), *Women and Revolution: A Discussion of the Unhappy Marriage of Marxism and Feminism*, Montreal, Black Rose Books.

Bruch, C. (1978) 'Making visitation work: dual parenting orders', *Family Advocate*, vol. 1, no. 1.

Bryson, L. (1983) 'Women as welfare recipients. Women, poverty and the state', in Baldock and Cass (1983).

Bryson, L. (1985) 'Sharing the caring: overcoming barriers to gender equality', *Australian Quarterly*, vol. 57, p. 300.

Buckley, J. F. and O'Mahoney, M. V. (1982) 'Recognition of foreign divorces: a further gloss', *Incorporated Law Society of Ireland Gazette*, vol. 76 (8), pp. 211–12.

Bunreacht na h-Eireann (1937) Stationery Office, Dublin.

Burton, C. (1987) 'Equal pay: a comment', *Australian Feminist Studies*, vol. 4, pp. 107–13.

Burton, C. Hag, G. and Thompson, G. (1987) *Women's Worth: Pay Equity and Job Evaluation in Australia*, Canberra, Australian Government Publishing Services.

Cabinet Sub-Committee on Maintenance (1986) *Child Support: A Discussion Paper on Child Maintenance*, Canberra, Australian Government Publishing Services.

CAHBI (1986) Council of Europe, Ad Hoc Committee of Experts on Progress in the Biomedical Sciences, *Provisional Principles on the Techniques of Human Artificial Procreation*, Strasbourg, CE.

Carbonnier, J. (1962) 'Note sous TGI Versailles', 24 September, *Dalloz*, 1962, p. 54.

Centraal Bureau der Statistiek (1987) *Statistisch Zakboek 1987*, den Haag, SDU/Staatsuitgeverij.

Chambers, D. L. (1979) *Making Fathers Pay*, Chicago, University of Chicago Press.

Chambers, D. L. (1984) 'Rethinking the substantive rules for custody disputes in divorce', *Michigan Law Review*, vol. 83, pp. 477–569.

Chancellor, A. (1987) 'Ethics of second place as "Baby M" hearing ends', the *Independent*, 13 March.

Chauviere, M. (1982) 'L' introuvable intéret de l'enfance', in *Le Droit Face Aux Politiques Familiales*, actes du colloque du 30.1.82 Laboratoire d'analyse critique des pratiques juridiques, Université Paris VII (Ronéo), pp. 53–63.

Chesler, P. (1986) *Mothers on Trial: The Battle for Children and Custody*, New York, McGraw-Hill.

Chisholm, R. (ed.) (1987) *Australian Family Law*, Butterworths, Sydney.

Chisholm, R. and Jessep, O. (1985) 'Sir Harry Gibbs and the Family Court', *Australian Family Lawyer*, 1 November.

Christiaens, M. (1986) 'Ouders wensen kinderen wensen ouders', in Kirkels, V. G. H. J. (ed.) *Verslag Studiedag Recht op een Kind? Ethiek, geloof en praktijk*, Nijmegen, Medische Afdeling Thijmgenootschap.

Christie, G. L. (1980) 'The psychological and social management of the infertile couple', in Pepperell, R. J., Hudson, B. and Wood, C. (eds), *The Infertile Couple*, Edinburgh, Churchill Livingstone.

Clark, D. (1987) *Australian Financial Review*, 12 January, article.

Clark, M. H. (1980) *The Cradle Will Fall*, Glasgow, William Collins.

Coester-Waltjen, D. (1983) 'Die Vaterschaft für ein durch künstlichen Insemination gezeugtes Kind', *Neue Juristische Wochenschrift*, vol. 36, no. 37, pp. 2073–81.

Cohen, B. and Clarke, K. (eds) (1987) *Childcare and Equal Opportunities: Some Policy Perspectives*, Equal Opportunities Commission, London, HMSO.

Commaille, J. (1982) *Familles sans justice?*, Paris, Le Centurion.

Cotton, K. and Winn, D. (1985) *For Love and Money*, London, The *Daily Star*/ABC Press.

Cox, E. (1983) 'Beyond community of property: a plea for equality', *Australian Journal of Social Issues*, vol. 18, pp. 142–6.

Cox, E. (1985) 'Matrimonial property scuttled', *Legal Service Bulletin*, vol. 10, pp. 192–4.

Cox, E. (1987) Paper (untitled) delivered at Human Rights Congress, 25–8 September, Sydney.

Cretney, S. M. (1984) *Principles of Family Law*, London, Sweet & Maxwell.

Currie, D. (forthcoming) 'State intervention and the "liberation" of women: a feminist exploration of family law', in Caputo, T. and Reasons, C. (eds) *Law and Society*, Toronto, Harcourt Brace Jovanovich.

D'Adler, M. A. and Teulade, M. (1986) *Les sorciers de la vie*, Paris, Galimard.

Dahl, T. S. (1987) *Women's Law: An Introduction to Feminist Jurisprudence*, Oslo, Norwegian University Press.

Dally, E. (1985) 'The story of a surrogate mother', the *Observer*, 13 January.

Dam, G. Ten and Wegelin, M. (1984) 'Omgangsrecht en de ideologische konstruktie van het vaderschap', *Psychologie en Maatschappij*, vol. 8, no. 1, pp. 32-48.

David, M. (1986) 'Moral and maternal: the family in the Right', in R. Levitas (ed.), *The Ideology of the New Right*, Oxford, Polity Press.

David, M. and New, C. (1987) 'Feminist perspectives on childcare policy', in Cohen and Clarke (1987).

Davin, A. (1978) 'Imperialism and motherhood', *History Workshop Journal*, no. 5, pp. 9-65.

Davis, G., Macleod, A. and Murch, A. (1983) 'Undefended divorce: should s.41 of the Matrimonial Causes Act 1978 be repealed?', *Modern Law Journal*, vol. 46, no. 2, pp. 121-46.

Davis, K. (1987) 'The Janus-face of power', paper presented at the symposium 'The Gender of Power', Leiden, 24-5 September 1987.

Davis, P. C. (1987) '"There is a book out..." An analysis of judicial absorption of legislative facts', *Harvard Law Review*, vol. 100, pp. 1,539-1,604.

Day, S. (1985) 'The Charter and family law', in Sloss, E. (ed.) *Family Law in Canada: New Directions*, Ottawa, Canadian Advisory Council on the Status of Women.

De Hondt, I. and Holtrust, N. (1985) 'Kunstmatig bevruchting. De invloed van de vierde macht', *Nemesis*, vol. 2, no. 2, pp. 72-3.

De Hondt, I. and Holtrust, N. (1986a) 'Draagmoederschap: Morele paniek waarover?', *Nemesis*, vol. 2, no. 3, pp. 117-19.

De Hondt, I. and Holtrust, N. (1986b) 'The European Convention and the Marckx-Judgement effect', *International Journal of the Sociology of Law*, vol. 14, no. 3/4, pp. 317-28.

De Jong, G. T., (1981) 'Voetje voor voetje', *Nederlands Juristenblad*, vol. 56, no. 34, pp. 817-907.

De Langen, M. (1982) 'Gezamenlijk ouderlijk gezag voor ongehuwden', in *Nederlands Juristenblad*, vol. 57, no. 42, pp. 1,135-6.

De Vries, A. D. W. and Van Tricht, F. J. G. (1903) *Geschiedenis der wet op de ouderlijke macht en de voogdij*, Part 1, Groningen, J. B. Wolters.

Delphy, C. (1974) 'Marriage et divorce, l'impasse à double face', *Les Temps Modernes*, no. 333-4, pp. 1,815-29.

Denning, Mr Justice (1947) *Report of the Committee on Procedure in Matrimonial Causes*, Cmnd 7,024, London, HMSO.

Department of Social Security (1987) *Annual Report: 1986-1987*,

Canberra, Australian Government Publishing Services.

Dhavernas, O. (1978) *Droits des femmes, pouvoir des hommes*, Paris, Seuil.

Dickey, A. (1985) *Family Law*, Sydney, Law Book Company.

Dijkstra, T. and Swiebel, J. (1982) 'De overheid en het vrouwenvraagstuk: emancipatiebeleid als mode en taboe', in S. Sevenhuijsen *et al.* (eds) *Socialisties-Feministiese Teksten*, vol. 7, pp. 42-64.

Dodds, M. (1983) 'Children and divorce', *Journal of Social Welfare Law*, July, pp. 228-37.

Doek, J. E. (1985) 'Een schok in het familie – en jeugdrecht: iets over de scheuren en de barsten', *Nederlands Juristenblad*, vol. 60, no. 7, pp. 213-17.

Donzelot, J. (1977) *La police des familles*, Paris, Minuit.

Donzelot, J. (1980) *The Policing of Families*, London, Hutchinson.

Drian, R. (1962) 'The rights of children in modern American family law', *Journal of Family Law*, vol. 2, 101-9.

Duncan, W. R. (1978) 'Second marriage after church annulments: a problem of legal policy', *Incorporated Law Society of Ireland Gazette*, vol. 77, no. 6, pp. 165-6.

Earle, J. and Graycar, R. (1987) 'A new dependence?', *Australian Society*, February, pp. 37-8.

Earle, J. and Jacobs, L. (producers) (1987) 'Men as fathers: care or control?', 'Coming Out Show', ABC National Radio, Australian Women's Broadcasting Co-operative, 21 February.

Edelman, M. (1974) 'The political language of the helping professions', *Politics and Society*, vol. 4 (3), 295-310.

Edgar, D. (1986) *Marriage, the Family and Family Law In Australia*, Discussion Paper no. 13, Australian Institute of Family Studies, Melbourne.

Eekelaar, J. (1984) *Family Law and Social Policy*, 2nd edition, London, Weidenfeld & Nicolson.

Eekelaar, J. and Clive, E., with Clark, K. and Raikes, S. (1977) *Custody After Divorce*, Oxford, Centre for Sociolegal Studies, Wolfson College.

Eekelaar, J. and Maclean, M. (1982) *Children and Divorce: The Economic Factors*, Oxford, Centre for Sociolegal Studies, Wolfson College.

Ehrenreich, B. (1983) *The Hearts of Men*, London, Pluto.

Eisenstein, Z. (1983) 'The state, the patriarchal family and working mothers', in Irene Diamond (ed.) *Families, Politics and Public Policy: A Feminist Dialogue on Women and the State*, New York, Longman.

Elkin, M. (1987) 'Joint custody: affirming that parents and families are forever', *Social Work*, January, pp. 18-24.

Ellis-Jones, A. (1986) *Focus on Family: Towards a Coherent Family Policy*, London, Bow Group.

Elster, J. (1987) 'Solomonic judgements', *The University of Chicago Law Review*, vol. 54, no. 1, pp. 1-45.

Elzinga, W. (1984) 'Note on Supreme Court decision May 4, 1984', *Nederlands Juristen Comite Mensenrechten-bulletin*, vol. 9, no. 5, pp. 357-61.

Equal Opportunities Commission (1986) *Legislating for Change: Review of the Sex Discrimination Legislation*, Consultative Document, London, HMSO.

Equal Opportunities Commission (1988) *Equal Treatment for Men and Women: Strengthening the Acts*, Formal Proposals, London, HMSO.

Family Law Council (1987) *Access – Some Options for Reform*, Canberra, Australian Government Publishing Services.

Feminist Legal Issues Group (NSW) (1986) *Submission to Cabinet Sub-Committee on Maintenance*.

Feversham, Earl of (1960) *Report of the Departmental Committee on Human Artificial Insemination*, Cmnd 1,105, London, HMSO.

Fineman, M. (1980) 'Beginnings and endings: the effect of the law on forms and consequences of family relations', in Nickols, S. and Engelbrecht, J. (eds) *Challenges of the 80s: Families Face the Future*, Proceedings of the Fourth Annual Conference of the Family Study Center, Stillwater, Oklahoma State University.

Fineman, M. (1983) 'Implementing equality: ideology, contradiction and social change. A study of rhetoric and results in the regulation of the consequences of divorce', *Wisconsin Law Review*, vol. 1983, no. 4, pp. 789–886.

Fineman, M. (1986) 'Illusive equality: on Weitzman's divorce revolution', *American Bar Foundation Research Journal*, vol. 4, pp. 781–90.

Fineman, M. (1987) 'Dominant Discourse: the Professional Appropriation of Child Custody Decision-Making', *Working Paper* 2:7, Institute for Legal Studies, University of Wisconsin, Madison Law School.

Fineman, M. (1988) 'Dominant discourse, professional language and legal change', *Harvard Law Review*, vol. 101, no. 4, pp. 727–74.

Fineman, M. and Opie, A. (1987) 'The uses of social science data in legal policymaking: custody determinations at divorce', *Wisconsin Law Review*, vol. 1987, no. 1, pp. 107–58.

Finger, P. (1983) 'Die Beëndigung der Amtsplegschaft des Jugendamtes nach par. 1707 BGB', *Zeitschrift fur das gesamte Familienrecht*, vol. 30, no. 2, pp. 429–33.

Finlay, H. A. (1983) *Family Law in Australia*, Sydney, Butterworths.

Folberg, J. (ed.) (1984) *Joint Custody and Shared Parenting*, Washington, DC: Bureau of National Affairs.

Foster, H. and Freed, D. (1972) 'Bill of rights for children', *Family Law Quarterly*, vol. 6, 343–75.

Foucault, M. (1976) *Histoire de la sexualité I, La volonté de savoir*, Paris, Gallimard.

Freeman, M. D. A. (1983) *The Rights and Wrongs of Children*, London, Frances Pinter.

Gallagher, J. (1987) 'Prenatal invasions and interpretations: What's wrong with fetal rights?', *Harvard Women's Law Journal*, vol. 10, Spring, pp. 9–58.

Game, A. and Pringle, R. (1984) 'Production and consumption', in Broom (1984).

Gavigan, S. A. M. (1986a) 'On "bringing on the menses": the criminal liability of women and the therapeutic exception in Canadian abortion law', *Canadian Journal of Women and the Law*, vol. 1, no. 2, p. 279.

Gavigan, S. A. M. (1986b) 'Women, law and patriarchal relations: perspectives within the sociology of law', in Boyd, N. (ed.) *The Social Dimensions of Law*, Scarborough, Prentice-Hall Canada.

Gavigan, S. A. M. (1988) 'Law, gender and ideology', in Bayefsky, A. (ed.) *Legal Theory Meets Legal Practice*, Edmonton, Academic Printing and Publishing, pp. 283-95.

Germane, C., Johnson, M. and Lemon, N. (1985) 'Mandatory custody mediation and joint custody orders in California: the danger for victims of domestic violence', *Berkeley Women's Law Journal*, vol. 1, pp. 175-200.

Gezondheidsraad (1986) *Advies inzake kunstmatige voortplanting*, Den Haag, Gezondheidsraad.

Gibson, C. (1982) 'Maintenance in the magistrates' courts in 1980', *Family Law*, vol. 12, no. 6, pp. 138-41.

Girdner, L. (1986) 'Child custody determination: ideological dimensions of a social problem', in Seidmand, E. and Rappaport, J. (eds) *Redefining Social Problems*, New York, Plenum.

Gisolf, R. C. and Blankman, K. (1980) 'Scheidingen in cijfers', *Tijdschrift voor Familie- en Jeugdrecht*, vol. 2, no. 2, pp. 37-47.

Glendinning, C. and Millar, J. (eds) (1987) *Women and Poverty in Britain*, Brighton, Wheatsheaf.

Goldstein, J., Freud, A. and Solnit, A. J. (1973) *Beyond the Best Interests of the Child*, New York, Free Press.

Goldstein, J., Freud, A. and Solnit, A. J. (1979) *Before the Best Interests of the Child*, New York, Free Press.

Goldstein, J., Freud, A. and Solnit, A. J. (1980) *Retten til barnet – eller barnets rett?*, Universitetsforlaget, Oslo (Norwegian translation of Goldstein *et al* (1973)).

Goode, W. J. (1965) *Women in Divorce*, New York, Free Press.

Goode, W. J. (1982) 'Why men resist', in Thorne, B. and Yalom, M. (eds) *Rethinking the Family; Some Feminist Questions*, New York/London, Longman.

Gordon, C. (1980) *Michel Foucault: Power/Knowledge*, Brighton, Harvester Press.

Graycar, R. (1985a) 'Compensation for loss of capacity to work in the home', *Sydney Law Review*, vol. 10, pp. 528-67.

Graycar, R. (1985b) 'Hoovering as a hobby: the common law's approach to work in the home', *Refractory Girl*, vol. 28, pp. 22-6.

Graycar, R. (1987a) 'Social security and personal income taxation', in Graycar and Shiff (1987).

Graycar, R. (1987b) 'Towards a feminist position on maintenance', *Refractory Girl*, vol. 30, pp. 7-11.

Graycar, R. and Shiff, D. (eds) (1987) *Life Without Marriage: A Woman's Guide to the Law*, Sydney, Pluto Press.

Green, M. (1976) *Goodbye Father*, London, Routledge & Kegan Paul.

Green, D. (1987) *The New Right*, Brighton, Wheatsheaf.

Green, V. and Gurr, R. (1987) 'A marriage of inconvenience? The media and the Family Court of Australia', *Legal Service Bulletin*, vol. 12, p. 243.

Greif, J. (1979) 'Fathers, children and joint custody', *American Journal of Orthopsychiatry*, vol. 49, pp. 311-19.

Grossbard, M. (1982) 'Fathers or mothers? The disputed custody case', *New Law Journal* (May), pp. 518-19.

Grossberg, M. (1983) 'Who gets the child? Custody, guardianship, and the rise of a judicial patriarchy in nineteenth-century America', *Feminist Studies*, vol. 9, no. 2, pp. 235-60.

Grossberg, M. (1985) *Governing the Hearth*, Chapel Hill, The University of North Carolina Press.

Guardian, the (1987) 'Man fails in final attempt to halt abortion', 'Life in a gown'; 'Painful but needed legal clarification', 25 February.

Gulbrandsen, L. and Hoel, M. (1986) *Morske kvinners yrkesdeltakelse pa 80-tallet*, INAS-rapport 86:7, Oslo (with English summary).

Guthrie, B. and Kingshott, M. (1987) 'Child care', in Graycar and Shiff (1987).

Hammerstein-Schoonderwoerd, W. C. E. (1982) 'Het onwettige kind', *Nederlands Juristenblad*, vol 57, no. 24, pp. 704-7.

Hammerstein-Schoonderwoerd, W. C. E. (1984) 'Ouderlijk gezag en echtscheiding', *Weekblad voor Privaatrecht, Notarisambt en Registratie*, vol. 115, no. 5,715, pp. 621-5.

Hammerstein-Schoonderwoerd, W. C. E., Mourik, M. van, and Robert, W. (eds) (1986) *Bijzondere wijzen van voortplanting, draagmoederschap en de juridische problematiek*, Zwolle, Tjeenk Willink.

Hampshire, S. (1984) *The Maternal Instinct*, London, Sidgwick & Jackson.

Hansen, R. (1966) 'The role and rights of children in divorce actions', *Journal of Family Law*, vol. 6 (1), 1-14.

Harrison, K. (1980) 'Child custody and parental sexuality', *Refractory Girl*, vol. 21, pp. 7-14.

Heida, A. (1984) 'Juridische perikelen rond draagmoederschap', *Weekblad voor Privaatrecht, Notariaat en Registratie*, vol. 5,716, no. 115, pp. 649-53.

Heida, A. (1986) 'Reageerbuisbevruchting, een taak voor de wetgever?', *Nederlands Juristenblad*, no. 25, pp. 769-72.

Heida, A. (1987) 'De Engelse wet betreffende draagmoederregelingen (Surrogacy Arrangements Act 1985)', *Nederlands Juristenblad*, pp. 12-14.

Henwood, M., Rimmer, L. and Wicks, M. (1987) *Inside the Family*, Ocassional Paper no. 6, London, Family Policy Studies Centre.

Heron, A. (1987) 'Child support – making fathers pay?', *Legal Service Bulletin*, vol. 12, p. 17.

Herziening van het Afstammingsrecht (1981) Draft Bill, Den Haag, Ministry of Justice.

Hijmans, A. (1958) 'Kunstmatige inseminatie bij de mens; een protestants-christelijke visie', *Socialisme en Democratie*, July, pp. 439-50.

Holtrop, A. and Scherphuis, A. (1985) 'In-vitro fertilisatie; naar Wenen voor een "reageerbuisbaby"', *Vrij Nederland*, 8 December, pp. 18–19.

Holtrust, N. (1986) 'Draagmoeders en wensvaders', *Nederlands Juristenblad*, no. 24, pp. 774-7

Holtrust, N. and De Hondt, W. A. (1987) *Bewust Ongehuwd Moeder*, Baarn, AMBO.

Holtrust, N. and Sevenhuijsen, S. L. (1986) 'Het nieuwe wetsvoorstel omgangsrecht', *Nederlands Juristenblad*, vol. 61, no. 18, pp. 545-9.

Horwill, F. and Bordow, S. (1983) *The Outcome of Defended Custody Cases in the Family Court of Australia*, Research Report no. 4, Family Court of Australia.

Howe, B. (1987) 'Reforms to child support', Ministerial Statement to Parliament, House of Representatives, 24 March, pp. 1,368–1,370.

Hunt, A. (1985) 'The ideology of law: advances and problems in recent applications of the concept of ideology to the analysis of law', *Law and Society Review*, vol. 19, no. 1, pp. 11–37.

Ietswaart, H. (1980) *Delegalization and the Family. A Review of Current American Literature*, SCR Ministère de la justice (ronéo), Paris.

Innes, J. (1986) 'Equal pay and the Sex Discrimination Act', *Legal Service Bulletin*, vol. 11, pp. 254-8.

Irving, H. H. and Benjamin, M. (1987) *Family Mediation: Theory and Practice of Dispute Resolution*, Toronto, Carswell.

Jansen, I. (1985) 'Over afstamming en ouderrechten', *Nederlands Juristenblad*, vol. 60, no. 7, pp. 207-13.

Jessep, O. and Chisholm, R. (1985) 'Children, the constitution and the Family Court', *University of NSW Law Journal*, vol. 8, pp. 152-82.

Johnson, C. and Wajcman, J. (1986) Comment on 'A comparative analysis of equal pay in the US, Britain and America', *Australian Feminist Studies*, vol. 3, pp. 91-5.

Joshi, H. (1985) *The Price of Parenting*, London, Centre for Population Studies.

Joshi, H. (1987) 'The cost of caring', in Glendinning and Millar (1987).

Jowell, R. and Witherspoon, S. (eds) (1985) *British Social Attitudes, The 1985 Report*, London, Gower.

Kelly, J. B. (1984) 'Post-divorce parent–child relationship: the effect of mediation on parental attitudes and visitation plans', in *Parent–Child Relationship Post-Divorce. A Seminar Report*, The Danish Institute of Social Research, Copenhagen, pp. 198-215.

Kemeter, P. *et al.* (1985) 'Psychosocial testing and pretreatment of women for in vitro fertilization', in Sepällä, M. and Edwards, R. G. (eds) *In Vitro Fertilization and Embryo Transfer*, Annals of the New York Academy of Science, vol. 442, pp. 523-32.

Kingdom, E. (1985) 'Legal recognition of a woman's right to choose', in Brophy and Smart (1985).

Klein, D. M. (1980) *Embryo*, New York, Doubleday.

Klein, S. S. (1985) 'Individualism, liberalism and the new family law', *University of Toronto Faculty Law Review*, vol. 43, pp. 116-35.

Knijn, T. and Mulder, A. C. (1987) *Unravelling Fatherhood*, Dordrecht/ Providence, USA, Foris Publications.

Komité Vrouwen en Familierecht (1982) 'De strijd om het omgangsrecht', in Anet Bleich (ed.) *Feminisme en politieke macht*, Part 1, Amsterdam, De Populier, pp. 87–95.

Lamb, L. (1987) 'Involuntary joint custody', *Horizons*, vol. 5, (1), pp. 20–3.

Law Commission (1986) *Family Law Review of Child Law: Child Custody*, Working Paper no. 96, London, HMSO.

Law Commission (1988) *Family Law Review of Child Law: Guardianship and Custody*, Law Commission no. 172, London, HMSO.

Leenen, H. J. J. (1980) 'Problemen rond het recht op informatie en het recht op geheim; over botsing van rechten', *Tijdschrift voor Gezondheidsrecht*, July/August, pp. 207–13.

Lees, S. (1972) 'Custody without care', *New Society*, June, vol. 6, p. 72.

Le Guidec, R. (1973) 'L'intéret de l'enfant en droit civil français', Thèse de doctorat en droit, Universite de Nantes, France.

Lehmann, G. (1983) 'The case for joint custody', *Quadrant*, vol. 27 (6), pp. 60–6.

Lettington, B. (1983) 'The fatherhood crisis', *Newsletter*, Winter, London, Families Need Fathers.

Levine, J. (1987) 'Motherhood is powerless. How the Baby M decision screws women', *The Village Voice*, vol. XXXII, no. 15, April, pp. 15–16.

Levy, R. (1985) 'Custody investigations in divorce cases', *American Bar Foundation Research Journal*, vol. 1985, 4; pp. 713–97.

Lewis, C. and O'Brien, M. (eds) (1987) *Reassessing Fatherhood*, London, Sage.

Lijphart, A. (1968) *The Politics of Accommodation; Pluralism and Democracy in the Netherlands*, Berkeley, University of California Press.

Litwack, T., Gerberg, G., and Fenster, C. A. (1979–80) 'The proper role of psychology in child custody disputes', *Journal of Family Law*, vol. 18 (2), pp. 269–300.

Lord Chancellor's Department (1988) *Annual Report*, London, HMSO.

Luthin, H. (1984) 'Elterlichte sorge, umgangsbefugnis und kindeswohl', *Zeitschrift fur das gesamte Familienrecht*, vol. 31, no. 8, pp. 114–17.

Luxton, M. and Rosenberg, H. (1986) *Through the Kitchen Window: The Politics of Home and Family*, Toronto, Garamond Press.

McBean, J. (1987) 'The myth of maternal preference in child custody cases', in Martin and Mahoney (1987).

McDonald, P. J. (ed.) and The National Institute of Family Studies (1986) *Settling Up: Property and Income Distribution on Divorce in Australia*, Melbourne, Prentice-Hall.

McKee, L. and O'Brien, M. (eds) (1982) *The Father Figure*, London, Tavistock.

MacKinnon, C. A. (1987) *Feminism Unmodified: Discourses on Life and Law*, Cambridge, Mass., Harvard University Press.

Maclean, M. (1987) 'Households after divorce: the availability of resources and their impact on children', in Brannen, J. and Wilson, G. (eds) *Give and Take in Families*, London, Allen & Unwin.

Maidment, S. (1976) 'A study in child custody', *Family Law*, vol. 6, pp. 195-200; 236-41.

Maidment, S. (1981) *Child Custody: What Chance for Fathers?*, London, National Council for One Parent Families.

Maidment, S. (1982) 'Law and justice: the case for family law reform', *Family Law*, vol. 12, pp. 229-32.

Maidment, S. (1984) *Child Custody and Divorce: The Law in Social Context*, London, Croom Helm.

Mark, P. (1987) 'In praise of parents - a view of separation pathways and positive outcomes', *Australian Journal of Family Law*, vol. 2, pp. 51-62.

Martin, S. and Mahoney, K. E. (eds) (1987) *Equality and Judicial Neutrality*, Calgary, Carswell.

Martin, S. L. and Roberts, C. M. (1984) *Women and Employment: A Lifetime Perspective*, London, HMSO.

Meer, J. H. B. van der (1986) *Nieuw leven - ander recht. Ethische, medische en juridische aspecten rond bevruchtingstechnieken*, Brielle, Prins.

Men's Confraternity (1985?) 'Submission to the Australian Law Reform Commission on Matrimonial Property' (unpublished).

Meyer, P. H. (1977) *L'enfant et la raison d'état*, Paris, Seuil.

Miller, D. J. (1979) 'Joint custody', *Family Law Quarterly*, vol. 18, no. 3, pp. 345-412.

Minkenhof, A. A. L. (1982) 'Over het Voorontwerp Afstammingsrecht', *Nederlands Juristenblad*, vol. 57, no. 29, pp. 826-33.

Minow, M. (1986) 'Consider the consequences', *Michigan Law Review*, vol. 84, pp. 900-18.

Mitchell, A. (1985) *Children in the Middle - Living With Divorce*, London, Tavistock.

Mnookin, R. H. (1975) 'Child-custody adjudication: judicial functions in the face of indeterminancy', *Law and Contemporary Problems*, vol. 39 (3), pp. 226-93.

Mnookin, R. H. (1979) *Bargaining in the Shadow of Divorce*, Working Paper no. 5, Oxford, Centre for Sociolegal Studies, Wolfson College.

Moggach, D. (1986) *To Have and To Hold*, Harmondsworth, Penguin.

Montague, M. and Stephens, J. (1985) *Paying the Price for Sugar and Spice: A Study of Women's Pathways into Social Security Recipiency*, Brotherhood of St Laurence and National Women's Advisory Council, Canberra, Australian Government Publishing Services.

Morgan, P. (1986) 'Feminist attempts to sack father: a case of unfair dismissal?', in Anderson, D. and Dawson, G. (eds) *Family Portraits*, London, Social Affairs Unit.

Morton, Lord (1956) *Royal Commission on Marriage and Divorce*, 1951-5, Cmnd 9,678, London, HMSO.

Moss, P. (1987) 'Some principles for childcare services for working parents', in Cohen and Clarke (1987).

Mossman, M. J. and Maclean, M. (1986) 'Family law and social welfare: toward a new equality', *Canadian Journal of Family Law*, vol. 5, no. 1, pp. 79–110.

Mottershead, P. (1987) 'Resource implications of childcare policy: a discussion paper', in Cohen and Clarke (1987).

Næss, P. O. and Undersrud, G. (1987) *Barnefordeling ved separasjon og skilsmisse*, Oslo, Tano.

National Association of Women and the Law (1985) *Bill C-47: Joint Custody, Child Support, Maintenance Enforcement and Related Issues*, A Submission to the Senate Standing Committee on Legal and Constitutional Affairs, Ottawa, National Association of Women and the Law.

National Council for One Parent Families (1985-6) *Annual Report*, London, The National Council for One Parent Families.

Nava, M. (1983) 'From utopian to scientific feminism', in Segal, L. (ed.) *What is to be Done About the Family?* Harmondsworth, Penguin.

Neely, R. (1984) 'The primary caretaker parent rule: child custody and the dynamics of greed', *Yale Law and Policy Review*, vol. 3, pp. 168-85.

Newell, M. L. and Joshi, H. (1986) *The First Job After the First Baby, Occupational Transition Among Women in 1946*, London, Centre for Population Studies.

New York Task Force on Women in the Courts (1987) 'Report', *Fordham Urban Law Journal*, vol. 15, pp. 11-198.

Noorman, L. (1987) 'Miracle babies', *Vrij Nederland*, 24 October, p. 7.

Norton, C. (1982) *Caroline Norton's Defence*, Chicago, Academy Chicago.

Nygh, J. P. (1985) 'Sexual discrimination in the Family Court', *University of New South Wales Law Journal*, vol. 8, pp. 62-79.

Oberg, B. and Oberg, G. (1984) 'Crisis therapy in custody disputes' in *Parent–Child Relationship Post-Divorce. A Seminar Report*, The Danish Institute of Social Research, Copenhagen, pp. 216-30.

Oberlies, D. (1983) 'Zu den Konsequenzen des Schweigens einer nichtehelichen Mutter uber den Kindesvater', in *STREIT, Feministische Rechtszeitschrift*, vol. 1, no. 2, pp. 19-25.

O'Brien, M. and McIntyre, S. (1986) 'Patriarchal hegemony and legal education', *Canadian Journal of Women and the Law*, vol. 2, no. 1, pp. 69-95.

O'Donnell, C. and Golder, N. (1986) 'A comparative analysis of equal pay in the US, Britain and Australia', *Australian Feminist Studies*, vol. 3, pp. 59-90.

O'Donovan, K. (1984) 'Protection and paternalism', in Freeman, M. D. (ed.) *State, Law and the Family: Critical Perspectives*, London, Tavistock.

O'Donovan, K. (1985) *Sexual Divisions of Law*, London, Weidenfeld & Nicolson.

O'Keefe, E. (1983) 'Property rights on marriage and property distribution on divorce: room for manoeuvre', *Australian Journal of Social Issues*, vol. 18, 2, pp. 136–41.

Okpaku, S. (1976) 'Psychology: impediment or aid in child custody cases', *Rutgers Law Review*, vol. 29, 5, pp. 1,117–53.

Olsen, F. (1984a) 'Statutory rape: a feminist critique of rights analysis', *Texas Law Review*, vol. 63, no. 3, pp. 387–432.

Olsen, F. (1984b) 'The politics of family law', *Law and Inequality*, vol. 2, no. 1, pp. 1–19.

Olsen, F. (1986) 'From false paternalism to false equality; judicial assaults on feminist community, Illinois 1869–1895', *Michigan Law Review*, vol. 84, pp. 1518–41.

O'Reilly, J. (1977) 'Custody disputes in the Irish Republic: the uncertain search for the welfare of the child', *The Irish Jurist*, vol. 12, pp. 38–65.

Parkinson, L. (1981) 'Joint custody', *One Parent Times*, no. 7, London, National Council for One Parent Families.

Parkinson, L. (1983a) 'Conciliation: pros and cons' (I), *Family Law*, vol. 13, pp. 22–5.

Parkinson, L. (1983b) 'Conciliation: pros and cons' (II), *Family Law*, vol. 13, pp. 183–6.

Parkinson, L. (1983c) 'Conciliation – a new approach to family conflict resolution', *British Journal of Social Work*, vol. 13, pp. 19–37.

Parkinson, L. (1986) *Conciliation in Separation and Divorce*, London, Croom Helm.

Parkinson, L. (1988) 'Child custody orders: a legal lottery', *Family Law*, vol. 18, pp. 26–30.

Parliamentry Debate (1985) *HC Hansard*, 26 November.

Pashukanis, E. (1979) *Toward a Theory of Law and Marxism*, London, Ink Links.

Pateman, C. (1980) 'Women and consent', *Political Theory*, May, vol. 8, no. 2, pp. 149–68.

Pateman, C. (1983) 'Feminist critiques of the public/private dichotomy', in Benn, S. I. and Gaus, G. (eds) *Public and Private in Social Life*, London, Croom Helm.

Pawson, M. E. (1981) 'The infertile patient – does she always want a baby?', in Cortes-Prieto, J. *et al.*, (eds) *Research On Fertility and Sterility*, Lancaster, MTP Press.

Payne, V. N. (1987) 'The regulation of surrogate motherhood', *Family Law*, vol. 17, May, pp. 178–80.

Pearson, J. and Thoennes, N. (1985) 'Child custody, child support arrangements and child support payment patterns', paper presented at the Fifth World Conference of the International Society of Family Law, Brussels, July.

Perrin, J. F. (1983) 'Tendence des changements législatifs en matière de divorce en Europe occidentale', in *Le Divorce en Europe Occidentale: La Loi et Le Nombre*, GIRD, CETEL, INED, Genève/Paris.

Perrot, M. (1982) 'Sur la notion d'intéret de l'enfant et son émergence au XIXeme siècle, in *Le Droit Face Aux Politiques Familiales*, Actes du colloque du 30.1.1982, Laboratoire d'analyse critique des pratiques juridiques, Université Paris VII (Ronéo), pp. 3–10.

Petchesky, R. P. (1984) *Abortion and Woman's Choice. The State, Sexuality and Reproductive Freedom*, London, Verso.

Petit, Ch. J. J. M. (1961) *Kunstmatige inseminatie bij de mens. Wenselijkheid en wettelijke maatregelen*, 's Gravenhage, Centrum voor Staatkundig Vorming.

Pfeffer, N. and Woollett, A. (1983) *The Experience of Infertility*, London, Virago.

Piachaud, D. (1981) *The Cost of A Child*, London, Child Poverty Action Group.

Piachaud, D. (1984) *Round About Fifty Hours A Week*, London, Child Poverty Action Group.

Pinchbeck, I. and Hewitt, M. (1973) *Children in English Society*, vol. II, London, Routledge & Kegan Paul.

Piper, C. (1985) 'Nice for the sake of the children', unpublished paper, Department of Law, Brunel University.

Polatnik, M. R. (1984) 'Why men don't rear children: a power analysis' in Trebilcot, J. (ed.) *Mothering: Essays in Feminist Theory*, New Jersey, Rowman & Allanheld.

Polikoff, N. (1982) 'Why are mothers losing: a brief analysis of criteria used in child custody determinations', *Women's Rights Law Reporter*, vol. 7, no. 3, pp. 235–49.

Polikoff, N. (1983) 'Gender and child-custody determinations: exploding the myths', in Diamond, I. (ed.) *Families, Politics and Public Policy: A Feminist Dialogue on Women and the State*, New York, Longman.

Priest, J. A. and, Whybrow, J. C. (1986) *Child Law in Practice in the Divorce and Domestic Courts*, Supplement to the Law Commission Working Paper no. 96, London, HMSO.

Rassaby, A. A. (1982) 'Surrogate motherhood: the position and problems of substitutes', in Walters, W. and Singer, P. (eds), *Test-Tube Babies; A Guide to Moral Questions, Present Techniques and Future Possibilities*, Melbourne, Oxford University Press.

Ratzinger, Cardinal J. and Bovone, Archbishop A. (1987) *Instructie Donum Vitae over de eerbied voor het beginnend menselijk leven en de waardigheid van de voorplanting*, Leusden, Stichting 'Ark' (translation of *Istruzione su: il rispetto della vita umana nascente e la dignita delle procreazione*).

Raymond, J. (1987) 'Bringing up children alone: policies for sole parents', *Social Security Review*, Issues Paper no. 3, Dept. of Social Security, Woden, Australian Capital Territory.

Report of the Joint Committee on Marriage Breakdown (1985), Stationery Office, Dublin.

Richards, M. (1982) 'Post-divorce arrangements for children: a psychological perspective', *Journal of Social Welfare Law*, May, pp. 133–51.

Richards, M. and Dyson, M. (1982) 'Separation, divorce and the development of children: a review', University of Cambridge, Child Care and Development Group.

Rights of Women (1984) *Response of the Family Law Group to the*

Consultative Document of the Matrimonial Procedures Committee (Booth Committee), London, Rights of Women.

Rights of Women Lesbian Custody Group (1986) *Lesbian Mothers' Legal Handbook*, London, Women's Press.

Riley, D. and Shaw, M. (1985) *Parental Supervision and Juvenile Delinquency*, Home Office Research, London, HMSO.

Robinson, J. and Griffiths, B. (1986) 'Australian families: current situation and trends; 1969–1985', *Social Security Review*, Background Paper no. 10, Dept. of Social Security, Woden, Australian Capital Territory.

Robinson, S. and Pizer, H. F. (1985) *Having a Baby Without a Man*, New York, Fireside/Simon & Schuster.

Rogerson, C. (1988) 'Winning the battle; losing the war: the plight of the custodial mother after judgement', in Hughes, M. E. and Pask, E. D. (eds) *National Themes in Canadian Family Law*, Calgary, Carswell, pp. 21–54.

Roll, J. (1986) *Babies and Money: Birth Trends and Costs*, Occupational Paper no. 4, London, Family Policy Studies Centre.

Ronalds, C. (1987) *Affirmative Action and Sex Discrimination: A Handbook on Legal Rights for Women*, Sydney, Pluto Press.

Rondeau-Rivier, M. C. (1981) 'Le remariage', Thèse de doctorate en droit, Université de Lyon III, France.

Rood-de Boer, M. (1984a) 'Een schok in het familie- en jeugdrecht', *Nederlands Juristenblad*, vol. 59, no. 41, pp. 1,277–82.

Rood-de Boer, M. (1984b) 'Rechtsvragen met betrekking tot moederschap', *Tijdschrift voor Familie en Jeugdrecht*, vol. 6–8, pp. 232–8.

Rorvik, D. (1978) *In His Image. The Cloning of a Man*, London, Sphere Books.

Roussel, L., Commaille, J., Kellerhalls, J. and Perrin, J. F. (1983) 'Le divorce en Europe occidentale: la loi et le nombre', GIRD, CETEL, INED, Genève/Paris.

Russell, G. (1983) *The Changing Role of Fathers?*, St Lucia, University of Queensland Press.

Ryan, J. P. (1986) 'Joint custody in Canada: time for a second look', *Reports of Family Law* (2d) vol. 49, p. 119.

Saffron, L. (1986) *Getting Pregnant Our Own Way: A Guide to Alternative Insemination*, London, Women's Health Information Centre.

Samuels, J. G. (1982) Comments reproduced in *Assessment of Damages*, Committee for Post-Graduate Studies in the Department of Law, Sydney University, November.

Schneider, E. (1986) 'The dialectic of rights and politics: perspectives from the women's movement', *New York University Law Review*, vol. 61, pp. 589–652.

Schulman, J. and Pitt, V. (1982) 'Second thoughts on joint custody: analysis of legislation and its implications for women and children', *Golden Gate University Law Review*, vol. 12, no. 3, pp. 538–77.

Scott, H. (1984) *Working Your Way to the Bottom*, London, Pandora Press.

285

Scutt, J. A. (1983) 'Equal marital property rights, *Australian Journal of Social Issues*, vol. 18, p. 128.

Scutt, J. and Graham, D. (1984) *For Richer For Poorer*, Melbourne, Penguin.

Segal, L. (1987) *Is The Future Female?* London, Virago.

Sevenhuijsen, S. (1985) 'Feminism, Illegitimacy and Affiliation Law in the Netherlands', Paper for the Summer Symposium on the Legal History of the American Family, Legal History Program, University of Madison.

Sevenhuijsen, S. (1986) 'Fatherhood and the political theory of rights: theoretical perspectives of feminism', *The International Journal of the Sociology of Law*, vol. 14, no. 3/4, pp. 329-40.

Sevenhuijsen, S. (1987) *De orde van het vaderschap. Politieke debatten over ongehuwd moederschap, afstamming en het huwelijk in Nederland 1870-1900*, Amsterdam, Stichting Beheer IISG.

Shatter, A. (1977) *Family Law in the Republic of Ireland*, Dublin, Wolfhound Press.

Shaver, S. (1983) 'Sex and money in the welfare state', in Baldock and Cass (1983).

Sheppard, A. T. (1983) 'Unspoken premises in custody litigation', *Women's Rights Law Reporter*, vol. 7, no. 3, pp. 229-34.

Sheridan, A. (1980) *Michel Foucault: The Will to Truth*, London, Tavistock.

Shiff, D. and MacIllhatton, S. (1985) 'Review of *For Richer, For Poorer*', *Legal Service Bulletin*, vol. 10, pp. 29-32.

Shrofel, S. M. (1985) 'Equality rights and law reform in Saskatchewan: an assessment of the Charter compliance process', *Canadian Journal of Women and the Law*, vol. 1, no. 1, pp. 109-18.

Singer, P. and Wells, D. (1984) *The Reproductive Revolution: New Ways of Making Babies*, Oxford, Oxford University Press.

Smart, C. (1982) 'Regulating families or legitimating patriarchy? Family law in Britain', *International Journal of the Sociology of Law*, vol. 10, no. 2, pp. 129-47.

Smart, C. (1984) *The Ties That Bind: Law, Marriage and the Reproduction of Patriarchal Relations*, London, Routledge & Kegan Paul.

Smart, C. (1986a) 'Book review: *Family Law in Canada: New Directions* (Elizabeth Sloss, ed.)', *International Journal of the Sociology of Law*, vol. 14, no. 3/4, pp. 419-20.

Smart, C. (1986b) 'Feminism and law: some problems of anlaysis and strategy', *International Journal of the Sociology of Law*, vol. 14, no. 2, pp. 109-23.

Smart, C. (1987) '"There is of course the distinction dictated by nature": law and the nature of paternity', in Stanworth, M. (ed.) *Reproductive Technologies. Gender, Motherhood and Medicine*, Oxford, Polity Press.

Smart, C. and Brophy, J. (1985) 'Locating the law: a discussion of the place of law in feminism', in Brophy and Smart (1985).

Smith, L., Côté-Harper, G., Elliot, R. and Seydegart, M. (eds) (1986) *Righting the Balance: Canada's New Equality Rights*, Saskatoon, The Canadian Human Rights Reporter.

Social Security Review (1986) *Income Support For Families With Children*, Issue Paper no. 1, Woden, Department of Social Security.

Social Survey (1983) Statistical Bureau of Statistics of Norway, Oslo-Kongsvinger (in Norwegian with English translations of the tables).

Staines, M. (1976) 'The concept of "The Family" under the Irish constitution', *The Irish Jurist*, vol. 11, pp. 223-42.

Statistics Canada (1983) *Divorce: Law and the Family in Canada*, Ottawa, Supply & Services.

Statistics Canada (1985) *Women in Canada: A Statistical Report*, Ottawa, Supply & Services.

Steel, F. (1987) 'Alimony and maintenance orders', in Martin and Mahoney (1987).

Steinman, S. (1981) 'The experience of children in a joint custody arrangement: a report of a study', *American Journal of Orthopsychiatry*, vol. 51, no. 3, pp. 739-62.

Steinman, S. (1983) 'Joint custody: what we know, what we have yet to learn and the judicial and legislative implications', *U. C. Davis Review*, vol. 16, no. 3.

Stetson, D. M. (1982) *A Woman's Issue: The Politics of Family Law Reform in England*, London, Greenwood Press.

Stevens, K. (1985) *Surrogate Mother; One Woman's Story*, London, Century.

Stone, O. (1982) *Child's Voice in the Court of Law*, Toronto, Butterworths.

Sumner, C., (1979) *Reading Ideologies: An Investigation into the Marxist Theory of Ideology and Law*, London, Academic Press.

Supreme Court (1984) 4 May, *Nederlandse Jurisprudentie*, p. 510.

Supreme Court (1986) 21 March, *Nederlandse Jurispurdentie*, p. 585.

Testart, J. (1986) *L'Oeuf Transparent*, Paris, Flammarion.

Thèry, I. (1983) *La référence à l'intéret de l'enfant dans la modification du droit de garde après le divorce*, Thèse de IIIeme cycle en démographie, Université Paris V – René Descartes.

Thèry, I. (1984) 'Les parents divorcés, nouvelles normes, nouveaux tabous', *Dialogue*, no. 86.

Thèry, I. (1985) 'La réference à l'intéret de l'enfant, usage judiciaire et ambiguités', in Bourguignon, O, Rallu, J. L. and Thèry, I. (eds) *Du divorce et des enfants*, Paris, PUF-INED, pp. 33-114.

Thorne, B. (1982) 'Feminist rethinking of the family: an over-view', in Thorne, B. and Yalom, M. (eds) *Rethinking the Family; Some Feminist Questions*, New York/London, Longman.

Trouw (1985) 'Werkgroep wil verbod van commerciele draagmoeder', 23 November.

Trouw (1986) 'Een gewenst kind, een twijfelachtige methode', 15 October.

Ursel, J. (1986) 'The state and the maintenance of patriarchy: a case study of family, labour and welfare legislation in Canada', in Dickinson, J.

and Russell, B. (eds) *Family, Economy and State: The Social Reproduction Process Under Capitalism*, Toronto, Garamond Press.

Uviller, R. K. (1978) 'Fathers' rights and feminism: the maternal presumption revisited', *Harvard Women's Law Journal*, vol. 1, p. 107.

Verbraken, A. M. (1981) 'Wordt vaders wil wet? Ontwikkelinger in het omgangsrecht', in S. Sevenhuijsen *et al.* (eds), *Socialisties-Feministiese Teksten* 6, pp. 17-43.

Verveen, B. F. (1965) *Rapport van de commissie Kumstmatige inseminatie bij de mens*, 's-Gravenhage, Ministerie van Justitie.

Vilaine, A. M. de *et al.* (1986) *Maternité en mouvement; les femmes, la re/production et les hommes de science*, Montreal, Presses Universitaires de Grenoble.

Viva (1986) 'Draagmoeder: Eigenlijk wist ik meteen al dat ik die baby wilde houden', 21 February, no. 9, pp. 18-20.

Vliet, F. van (1987) 'Afstamming en ouderlijke zorg: wie niet zaait, zal niet oogsten?', *Nederlands Juristenblad*, no. 26, pp. 814-17.

Volkskrant, de (1987) 'Draagmoedercontract in Nederland niet geldig', 2 April.

Waarheid, De (1988) 'Draagmoeders', 7 January.

Walczak, Y. and Burns, S. (1984) *Divorce: The Child's Point of View*, London, Harper & Row.

Wallerstein, J. and Corbin, S. (1986) 'Father–child relationships after divorce: child support and educational opportunity', *Family Law Quarterly*, vol. 20, no. 2, pp. 109-28.

Wallerstein, J. and Kelly, J. (1979) 'Children and divorce: a review', *Social Work*, vol. 24 (6)1, pp. 468-75.

Wallerstein, J. and Kelly, J. (1980) *Surviving the Breakup*, New York, Basic Books.

Warnock, M. (1985) *A Question of Life: The Warnock Report on Human Fertilisation and Embryology*, Oxford, Basil Blackwell. Originally (1984) *Report of the Committee of Inquiry into Human Fertilisation and Embryology*, Cmnd 9,314, London, HMSO.

Wearing, B. (1984) *The Ideology of Motherhood*, Sydney, George Allen & Unwin.

Weitzman, L. (1981) 'The economics of divorce: social and economic consequences of property, alimony and child support awards', *UCLA Law Review*, vol. 28, no. 6, pp. 1,181-268.

Weitzman, L. (1985) *The Divorce Revolution: The Unexpected Social and Economic Consequences for Women and Children in America*, New York, Free Press.

Westcott, J., Mills, V. and Reader, A. (1988) 'Joint custody orders', *Family Law*, vol. 18, pp. 95-7.

Wetsvoorstel Nadere regeling van de omgang in verband met scheiding (1986) Tweede Kamer 1986-7, no. 18 964.

Whyte, J. H. (1971) *Church and State in Modern Ireland*, Dublin, Gill & Macmillan.

Wilson, E. (1980) *Only Halfway to Paradise; Women in Postwar Britain: 1945-1968*, London, Tavistock.

WING (Women Immigration and Nationality Group) (1985) *Worlds Apart: Women Under Immigration and Nationality Law*, London, Pluto.

Women's Electoral Lobby NSW, Family Law Action Group (WEL) (1981) 'Discussion Paper on Reform of Marital Property Laws in Australia by Means of a System of Community of Property'. (Unpublished, on file at the Australian Law Reform Commission.)

Women's Electoral Lobby NSW, Family Law Action Group (WEL) (1985) 'Equal Rights To Marital Assets', Submission to the Australian Law Reform Commission and the Australian Attorney General. (Unpublished, on file at the Australian Law Reform Commission.)

Woods, L., Been, V., and Schulman, J. (1983) 'Sex and economic discrimination in child custody awards', *Clearinghouse Review*, vol. 16, pp. 1,130–4.

Zaborszky, D. E. (1984) 'Domestic anarchy and the destruction of the family, Caroline Norton and the Custody of Infants Bill', *International Journal of Women's Studies*, vol. 7, no. 5, pp. 397–411.

Zipper, J. (1986) *Het Zaad der Twijfel. Politieke debatten over kunstmatige inseminatie in de jaren '50-'65*, Amsterdam, University of Amsterdam, Subfaculteit der Algemene Politieke en Sociale Wetenschappen.

Zipper, J. (1987) 'Dilemma's rondom prenatale diagnostiek', *Politieke en Sociale Vorming*, vol. 5, no. 18, pp. 10–12.

Zipper, J. and Sevenhuijsen, S. (1987) 'Surrogacy: feminist notions of motherhood reconsidered', in Stanworth, M. (ed.) *Reproductive Technologies. Gender, Motherhood and Medicine*, Oxford, Polity Press.

NAME INDEX

SUBJECT INDEX